Firearms & the Fortress

A New Theory of Historical
Materialism and Some Reflections
on the Road to Communism

James Ward

COOL MILLENNIUM BOOKS

1

A CIP catalogue record for this book is available from the British library.

ISBN: 978-1-913851-65-1

This novel was produced in the UK and uses British-English language conventions ('authorise' instead of 'authorize', 'The government are' instead of 'the government is', etc.)

To my wife

CONTENTS

Introduction

This whole book might be described as an attempt to set history on a different trajectory from the one it is now following.

Which might look like a hopeless task: how on earth to bring about a 'revolution', in the middle of the 21st century, when it is supposedly easier to imagine the end of the world than a radically better society?

In order to address a difficult problem, sometimes it helps to see it as a puzzle - at least to begin with. Some of the pieces are: the darkness of human nature, our separation as, and by, nations, war, prejudice, discrimination, education (or lack of it), corruption. Most people despair of radical change because they cannot see how to complete the jigsaw, or even that it *is* a jigsaw. Part of the remedy may consist in hybridising right- and left-wing politics. But there are things in what follows that will alienate both sides.

'What follows' is, to begin with, a radical revision of Marx's theory of historical materialism as presented in *The German Ideology,* the Preface to his 1859, *A Contribution to the Critique of Political Economy,* and elsewhere. It proceeds from the contention that Marx omitted something crucial – a pre-condition for the entire edifice of means of production, relations of production, private property & division of labour, etc. – which I have called *the means of securitisation*.

But the Marxian theory also fails in other crucial respects. Among its most glaring wrong-turns was its assertion that the malignity of capitalism lies in objective 'shop-floor' relations (surplus value, or the alienation of the labourer from the product, etc. – neither of which captures the problem).

My aim for *Firearms & the Fortress* was that it should be clear, well-argued and relatively brief. Revolution and reform are not alternatives; they are two points on the same spectrum (thus, mistakenly or not, Marx once said Britain could make the transition to Communism by peaceful means). There is rarely an authentic 'violent revolution'. Events characterised as such are typically *coups d'état* followed by an extensive culling of undesirables, and, in the long run, society stays the same or gets worse.

I hope the material below will contain all I have to say on its title-subject, but obviously, I cannot be sure: to write two books on the same topic - and even to have to 'explain' one's book - should probably be regarded as a failure. Nevertheless, things have now reached such a point, and past exploration of our shared predicament has been so inadequate, that all the present analysis can do is point the way to what *may* be an exit; to re-orient us so that we point in the right direction. In which case, some sort of future re-elaboration may, regrettably, be unavoidable.

To some extent, it may read like a collection of references to other people's texts; texts containing arguments that have persuaded me, and which, for want of space, I cannot usually summarise as effectively as I would like; and for which I am not entitled to take any credit. "As [author] says, in her [date] book, [title]" unavoidably recurs. The bibliography at the end contains all and only the texts that I directly refer to in these pages. It is not a scattergun reading list for students.

Firearms & the Fortress was partly inspired by Mark Fisher's 2009, *Capitalist Realism,* in particular, the discovery that he intended to follow it up with a more substantial book of theory. Obviously, following his death in 2017, that never happened. In 2023, I posted a TikTok video in which I concluded, "It is impossible to read this book without wondering what the longer, theoretical work Fisher had in mind might have looked like. I have my own ideas about that."

My first guess was that he would have centralised Marx's notion of the *Fessel* (fetter): ie, that he would have claimed our imaginations have been 'fettered' by late capitalism, and that is the reason we are unable to conceive anything beyond it. One speculation led to another, and *Firearms & the Fortress* is the result. I wish I had been able to discuss it with Fisher himself, but that is inconsequential: even had he lived, it is highly unlikely our paths would ever have crossed.

To what extent the left is currently in the grip of so-called identity politics is an open question.[1] Fifty years ago, a person wanting to join its ranks simply turned up. Nowadays, one has to pay for the privilege by spending time with intellectual purists – often, in universities - whose default mode is mistrust.

Intersectionality is, as far as it goes, a good idea - obviously it is. However, it was never intended as a philosophical system. Arguably, it fails as such; it treats all intersections as what we might call reinforcing, and ignores the collapsing ones.

A good example of a 'reinforcing' intersection occurs when an individual is overlooked because she belongs to two or more minority groups. The injustice of being, eg, disabled reinforces her exclusion from mainstream society as a result of possessing, eg, a particular ethnicity. But there is also a certain *a priorism* in moral evaluations here: when A and B get into an altercation, the question of who is the more 'privileged' is never irrelevant, and may even play a purely deductive role in any attempted resolution.

A 'collapsing' intersection occurs when a minority group, or a member of one, excludes another minority as a matter of

---

[1] Musa Al-Gharbi (2024) puts much of it down to a new form of capitalism which is determined to flaunt its 'egalitarian' credentials. We might be sceptical of this, given the speed with which Facebook, Amazon and Google cut back or abolished their diversity policies in the wake of Trump's second-term win.

principle or policy. Intersectionalists have had difficulty dealing with the fact that the economies of most African kingdoms in the pre-modern era – like pre-modern kingdoms everywhere - were based in slavery, since that makes the historical issue of slavery a 'collapsing' one: we have to deduct our embarrassment over the one from our indignation concerning the other, and we may end up with less than we thought. The seventeenth century Angolan Queen Nzinga, an intersectionalist role model, was undoubtedly brave, resourceful and, up to a point, compassionate, but she was also a slave trader. Her own mother was one of her father's slave-wives. Today, however, in practice, her status as a powerful black woman trumps her role as a slaver, so the latter is often passed over in silence.[2]

In recent years, the political right has had significantly more success in dealing with this sort of moral collision than the left, usually by adopting a nuanced position to the effect that while some things really are morally horrendous, everyone directly responsible is long dead, the idea of 'punishing the sins of the parents to the third and fourth generation' is rightfully obsolete, egregious injustice is a fact of pre-modern societies always and everywhere, and we cannot always judge the distant past by the standards of the immediate present. Ironically, this has had the effect of restoring the laudability of figures like Queen Nzinga, while not trying to 'smooth them out' for a particular kind of

---

[2] So, for example, the BBC tells us, amazingly, that she "was a key figure in resisting the expanding slave trade in central Africa" (https://www.bbc.co.uk/newsround/58899050#:~:text=Queen%20Nzinga%20Mba ndi), while the online Oxford Research Encyclopedia omits all mention of her connection with slavery.

modern fastidiousness. But its firm basis in common sense[3] has also made it a key component in election victories.[4]

In addition to its failure to distinguish reinforcing from collapsing intersections, however, intersectionality tends to take a movement over: the reinforcing intersections are necessarily different each time, and since exclusionary injustice supposedly occurs at precisely those less visible places, guarding against missing them can become an obsession. The problem can be forestalled by means of a principle to the effect that where an individual stands at the juncture of two or more disadvantages, *it must be assumed as a matter of principle, regardless of context and unless there is convincing evidence to the contrary, that that individual has been rendered invisible.* This, in combination with a new reading of 'The personal is political' to mean that one's private beliefs are always suspect, has produced a guilty-until-proven-innocent approach to diversity in which would-be leftists are routinely expected to undergo supervised auto-criticism in order to assess their level of credit with, or indebtedness to, the socially excluded. This 'Neo-Maoism', as I will call it, is perpetually on the lookout for deviationism: it is keen on no-platforming, silencing, and chasing individuals from their jobs. Its tendency to regard science and reason as 'heteronormative' and/or 'patriarchal' and/or 'colonialist'

---

[3] A term which goes back to Aristotle and appears as a significant consideration most recently in GE Moore, but which always has some thinkers reaching apoplectically for Gramsci. But Gramsci's discussion of common sense is considerably subtler than his supporters often insist. It does *not,* for example, consist of a vulgar assertion that it is manufactured entirely by the media (1971, p419-425).

[4] There is a strong resemblance here to the western left's attitude to the Soviet Union prior to 1989. The idea was that, yes, we know the USSR has lots of faults, but we should keep quiet about them, because the 'wrong' sort of people might use our words to further an anti-Soviet agenda. Nowadays, the idea is that, yes, we may know an oppressed minority group has lots of faults (eg, a longstanding homophobia), but we should keep quiet about that, because the 'wrong' sort of people might use our words to compound that minority's oppression.

makes it inward-looking[5] and arguably far too fractious to effect meaningful change in the real world.[6]

To some extent, the fault for all this lies with three members of the Frankfurt school. Theodor Adorno, Max Horkheimer and Herbert Marcuse invented a corrosive fusion of Marx and Freud in which there is nothing outside capitalism, so that civil rights, reason, science and morality are all equally 'bourgeois' and deserving of censure. 'Dialectics' – a term that rarely adds anything to a discussion, and usually obfuscates it – looms large, and all too often takes the form of 'negative dialectics', with predictably dour results.

The word 'communism' in this book is simply shorthand for a world in which people of all races, genders, ages and outlooks coexist harmoniously in a single, global society whose hallmarks are mutuality and justice. It is what Kant called 'The Kingdom of Ends'; it is implicit in all genuine moral behaviour, and pre-dates Marx by millennia. My strong feeling is that nearly all people on Earth are natural communists; or, at the very least, they would be, if they knew what it meant.

Some perfectly reasonable thinkers have advanced the claim that capitalism has made ours the best age there has ever been: it has bestowed numerous benefits upon us, and, for all its faults, no one has ever come up with anything better.

---

[5] A tendency which is reinforced by the need to keep an eye on party membership to ensure it is truly representative and diverse. ('Diversity' in this context is a biological term, and need have nothing whatsoever to do with variety of outlook or opinion).

[6] While we are on, we might as well mention the dubious notion of 'white privilege' (WP); for in a situation where a black person (A) experiences discrimination which a white person (B) avoids by virtue of her skin colour, there are two possible descriptions: (1) the WP description and (2) the human rights (HR) description are mutually exclusive, since rights and privileges are opposing concepts. (1) focuses on B and talks of B's WP. (2) focuses on A and talks of A's being denied basic HR. The problem is that privileges are favours that can, and in some circumstances should, be removed. In other words, WP introduces a new (and dangerous) conception of human rights as favours. B is not 'privileged' by virtue of having his basic human rights respected; no one is.

I deal with that claim in detail later. Although there is an apparent abundance of evidence for capitalism's munificence – 'global living standards have perpetually improved since around 1850', etc. – it is almost entirely spurious. Some of the upturn is down to a profoundly unsustainable plunder of the Earth's limited resources, otherwise it is science[7], trade unions, civil liberties and the rule of law we have to thank, not capitalism. Capitalism is now a global system, showing it can function perfectly well under despotic conditions; its propensity for 'bad science' is well known,[8] and when opportunity beckons, it rarely balks at breaking the law. Its highest development can currently be seen in Vladimir Putin's Russia: there, it has been allowed to run its course – it does have a specific 'course', just as an exponentially reproducing bacteria has a 'course', a process of using up its own sustenance – concluding with its implosion into unadulterated plutocracy, roughly as Karl Polanyi suggested an unimpeded free market always would, as long ago as 1944.

However, even if it *is* as broadly benign as just claimed, the conclusion 'so we should preserve things as they are' does not follow. Unless what we have is perfect, we can always, in principle, do better. At present, for example, we can all imagine a world without tax havens, without corruption, without cronyism. To get rid of these three things alone would be a revolution, and that could happen *within* capitalism.

Couldn't it?

Let us begin.

---

[7] The word 'science' in this book is nearly always shorthand for what, in the English-speaking world, is nowadays called 'STEM': science, technology, engineering and mathematics.

[8] Ben Goldacre's *Bad Science* (2008) and *Bad Pharma* (2012) can be read as descriptions of what frequently happens at the interface of science and capitalism.

PART ONE

1. The Means of Production and the Means of Securitisation

What *is* 'The Means of Production'?

Marx's theory of historical materialism begins with the means of production. Human beings must cooperate to produce goods that satisfy their basic needs of food, clothing and shelter. That requires technology, and technology requires that human beings enter into specific relations with it and with each other. So, the means of production gives you relations of production. As Marx famously put it in *The Poverty of Philosophy*, "The windmill gives you society with the feudal lord; the steam mill, society with the industrial capitalist." Relations of production involve a division of labour, and when crises occur, the myriad different occupations will distil into mutually antagonistic social classes. Those classes will carry on an "uninterrupted, now hidden, now open, fight", ending, each time, with either a revolutionary reconstitution of the social order, or mutual destruction. Ultimately, when the means of production has evolved sufficiently to abolish scarcity, there will be a socialist revolution: the workers will seize the means of production, private property and the division of labour will be abolished, and, after a relatively brief transitional period, society will become communist and everyone will live happily ever after.

There are all sorts of problems with this account. Given that everyone has to have some relation to the means of production, how and why does it end up being owned by one group rather than another? How does ownership arise? If the means of production drives history, what causes inventions? Why hasn't Communism existed from all eternity? Yes, past history has mostly been characterised by scarcity, but, except in its extreme form, where large swathes of a population are perpetually starving to death, scarcity doesn't necessarily imply inequality, and certainly not *gross* inequality, not unless some other factor is involved. On the contrary: the earliest hunter-gatherer societies were probably fairly egalitarian. It was when surplus crept in that authoritarianism appeared.

Above all, what *is* the means of production? For orthodox Marxism, it is the means by which we produce our subsistence of food, clothing, and shelter. But of course, nowadays, the technology that produces our food, essential clothing, and shelter is a tiny subset of goods-producing technology. What, if anything, sets that tiny subset apart for the purposes of conditioning social relations?

And yet, the theory undoubtedly *does* require this subset as a necessary condition of the entire edifice (we could eliminate Venetian blinds production from the current system without much effect, but not food production). In fact, it seems that, just as historical materialism involves levels of determination, so does the means of production - the most basic of which is untouched biology.

To put it another way, we get our subsistence from the land, but the Earth can produce it without any need for human intervention at all; it can, and does, produce plants and animals for us to eat, rain and river water to drink, animal hides for clothing and shelter, and so on. Historically, humans will begin by hunting and gathering those things, then cultivating them, but, even in the most advanced societies, that will still be what they ultimately depend on. The rest of the means of production is built on top of this *non-human means of production*, as a kind of second level, and cannot function without it.

Consider: if an extraterrestrial were to land on our planet and ask to see our means of production, what would we show him or her? Our best exhibit would probably be a farm, where we would exhibit combine harvesters, milking machines, tractors, land imprinters, seed drills, but also living organisms: cows, sheep, fields of wheat and barley.

Yet that would be inadequate too: most people in modern production roles have no direct contact with the subset of technology that produces life's basic necessities. It is difficult to claim that it is the principal conditioner of our entire way of life.

The alternative is that we would show our extraterrestrial *everything;* the equipment we use to manufacture every single one of our commodities: tin cans, yachts, bubble gum, trainers, pencils, phones, and so on.

Perhaps *that* is the means of production. But it makes it such a wide and varied phenomenon that the task of saying precisely how it engenders the social relations looks impossible. On that understanding, both sides of the equation – the means of production and the social relations – are arguably beyond circumscribing any longer.[9] Thus the idea that the means of production produces the social relations becomes just another dogma.

To help solve this problem, we might distinguish four levels of the means of production:

(1) The non-human means of production. The *growth* of plants and animals, fully independently of any use humans might make of them;

---

[9] In *Postmodernism*, Fredric Jameson claims that base and superstructure have recently become indistinguishable from one another. This goes too far: economists still have no difficulty distinguishing productive forces, nor aesthetic commentators, arts, literature and philosophy.

(2) The *harvesting* of the product of (1) by humans, either (a) by hunting-gathering or (b) on farms, using farming technology;

(3) The *processing* of food for consumption by industries alongside or outside the farming industry;

(4) The *production of everything else* – shoes, batteries, clocks, etc. - which obviously requires the production of food in (1) as its precondition.[10]

As soon as humans become involved in production, in (2), the process becomes inherently violent. Even (if there is such a scenario) where humans merely gather, without hunting, they will find themselves in competition with others – other humans, other animals. How far the violence inherent in (2) can be mitigated by the higher levels, 3 and 4, is an open question.

Secondly, the means of production involves relations of production. But there is a sense that in Marx, the way people relate to each other in any given society is entirely an expression of the production relations, which means that other, non-productive technology must be discounted. But it is obvious that inventions like the steam engine, the camera, the telephone, the video recorder, etc. changed the way people related to each other in society *after those products had left the factory floor*. We can, if we are determined to defend Marx, assimilate the means of communication, the means of transportation and the means of entertainment to the means of production, but only very artificially.[11]

---

[10] The production of shelter would be part of (4). Shelter is a part of the means of securitisation, and does not strictly belong to the means of production.

[11] In his *Fifty Machines That Changed the Course of History* (Quid 2014), Eric Chaline rightly includes the typewriter, the gramophone, the safety bicycle, the Hoover Suction Sweeper, the Graf Zeppelin, the microscope, the Hubble Space Telescope, and a host of other inventions that can only at a huge stretch be considered part of the means of production.

Relevant in this context (though it is rarely presented as such) is Martin Heidegger's discussion of 'equipment' (*Zeug*) beginning in section 68 of *Being and Time*. We are surrounded by equipment which "always belongs to a totality of equipment … ink-stand, pen, ink, paper, blotting pad, table, lamp, furniture, windows, doors, room … Out of this, the 'arrangement' emerges, and it is in this that any 'individual' item of equipment shows itself. *Before* it does so, a totality of equipment has already been discovered."[12] Equipment is definitely a medium through which *Dasein* relates itself to itself, and to others, and it seems to play roughly the same role in Heidegger as the means of production does in Marx. Moreover, Heidegger's account is highly plausible. But to what extent are those two key concepts translatable into each other?

As if these were not problems enough, we also have the so-called problem of legality. In his 1955, *The Illusion of the Epoch*, HB Acton pointed out that production was only possible within a given legal framework, and that Marx's theory of history, which placed the means of production at the basic causal level, and ideas – including legal ones – at the 'superstructural' level, was therefore faced with a problem.

In his 1978 *Karl Marx's Theory of History*, the analytical Marxist, GA Cohen, tried to solve that problem by providing what he called a *rechtsfrei* interpretation of the means of production, in which its socially endorsed operation is grounded in *de facto powers*, rather than legal entitlements. The superstructure, where such entitlements properly belong, simply ratifies the powers at the basic level; it does not create them.

It is an ingenious response, but it raises the question of whether those *de facto* powers are sufficient in themselves. If they are, then the superstructural rights are redundant; if they

---

[12] Heidegger, Martin (1980), p97-98.

are not, the problem remains. To put it another way, do the powers need the rights to give them power?

Firearms & the Fortress *or* The Means of Securitisation

In fact, Marx's theory, on its own, cannot explain how history works because it is missing a level. Production is always production *for* some community or other, and the means of production can only function as such insofar as the community takes steps to shield it from attack. Before a community can begin to produce in any systematic, enduring way, it needs to have considered what I will call *the means of securitisation*: how it will protect

(1) the means of production and
(2) the product of production

from seizure or destruction by hostile forces.

Until this question is satisfactorily answered, the means of production cannot come into existence, or its use will be pointless.[13] As regards (1), the instruments themselves will be stolen, or vandalised. As regards (2), the goods produced will be continually plundered or spoilt. No, the means of production, and its produce, has to be surrounded by, or contained within, a safe of some kind. Moreover, since the means of production is always, at least potentially, a means of creating indefinite private wealth, it will be subject to continual appropriation

---

[13] Those who disagree with this assertion may point to Abraham Maslow's 'hierarchy of needs' in which physiological needs like food and shelter trump security needs. But anyone who has ever fed a group of hungry animals a limited amount of food will notice that the animal that gets there first will attempt to find a safe space to consume it. Of course, once the procuring of food becomes a matter of social planning rather than luck, security becomes even more of a priority, and once the satisfaction of physiological needs is guaranteed, and other goods enter the equation, it arguably becomes foundational or at least indistinguishable from the 'lower'.

attempts, so the means of securitisation is never a once-and-for-all static thing: it must be perpetually maintained, and, as far as possible, it must improve. Its evolution is linked to the evolution of the means of production, and forms its precondition insofar as a more secure space makes procuring more up-to-date, and probably more costly, technology worth the risk.

The earliest safe may simply have been a hole in the ground, in which the surplus of the day's hunt or forage was kept overnight and covered over. The anticipated plunderers would be wild animals and rival tribes, and for practical purposes they were probably regarded as one and the same. Securitisation of the product of production was limited by biology; ultimately, by the inevitability of decomposition. The land could never be entirely securitised in the way that, later, a machine could. Even in relatively advanced agricultural societies, thieves and wild animals would break in and steal, and the biological depreciation of the product of production made sharing as much of a practical as a moral necessity ('Give X the unusable surplus, and next year, he may be in a position to return the favour').

When defensible safe technology advanced to the point where animals ceased to pose so much of a threat, only hostile humans remained; eventually, these stopped occupying territory outside the tribal boundaries and became incorporated into settled communities, at which point they changed from being a rival set of tribes to being a rival social class. Writing was originally a means of securitisation: a way of recording what was owed. Note that the ruling class was not so much the one that owned the *means of production* as the one that owned *the means of securitisation of the product of production*. The means of securitisation has always been a better way of explaining the phenomenon of social class than the means of production. Political power here, as elsewhere, is nothing more than the effective ownership of at least a share in that means.

To fully appreciate this, it is necessary to understand that the means of securitisation has a double aspect. In order to secure my goods, I need more than a safe/stronghold: that is merely *defensive* or passive securitisation. Such means will, at first, involve physical blows and kicks, projectiles and staves for defending the product of production against rival tribes and wild animals. But if it is to be effective, securitisation must always have a *proactive* or *offensive* aspect. It must recognise that attack is the best form of defence, and devise a means of meeting fire with fire. In historical order, spears, swords, bows and arrows, muskets, cannons, and machine guns have been used interchangeably between defence and attack.

In other words, the proactive means of securitisation has applications well beyond securitisation: it can also be used to plunder.[14] Nevertheless, the defensive means of securitisation must precede the proactive. Before a tribe can carry out raids and conquests, it must be relatively confident of its own ability to withstand attack. (It goes without saying that in war, attack and defence are often inseparable.)

Yet raiding hordes are probably the historical exception; far more common is the phenomenon of governments using the proactive means of securitisation to rob their own citizens. It is often said that the nation-state is an artificial, modern invention that still appears as an intrusion in some parts of the world. That may be true insofar as some human communities are nomadic, or subsist chiefly by raiding. But as soon as a community settles down, the nation-state is always implicit in its development.

---

[14] In my *A New Theory of Justice* (Cool Millennium 2012), I distinguish between 'harmonic' and 'emancipatory' justice. Roughly speaking, 'harmonic' would be the maximally effective *unified* use of the entirety of the available means of securitisation by one group against another, or (theoretically) by the whole of humankind to create a Utopia; 'emancipatory' would involve a distribution of the means of securitisation amongst antagonistic groups. It should never be forgotten that a pair of fists is, in domestic circumstances, often an effective means of securitisation, and in *A New Theory of Justice*, I use this to help explain the subjugation of women throughout history.

Cities emerge first, but ultimately they have to be walled to repel raiders; when raiders arrive, men and women from the surrounding countryside seek security within those walls: since the peasants are the foundation of the urban economy, and vital to its continuance should the crisis pass, they can hardly be left to fend for themselves, or turned away.

Of course, the wall also has proactive aspects. Both aspects combine to reshape human nature. As Bowyer puts it, "In addition to providing the greatest possible protection to its inhabitants, the city also offered the greatest opportunity to aggressive behaviour. While offering unparalleled freedom it also imposed a regulation of life which has, over the years, *become second nature to man*. Law and order supplanted brute force as the city took form around the Royal Citadel."[15]

But this shows that we already have the beginnings of a nation: a fortified city surrounded by a population which sees itself as 'belonging' to it, and whose sense of belonging is reciprocated. What must happen to make the idea more explicit is for the rural population to increase to the level at which 'our' citizens (those associated with our city) come up physically against 'theirs' (those associated with the nearest rival city), at which point a border – more or less fluid - will be established, either by convention or diplomacy or force. 'Our' population becomes a pool from which soldiers can be legitimately recruited. At this point, Anderson's 'imagined community'[16] begins to materialise: its sense of collective belonging is initially based in warfare: communal mourning, victory celebrations (which may become festivals), the identification and mythologization of heroes. To some extent, in a world of city-states something like the nation eventually emerges naturally from the notion of defensive securitisation, but it only gradually coalesces to the extent that the rivalry of Crown and

---

[15] Bowyer, Jack (1973) p180. Italics mine.
[16] Anderson, Benedict (1991)

Municipality is resolved, and its maintenance often requires proactive securitisation.

As the nation-state solidifies, differentials of wealth stabilise, and, given enough territory, these will be expressed in terms of locations and access. The means of securitisation is not ultimately firearms and fortresses *in themselves*, but the spaces they mark off from 'intrusion'. A well-organised militia – at first, local and baronial, but always ultimately tending towards an omnipresent police force - is necessary to prevent trespass, but it must be supplemented by a judicial system to punish trespass when it occurs. David Harvey probably saw this first, although Max Weber also wrote insightfully on the subject[17]: geography is always, on one level, a representation of securitisation. As Nick Hayes recently put it in the context of the English landscape: "Race, class, gender, health, income are all divisions imposed upon society by the power that operates on it; if this power is sourced in property, then the fences that divide England are not just symbols of the partition of people, but the very cause of it."[18] But of course, private property is impotent without an effective means of securitisation to support it. As Hayes goes on to point out, the English are excluded, by law of trespass, from 92% of their land and 97% of their waterways.

In any case, settled communities with strong economies and standing armies can only be developed on the basis of an effective defensive means of securitisation. The means of production must exist within some infrastructural framework of safekeeping.

We should also distinguish *attempts* at *securitisation* from the means of securitisation. The Norman invasion of England in 1066 was an attempt at securitisation; Norman forts and the Harrying of the North were the means that enabled it to succeed. The whole of human history can, in many ways, be understood

---

[17] Weber, Max (1966).
[18] Hayes, Nick (2020), p23.

as a series of attempts at securitisation by different groups, more or less successful depending on their possession of an effective means.

It is obvious that, once the means of securitisation is factored into the equation, we end up with a completely different outcome for the relations of production. The idea that those relations emerge as a straightforward function of the means of production, as nothing much more than an optimal division of labour required to effectively deploy the relevant technology, is implausible: it cannot explain social classes except on the understanding that candidates for the skilled roles within the division of labour will be rarer, thus in greater demand, and thus better remunerated, giving rise to differentials of wealth. In Marxism, this is known as the problem of 'primitive accumulation': the question of how some people, in an originary world of rough equality, manage to end up owning capital while others do not. For Adam Smith, the solution lay in the fact that some workers put in longer hours, and so earn more money, which they then invest.

Marx dismissed this explanation as 'childish', and we only need look about us to see that workers are not necessarily rewarded according to hard work or even skill.[19] And in any case, differentials of wealth can never, in themselves, explain the emergence of an owning class, who do little except live off the fruits of others' labour. As David Harvey pointed out in 2003[20], primitive accumulation may have peaked during the transition from feudalism to capitalism, but it is an ongoing process: it occurs, for example, every time a playing field is sold to private developers. And yet the 'primitive accumulators' in any society never look like hard workers or skilled tradespeople. They usually look more like thieves. Possession is nine-tenths of the

---

[19] See, eg, the 2022 Deloitte report, 'Building tomorrow's skills-based organization: jobs aren't working anymore'.
[20] In *The New Imperialism*.

law, and private property, which is supposed to be predicated on alienated labour in (the early) Marx, is simply the securitisation of significant goods by powerful elites, and has existed since ancient times.

And in fact, it is this very solution that Marx himself endorses. Primitive accumulation is the fruit of violence, effectively applied. In other words, it cannot be explained by the means of production, but only by the proactive means of securitisation: guns, swords, clubs, armies. And what is accumulated is retained by the defensive means of securitisation: guns, swords, clubs, armies, but also fortresses, palaces, banks.

More than that, it is not primarily the means of production that drives history, but the means of securitisation. It does so because the proactive and the defensive means of securitisation are locked in perpetual fecund conflict. When an effective defence is invented, an effective way of getting past it must be devised, which in turn requires an innovation in defence, and so on. In short, war drives technological innovation, and one (indirect) outcome of that will be an improvement in the means of producing food, and shelter. The other (direct) outcome will be an improvement in the means of securitisation. Obviously, the two are interlinked.

A good example of this can be found in Bowyer's analysis of the history of building, in a passage which also shows the impact of the means of securitisation on social institutions, types of informal assembly, and styles of architecture:

> "Up to the 15th century, defence was stronger than attack. The improvements in the production of cannon and the invention of the iron ball changed this... The effect of the attacker's artillery on stone walls and tiled roofs of the city was disastrous... New systems of fortification were devised with outworks, salient and

bastions in star formation, which for two centuries protected the cities of Europe. The cost of providing and maintaining these works cast a financial burden on the inhabitants which may well have contributed to the decline in living standards which ensued during this epoch. The restricting effect of the new fortifications was a planning disaster. New growth could only take place either by utilising the gardens and open spaces which were formerly so valuable as a safeguard to the health of the population, or by increasing the height of the buildings (up to 10 or 12 storeys in places such as Edinburgh). The intensive development of the art of fortification altered the pedestrian scene of the medieval city to the expanding world of the Baroque city with its long-range artillery and wheeled vehicles. The army became a new factor in city life, the barracks took the place of the medieval monastery, and the parade ground was conspicuous in the new city plan… In addition, avenues were a great military asset, not only for the rapid movement of troops from one section of the city to another, but also for contributing to the sense of power imparted by a matching column."[21]

Some readers may object, at this point, that the means of securitisation must itself be produced, and so cannot be primary: the means of production must be primary. The answer is (a) that the means of production can only be produced within a means of securitisation, so we have, at best, a circular chicken and egg situation, and (b) that most people will only come into contact with the means of production during their working hours. Throughout that time, they will be working with, and within, a system defined and conditioned by the means of

---

[21] Bowyer, Jack (1973), p185-86.

securitisation. But they will also be defined and conditioned by the means of securitisation when they get home, when they walk outdoors, when they eat and when they sleep. Mostly, they will literally bear a means of securitisation on their bodies (eg, a purse or a weapon to defend against attack). They will worry about the means of securitisation, because it is rarely perfect, and that process of concerned thinking will undoubtedly condition their self-understanding and their relationships with others. The same cannot be said of the means of production: it is nowhere near as pervasive.

Anyone who doubts this should read Robert Peckham's 2023, *Fear: An Alternative History of the World*. "Dynasties rise and fall," he writes, "religions are created, reform and break apart; modern states are born; profits are had, and markets implode; the world is made and unmade – and all, in part, because of fear and its offshoot, panic. Yet if you look up 'fear' in the index of most history books, it's doubtful you'll find it. Like the background noise in a film, it's part of the atmospherics. Something that happens incidentally, the most inaudible soundtrack of real life."[22] In another context, Germaine Greer wrote: "probably the only place a man can feel really secure is a maximum security prison."[23]

A focus on the means of securitisation allows us to bring psychology and sociology together as part of a single science, in a way that primary focus on the means of production does not. The Frankfurt School famously tried to meld Marxism and Freudian psychoanalysis, and in recent times, Slavoj Žižek has attempted the same thing, only with an emphasis on Jacques Lacan. But Freud and Lacan were arguably pseudoscientists (which is perhaps why Hannah Arendt was able to have such fun analysing the Frankfurters themselves in terms drawn from the Oedipus complex). The fact that human beings are highly

---

[22] Peckham, Robert (2023), p5.
[23] Greer, 1970, p270.

securitised in an ever-increasing number of ways under modern capitalism explains why we are so Janus-faced: simultaneously grateful for being so safe, yet acutely anxious that our safety might evaporate at any moment. The daily news produces the impression that the world outside is a dangerous place, and so we have become an 'indoor society' - which adds to our malaise. More about this later.

But even apart from all this, the primacy of the means of production, in the classical Marxist sense of the technology producing food and shelter, can be questioned. In her 2017, *Doughnut Economics*, Kate Raworth follows feminists like Neva Goodwin, Angela Davis and Silvia Federici in observing that:

> "Mainstream economic theory is obsessed with the productivity of waged labour while skipping right over the unpaid work that makes it all possible, as feminist economists have made clear for decades. That work is known by many names: unpaid caring work, the reproductive economy, the love economy, the second economy. However, as economist Neva Goodwin has pointed out, far from being secondary, it is actually the 'core economy' and it comes first every day, sustaining the essentials of family and social life."[24]

Nevertheless, all the tasks Raworth lists under this economy – 'making breakfast, washing the dishes, tidying the house, shopping for groceries, teaching the children to work and to share, washing clothes, caring for elderly parents, emptying the rubbish bins, collecting kids from school, helping the neighbours, making the dinner, sweeping the floor, and lending an ear' – require an effective means of securitisation if they are

---

[24] Raworth, Kate (2017), p79.

to make a difference. Once again, the means of securitisation is primary.

In his 1975, *Discipline and Punish*, Michel Foucault describes the societal transition, in the sixteenth and seventeenth centuries, from feudalism to what he calls a 'disciplinary' regime. Under the former, "Individualisation is greatest where sovereignty is exercised and in the higher echelons of power. The more one possesses power or privilege, the more one is marked as an individual… In a disciplinary regime, on the other hand, individualisation is 'descending': as power becomes more anonymous and more functional, those on whom it is exercised tend to become more individualised." What we gradually see is an increasing preponderance of fine-grained, military-type surveillance and control in schools, hospitals, prisons, and, of course, barracks.

Foucault does not ask where this comes from, although it can undoubtedly be re-described without loss as an intensification of the social means of securitisation; the securitisation of what we will call Productive Human Bodies. Barbara Ehrenreich, in her 2007, *Dancing in the Streets*, describes 'what looks, in today's terms like an epidemic of depression' occurring at the same time[25], which common sense suggests must be related.

The likely ultimate source of all this was the printing press: a way of securitising texts by reproducing them in such quantities that they would gain greater permanence. From that, came the Protestant Reformation and the religious wars that accompanied and followed it, above all (for the emergence of the 'disciplinary' society) the Thirty Years' War, one of the most violent and traumatic events in the continent's history. Suddenly, there were two camps in Europe whose intense mutual antagonism dwarfed anything the class system of the time could produce. No one was entirely safe: Protestants and

---

[25] Ehrenreich, Barbara (2008), p129f.

Catholics could be, and were, 'fifth columnists' in each others' countries.

As part of the same effect, as Benedict Anderson pointed out, the invention of printing gave rise to modern nation-states: firstly, by creating "unified fields of exchange and communication below Latin and above the spoken vernaculars"; secondly, by giving a "new fixity to language" which "helped to build that image of antiquity so central to the subjective idea of the nation"; thirdly, by creating "languages-of-power different to the older administrative vernaculars."[26] The nation-state is perhaps the chief means of securitisation in the capitalist world, as will be discussed below.

All the proximal factors behind Foucault's 'disciplinary' society are violent. In addition to the Thirty Years' War: the see-saw movement in England between Henry VIII and William III, and the accompanying threat from Spain; the Anglo-French War of 1627-29; the British 'Wars of the Three Kingdoms' between 1639 and 1653; the Nine Years' War of 1688 to 1697, and so on. All of which must have been alarming enough, but since Protestants and Catholics could be living in each other's midst, the need for the most exhaustive surveillance, and hence securitisation, of all societies everywhere must have seemed indispensable. In this context, it is interesting to note how often Foucault's own analysis mentions the intensity with which religious orthodoxy was scrutinised ('whoever did not have his rosary' (176), 'when a pupil has not retained the catechism from the previous day' (179), 'a pupil may be given four or six catechism questions to copy out as an imposition' (180), 'catechism in the morning' (186), 'whether they know their catechism and the prayers' (211), 'knowledge of prayers' (212), and so on).

---

[26] Anderson, Benedict (1991), p46-47.

Of course, once that 'discipline' (to return to Foucault's term) had been successfully imposed and accepted, and religious tensions had calmed down – beginning at the end of the eighteenth century and ending in 1815 with the defeat of Napoleon - the pacified, effectively securitised result constituted fertile conditions for the transformation of industrial production to power full steam ahead.

A theory in which history is driven by the means of securitisation rather than the means of production has no difficulty in explaining Acton's 'problem of legality': laws are institutional undertakings/threats to bring the means of securitisation to bear in specified circumstances, and since that means is prior to the means of production, of course laws can be too. It also has no difficulty accounting for Karl Polanyi's claim that, for most of human history, the economy has been subject to the broader requirements of society.[27] Indeed, the only circumstances in which the economy would drive history entirely unrestricted by politics would be under the kind of anarcho-capitalism favoured by Friedrich Hayek and Milton Friedman.

Above all, it explains something that appears in Marx, but which he underestimated: the 'fetter' (*fessel*), in which the ruling powers of one economic system try to prevent the classes constituting its successor from taking charge. Thus, in *The German Ideology:*

> "In the place of an earlier form of intercourse, which has become a fetter, a new one is put, corresponding to the more developed productive forces and, hence, to the advanced mode of the self-activity of individuals - a form which in its turn becomes a fetter and is then

---

[27] "The outstanding discovery of recent historical and anthropological research is that man's economy, as a rule, is submerged in his social relationships" Polanyi (2024), p53.

replaced by another. Since these conditions correspond at every stage to the simultaneous development of the productive forces, their history is at the same time the history of the evolving productive forces taken over by each new generation, and is, therefore, the history of the development of the forces of the individuals themselves."

And in the 1859 Preface:

"At a certain stage of development, the material productive forces of society come into conflict with the existing relations of production or – this merely expresses the same thing in legal terms – with the property relations within the framework of which they have operated hitherto. From forms of development of the productive forces these relations turn into their fetters. Then begins an era of social revolution. The changes in the economic foundation lead sooner or later to the transformation of the whole immense superstructure."

The fetter is a deployment of the means of securitisation – an impending revolution could best be stopped using police surveillance, armed military obstruction, and prisons - and, contra Marx, sometimes it may constitute a more or less permanent brake on social development.[28] It would be difficult,

---

[28] Polanyi discusses what is clearly a closely related phenomenon in *The Great Transformation:* "The theory of 'survivals' was sometimes adduced as an explanation according to which functionless institutions or traits may continue to exist by virtue of inertia. Yet it would be truer to say that no institution ever survives its function – when it seems to do so, it is because it serves in some other function or functions, which need not include the original one. Thus feudalism and landed conservatism retained their strength as long as they served a purpose that happened to be that of restricting the disastrous effects of the mobilisation of land." (2024, p213)

if not impossible, to deduce the different political systems of each of the current 195 nations in the world from an examination of the means of production within their borders, but a grasp of their means of securitisation, and especially the frequency and geographic scope of its deployment, would give a fairly accurate sense of their nature.

Affordable, effective securitisation gave us individualism, and eventually social atomism, with all its attendant mental health problems.

The Hundred Years War began with archers and ended with riflemen. The First World War began with dispatch riders and cavalry detachments and ended with field radios and tanks. The means of securitisation is an animal that reproduces by eating itself.

Productive Human Bodies

A crucial aspect of the means of securitisation is always the securitisation of what Marx called Labour Power, but which we shall call Productive Human Bodies. ('Labour Power' is too abstract: it hints at a precision of measurement that does not exist in practice). As we mentioned at the beginning of this chapter, at its most basic level, the means of production is purely biological: the Earth, the life-cycle of crops, the regularity of rain. But humans need to harness that if they are to survive. Once they do so methodically, they mostly settle into geographically fixed communities, and they build places to live. Besides necessity, they probably perceive this first and foremost as a matter of relative comfort and convenience, but it is also a matter of self-securitisation.

Which will usually require other-securitisation: in more complex settled societies, tools - including slaves, where they appear - need to be locked away, and/or locked out when they are not being used, farmers and their dependents need somewhere (like a walled city) to flee to when an invading army arrives. Productive Human Bodies are perhaps the most precious resource a community has, and though they may be brutally mistreated, they cannot be allowed to die off *en masse*.

But self-securitisation and other-securitisation pull in slightly different directions. As soon as the individual has achieved self-securitisation, providing he is not subject to restrictions imposed externally by certain kinds of other-securitisation, he might well ask himself what he can do to improve his living accommodation, especially if he has to spend a lot of time there. Thus, the house takes on a double aspect in which its function as a means of self-securitisation can be rivalled by its function as a status symbol and a source of luxury.

So private property enters the equation, and we begin to see the rise of a middle class. More about this in chapter 4.

2. Capitalism

Considerations of Terminology

Anyone acquainted with modern critical thought will inevitably notice that, for many authors, blaming a problem on capitalism is like waving a magic wand, in that it instantly terminates the need for analysis. The faults of capitalism are supposed to be so obvious that nothing more needs to be said, and in that guise, it is a disguised rallying cry, the sort of thing a philosophical Emotivist might recognise.

Accordingly, a more impartial spectator might well wonder what we are talking about when we talk about capitalism. We can distinguish at least seven current usages:

(A) 'Capitalism' is used as a descriptive, would-be scientific term to specify *a manufacturing process:* namely, the one described in chapter 4 of the first volume of Marx's *Capital*: "The exact form of [the capitalist] process is therefore $M-C-M'$, where $M' = M + \Delta M =$ the original sum advanced, plus an increment. This increment or excess over the original value I call 'surplus-value.' The value originally advanced, therefore, not only remains intact while in circulation, but adds to itself a surplus-value or expands itself. It is this movement that converts it into capital."[29]

(B) 'Capitalism' is used as a descriptive, would-be scientific term to specify *an entire economic system* predominantly characterised by the process outlined in (A).

---

[29] At: https://www.marxists.org/archive/marx/works/1867-c1/ch04.htm.

(C) 'Capitalism' is used as *a moralistic term* to appraise the economic system described in (B), above. Evaluations can be positive or negative, but most of the positive ones are apologetic (in the technical sense) reactions to the negative; the negative is primary.

(D) 'Capitalism' is used as a vague moralistic synonym for (i) *large multinational companies* and/or (ii) *the super-rich:* Amazon/Jeff Bezos and Tesla, Inc./Elon Musk exemplify 'capitalism' in this sense. Small businesses and their owners often escape censure, even though the latter may employ workers who create 'surplus value'. (D) is arguably behind the slogan 'We are the 99%'. It differs from (C) above in being purely evaluative: in (C), an evaluation supervenes on a perceived fact.

(E) 'Capitalism' is used as a vague moralistic synonym for *the collective shortcomings of the present age.* In this form, it can be blamed for all social ills, regardless of whether the accuser can demonstrate a connection. Thus conceived, it functions more as a proper noun than a common noun.

(F) 'Capitalism' is an item in the discourse of *radical chic.* An individual publicly claims to be 'anti-capitalist' as a means of self-advertisement. Its use here is essentially egoistic.

(G) As in Marx, 'capitalism' is a synonym for 'bourgeoisie', the middle classes. The word 'bourgeoisie' is largely absent from leftist discourse nowadays, and few thinkers consciously use the term 'capitalist' in this manner anymore. More about that later.

In addition to A-G, we have historical divisions of capitalism, for example, Werner Sombart's four stages: 'proto-', 'early', 'high' and 'late'. The notion of 'late capitalism' (*Spätkapitalismus*) – which entered the English language via

38

Ernest Mandel in the 1970s - has, of course, been very influential. The Frankfurt School's notion of 'advanced capitalism' is similar, but not wholly identical.

And we also have synchronous divisions of capitalism. To give just a few examples - industrial capitalism, finance capitalism, eco-capitalism, state capitalism, print capitalism, venture capitalism, crony capitalism, bailout capitalism, biopolitical capitalism, disaster capitalism, vulture capitalism, communicative capitalism, semiocapitalism, vector capitalism, oligarchic capitalism, state-guided capitalism, big-firm capitalism, entrepreneurial capitalism, anarcho-capitalism, crack-up capitalism, surveillance capitalism – which are not, by any means, mutually exclusive categories, but whose entanglement may be impossible to unpick with any precision. There is a sizeable academic industry, reminiscent of medieval scholasticism, devoted to the precise taxonomy of capitalism.

Despite all this, it is rare for people to find themselves at cross-purposes when they talk critically about 'capitalism' - which may suggest that the purpose of such talk is to signal that the speakers belong on a particular political wavelength. In many, but not all cases, it functions as a kind of tribal password.

Part of the problem is that, in classical Marxism, capitalism was one side of a dualistic conception of social relations: "society is more and more splitting up into two great hostile camps, into two great classes directly facing each other: Bourgeoisie and Proletariat."[30] The proletariat was, of course, the industrial working classes.

But in the 21st century, the industrial working classes have largely disappeared as a significant political force: in their place we are often presented with a broad spectrum of different disadvantaged or excluded groups that some leftists hope to meld into an anti-capitalist coalition, but which share no

---

[30] Marx, K and Engels, F (1967), p80.

unifying name – and perhaps very little intrinsic overlap. Added to which there is the difficulty of specifying – at least, for everyday polemical purposes - exactly how it is that each of these groups, separately or in combination, is adversely impacted by capitalism. It can be done, but it is not so glaringly obvious as it was for the proletariat in 1848.

Capitalism's '-ism' suffix compounds the difficulty, but perhaps also points the way out of the maze. It implicitly incorporates the term into a family whose members would include communism, socialism, anarchism, Calvinism, Hinduism, atheism, conservatism – in short, a family of ideological belief systems. The capital*ist* is primary here, as is the Calvinist, the atheist, etc: the *person* who believes in the moral and practical integrity of the thought-system in question.

In some ways, this *is* an accurate characterisation of 'capitalism', however: it really *is* an ideology. Like all ideologies it serves to both disclose and conceal the underlying reality of which it is the distorted expression. The disclosure consists in there being nothing intrinsically unjust about capitalism as outlined in (1) above; the concealment consists in (1) bearing hardly any resemblance to the underlying state of affairs.

(1) Capitalism's Supposed Modernity

Traditionally defined as the extraction of surplus value, there is nothing intrinsically *modern* about capitalism. In the first half of the twentieth century, Sombart identified a phenomenon which he called 'proto-capitalism', which ran from the close of the Middle Ages until the Industrial Revolution, but in fact, capitalism is much older than that. The vineyard owner in chapter 20 of Matthew's Gospel is recognisably a capitalist. And 'proto-capitalism' hardly differs from capitalism *per se*, except insofar as it is not widespread.

In practice, capitalism has been a more or less permanent presence in complex societies since ancient times. It occurs wherever there is money, because money always has the potential to be transformed into capital; when a farmer hires labourers and sells his produce, he is engaging in capitalism. Farmers and money have not existed together at all periods of history, but their occasional simultaneity goes back a long way. For that reason, capitalism has been a feature of much of written history.

Marx himself seemed to recognise that, and also to appreciate the intimate connection between money and capitalism. In the 1844 Manuscripts, he wrote:

> "Money is the alienated ability of mankind... It transforms fidelity into infidelity, love into hate, hate into love, virtue into vice, vice into virtue, servant into master, master into servant, idiocy into intelligence, and intelligence into idiocy. Since money, as the existing and active concept of value, confounds and confuses all things, it is the general confounding and confusing of all things – the world upside-down – the confounding and confusing of all natural and human qualities."[31]

In general, communists have been chary of underlining the interdependence of capitalism and money. The idea that capitalism, as an economic system, might one day be superseded strikes many people as just about conceivable; the idea that complex societies such as ours might no longer need money seems, at least to the layperson, less credible - although it may not be impossible.[32]

---

[31] Marx, Karl (1977), p124.
[32] Cf. eg, Holten, Matthew (2022), Nelson, Anitra (2022), Project Society After Money (2020)

This is partly because money is only, and has always been, the means of securitisation in abstract form. You use it to buy a way of protecting yourself, or arming yourself, or insuring yourself, or binding others to you, or symbolically elevating yourself, or securing a privileged route (either literally, from one geographical location to another, or figuratively, through life). Money is always, primarily, about *safety*, real or imagined. Its secondary uses have to do with bodily necessities and are such as any hunter-gatherer could fulfil.

Marxists, as everyone knows, see capitalism as having been preceded by 'the feudal system'. The idea is that vassals were exploited by lords of manors; the lord gave them his protection (up to a point); in return, they gave him fealty and a part of their produce.

The whole thing was essentially a system of securitisation: if Lynn White is correct,[33] it began with the invention of the stirrup, which was a device to maximise the potential of existing means of securitisation such as the lance, the trained horse and the suit of armour. In feudalism's developed form, the vassal would fight for the lord, and, in return, the lord would shield him from external aggression. The economy was organised to facilitate this arrangement, and its precise character was thus derivative; it supervened on the social relations, rather than the other way around. As Bloch says:

> "One of the most distinctive characteristics of feudal societies was the virtual identity of the class of chiefs with the class of professional warriors serving in the only way that then seemed effective, that is as heavily armed horsemen … Land itself was valued above all because it enabled a lord to provide himself with 'men' by supplying the remuneration for them. We want

---

[33] *Medieval Technology and Social Change* (Oxford 1966)

lands, said in effect the Norman lords who refused the gifts of jewels, arms, and horses offered by their duke. And they added among themselves: 'It will this be possible for us to maintain many knights, and the duke will no longer be able to do so.'"[34]

And Strayer concurs: "It is perfectly legitimate to speak of feudal society, or the feudal age, if we remember that it was the political-military structure that made the society and the age feudal."[35]

The explanation for the demise of feudalism is almost certainly to be found in the invention and development of artillery and standing armies. The Western cannon was invented in the early 1300s, with the Loshult gun appearing shortly afterwards, and the matchlock in approximately 1400; the French king, Charles VII recruited the first Christian standing army since ancient Roman times in the 1430s, and although it was originally equipped with traditional medieval armaments, after the decisive defeat of the English at Formigny in 1450 - in which culverins played a crucial role – guns and professional militiamen came together, and the fate of feudalism was sealed. Feudal securitisation had to a large extent been based on the horse, the suit of armour, the bow and arrow, the sword, siege engines, the fortress, and vassalage (Block points out that "a salary... was out of the question"[36]). Cannons and muskets and salaried soldiery gradually rendered all those obsolete.

---

[34] Bloch, Marc (1965), p444.
[35] Strayer, Joseph R (1965), p13. See also Stephenson, Carl (1956), p14: "By 'feudalism', we properly refer to the peculiar association of vassalage with fief-holding that was developed in the Carolingian Empire and thence spread to other parts of Europe. Insofar as this association was effected for governmental purposes, feudalism was essentially political. It should not be thought of as a necessary, or even usual stage, in economic history. Although feudal institutions presupposed certain agrarian arrangements, the latter were not themselves feudal."
[36] Ibid., p446.

The truth is that capitalism was lying low throughout the Middle Ages – as it has been for most of human history - waiting for its chance. Capitalism throughout was essentially a rival system of securitisation. First of all, it was primarily defensive: in the medieval period, for example, the accrual of gold would have allowed the capitalist to escape apprehension at short notice, to ransom himself or to obtain a pardon, perhaps even – if he could advance stealthily via the official channels – build a fortress of his own. But mostly, he would have had to hide his wealth, because the established powers were likely to see any hint of 'conspicuous consumption' as a veiled threat. He did not want to end up like Jacques de Molay and the Knights Templar, arrested by an envious king on false charges, then tortured and burnt at the stake. Throughout the Middle Ages, anti-Semitism was a symbolic expression of the dangers facing the too-brazen capitalist, re-directed at a minority group by racism.

Nevertheless, capitalism made gradual encroachments on the feudal system. As Ganshof tells us:

> "From the thirteenth century onwards, and no doubt even before that date, men of bourgeois origin were acquiring *fiefs* side by side with the nobility; they became so numerous that in France an unusually heavy form of payment known as *droit de franc-fief* was customarily exacted on such occasions. The acquisition of a *fief* was a regular way in which a man of the middle or lower classes could hope to rise in the social scale."[37]

With the arrival of firearms and standing armies, the rising bourgeoisie finally gained the power to challenge the feudal system. Henceforth, anyone with wealth could buy and equip an army; ties of fealty and grants of land had become irrelevant.

---

[37] Ganshof, FL (1964), p168-69.

The first English standing army was raised by Parliament in 1645, specifically to abolish in some of the excesses of feudalism. Bloch tells us that in England, "the first of the seventeenth-century Revolutions abolished all distinctions between tenure by knight-service and other forms of tenure."[38] And Shoard reminds us that, "Oliver Cromwell's Parliament was dominated by landowners. Half the members returned for the Midlands, for example, had been fined for depopulation [of the commons] or belonged to families which had recently been fined. And it soon became apparent that the English Revolution was to have the effect of strengthening the grip of the landowner over the landless."[39]

According to Ganshof, "Feudal institutions lasted in Europe until the end of the *Ancien Régime* and in some countries, elements of them survived into the nineteenth and even the twentieth centuries."[40] Nevertheless, the (false) idea that capitalism is an entirely modern phenomenon is worth remarking on, because it helps bolster the myth that it has single-handedly delivered immense benefits to humanity: massively better living standards, hugely improved health care, security, life-expectations, etc. A sceptic might unravel that claim by focusing on the suspicious fact that the birth, growth and maturity of 'capitalism', in this story, exactly coincides with the birth, growth and maturity of modern science - which might easily enable it (if it so desired) to take full credit for the achievements of the latter. Our sceptic might also note that Isaac Newton was not a capitalist, nor was Gregor Mendel, nor was Max Planck, nor was Albert Einstein, nor was Neils Bohr, nor were any of the great mathematicians of the modern era. By the same token, John D Rockefeller, Andrew Carnegie and Cornelius Vanderbilt made no contribution to the history of

---

[38] Bloch, Marc (1965), p448.
[39] Shoard, Marion (1987), p53.
[40] Ganshof, FL (1964), p168.

technology, and could have achieved nothing without the scientists they kept firmly in the background.[41] She might well conclude that we are not better off thanks to anything capitalism gave us – capitalists have always, and usually only, worked for themselves – but simply because scientists learned to manipulate the forces of nature.

The reason the left has had difficulty accepting any of this is partly down to a disastrous wrong-turn it took in 1947, with Max Horkheimer and Theodor W Adorno's *Dialectic of Enlightenment*. The authors swallowed the conflation of capitalism and science wholesale, and launched a sustained attack on Enlightenment rationalism.

> "Enlightenment stands in the same relationship to things as the dictator to human beings. He knows them to the extent that he can manipulate them. The man of science knows things to the extent that he can make them. Their 'in-itself' becomes 'for him.' In their transformation, the essence of things is revealed as always the same, a substrate of domination. This identity constitutes the unity of nature."[42]

---

[41] Related to this is a certain default public credibility concerning the claims of big capitalists to be high-achieving scientists: it used to be thought that Elon Musk was an expert in mechanical engineering, rocket science and AI. We know better partly because he made himself so unpopular that people began digging.

[42] Horkheimer, M and Adorno, T (2002), p6. The ultimate cause of this enmity might be traced to a particularly bruising encounter Horkheimer and his colleagues had with Sidney Hook and the 'New York Intellectuals' in 1936 and 1937. As Stuart Jeffries notes, "The championing of science as a tool for liberation rather than a tool of oppression was inimical to Horkheimer and his colleagues. Hook was insufficiently dialectical. Hook retorted to these charges by sarcastically asking Horkheimer and Marcuse what doctrines are dialectically true but scientifically false, or scientifically true but dialectically false. For Hook, the Frankfurt school's dystopian perspective on science was unwarranted." Jeffries, Stuart (2017) p202.

It did not occur to either thinker that something like the means of securitisation might be behind the working classes' failure to mount a revolution; instead, they thought state intervention had eliminated the structural tension between the means of production and the relations of production, making the masses more vulnerable to cultural manipulation. The inevitable conclusion of the Enlightenment was fascism, because reason had reduced the world to a collection of pure, mechanical, well-behaved and manageable categories. So when fascists celebrated the 'self-destruction' of the Enlightenment, they were only doing so 'hypocritically'.[43]

This was highly convenient, because none of the Frankfurt school to which Horkheimer and Adorno belonged were scientists; they were cultural critics. *The Dialectic of Enlightenment* opened an entire unmined seam of critical enquiry premised in the supposed identity of capitalism and science, and whose heirs include Paul Feyerabend, Michel Foucault, John Gray, Alasdair Macintyre, Luce Irigaray and much of Postmodernism.

The problem with demonising what some thinkers have called 'the Enlightenment project' is that, in the end, it has to use rational arguments to make any sort of case at all.[44] Appealing to the indisputable fact that some Enlightenment thinkers were flawed or inconsistent (turning a blind eye to slavery, for example) falls into the trap of treating 'enlightenment reason' as a thing, fixed forever in its instantiation in particular historical persons at a particular time and place. Isaac Newton was an alchemist, but that does not invalidate his laws of motion. Reason and science remain among humankind's best hopes for a better world – if used rightly. In themselves, they are neither

---

[43] Ibid., pxiv, 253.
[44] As Jeffries notes, Horkheimer and Adorno were "compelled to use the tools" of the Enlightenment to critique it. "Their book was, among other things, a virtuoso performance of immanent critique, one that used reason to critique the categorical reason of the Enlightenment." (2017) p235-36)

bad nor good. In any case, capitalism and science are different things.

(2) The Supposed Injustice of Capitalism, on the Marxist Model

An argument can be constructed to the effect that, on the Marxist model, there is nothing intrinsically unjust about capitalism. The model itself is well summed up by Erik Olin Wright:

> "Workers are paid a wage which covers the cost of production and their labour power; capitalists receive an income from the sale of the commodities produced by workers. The difference in these quantities constitutes the exploitative surplus appropriated by capitalists."[45]

A capitalist is someone who hires others to produce a commodity, which he or she then sells for a profit. The capitalist pays the others for their labour power; the profit comes from the value added to it - ie, from the 'surplus value' - by those others. To put it in the language of morality, the worker is allegedly 'exploited' by the capitalist.

But it is obvious that the entire process could be wholly consensual and entirely fair: the capitalist will, after all, provide the location and the raw materials, as well as gambling that the finished product will sell. The workers may not want that level of commitment. True, in practice, the process *may* be exploitative - the workers may have no choice but to sell their labour power – but equally, they may *not* be in that position.[46]

---

[45] Roemer, John (Ed.) (1986), p124.
[46] It is worth noting that, arguably, on John Locke's account of the legitimacy of property in *The Second Treatise of Government* (1690), the situation *is* unjust: the workers have 'mixed' their labour with the raw materials to create the commodity

But this is far from the whole picture. Marx thinks he can discern what is wrong with capitalism by reductionism: he imagines a single capitalist investing a single sum of money, M, producing a single commodity, C, and selling it at a profit, M^1. The problem is that capitalism creates a system and it can only be understood in holistic terms. The capitalist rarely embarks on a commercial enterprise in a vacuum. To fully succeed, he needs to drive his rivals out of the market: simply taking a share of the market is never a prudent long-term aim, because the competition can always come back. He must go for broke. Ultimately, he has to aim – whether he realises it or not (in some ways we are dealing with a kind of 'postulate of the capitalist enterprise' here, analogous to Kant's three 'postulates of the moral life') – to deprive his competitors of their livelihoods.

But surely all sides know what is at stake in the contest? To the extent that their consent is fully informed, no one has the right to interfere. It is like a game.

It is not a team game, however, and there are no intrinsic rules. If the capitalist is to survive for any length of time, at some point he will have to exaggerate the virtues of his product, destabilise his competitors, cut corners when it comes to his environmental impact, conceal any duplicity, charge the customer as much as he thinks he can get away with. Morally good capitalists do survive, but they are like mutations whose novel qualities make them less fit for their environment. In the long run, they tend to go under. In small capitalist enterprises, the deceit will be small, and perhaps society at large will think it worth tolerating in order to get access to certain non-essential goods.

However, Adam Smith's 'perfect competition' does not exist. Competition means that there will be winners and losers, and the winners will become stronger. Monopolies or near-

---

in a way that the capitalist has not. They have acquired property rights over it. The capitalist has not.

monopolies will always be implicit in the system, and regulatory bodies can always be suborned. Capitalism is a system of different-sized enterprises in which real power lies at the top, where the enterprises are largest. There, the damage can be, and is, very significant indeed. It is why we are living in an era of planetary destruction.[47]

Unfortunately, capitalism is a system whose nature cannot be discerned by examining its inchoate form, any more than one can discern the nature of a killer from his infant school report. Capitalism is a half-integrated, half-internecine system with millions of players; it infuses the whole of society, and its net influence there is almost always malign.

It saturates society with the overriding goal of *becoming rich*, which is one of the most destructive of all life-purposes. It ruins otherwise creative talents. In a capitalist society, the natural world gradually deteriorates and citizens see the goal of life in terms of ownership of prestigious, non-essential material goods. To get the 'best' of those things, one usually has to cheat somewhere along the line.

We are now in a position to give our own definition of capitalism. It is *an inadvertent economic system premised on the private pursuit of unlimited monetary wealth by means, at least to begin with, of the scalable production of commodities, in the form either of goods or services, and the hypothetical perfectibility of the means of securitisation.*

It is 'inadvertent' because the circumstances which put capitalists into competition with each other arise not from within the individual capitalist enterprise, but from forces of attraction which have their origin outside: competition always arrives as a spectre at the feast.

---

[47] According to Naomi Klein in *The Shock Doctrine: The Rise of Disaster Capitalism* (Penguin 2008), modern capitalism deliberately provokes international catastrophes which become market opportunities.

The clause 'at least to begin with' appears because, after a significant period of success, the capitalist may increasingly deploy alternative means of accumulating wealth, some of which (like buy-outs and buy-ins, share dealing, property investment and tax avoidance) lie within the law, others of which (like false accounting, antitrust violations and tax evasion) lie outside it. The -ism of 'capitalism' asserts the capitalist's claimed right to make an infinite amount of money (and thus accrue an infinite amount of power over others) as a consequence of a finite set of achievements: it involves a belief, explicit or not.

The 'hypothetical perfectibility of the means of securitisation' appears because the pursuit of unlimited wealth is not worth embarking on if one cannot retain it with complete confidence. For this reason, banks, safes, money laundering schemes, police stations, prisons, and tax havens are not an adjunct to capitalism, they are an integral part of it.

The superiority of this definition of capitalism to any that sees it in terms of relations between the worker (W) and the owner of the means of production (O) can be demonstrated thus: if all the workers in such a system were to be replaced by self-replicating, self-repairing machines (M), then, on the W-O model, capitalism would have ended.

For this reason, we are better off characterising the problem of capitalism in terms of *damage* than exploitation. In the M-O world, where W is excluded, there is arguably no exploitation, because O and W need not even meet. But there will always be damage. Why? Because, on our definition, capitalism is 'premised on the private pursuit of unlimited monetary wealth'. Money is a form of power (and both are reducible to access to the means of securitisation); to the extent that an individual pursues unlimited quantities of it, he or she is pursuing unlimited power. But two people cannot have unlimited power, since each would act as a check on the other. For any one person to have unlimited power, everyone else must be defenceless. But no one will voluntarily consent to become defenceless. Hence capitalism must always, at some point, inflict damage on others; and the more powerful the capitalist becomes, the greater the damage.

Hopefully, the reader can see what was meant, above, by the claim that capitalism's '-ism' suffix points the way to its definition. The capital*ist* is primary, because capitalism is premised on the hypothetical possibility – which is also an ideal – of monopoly. Ultimately, there can only be one winner, and capitalism calls individuals to become that winner.

It should be noted that this idea of capitalism as essentially monopolistic rather than competitive is not new: it appears in Ferdinand Braudel's *Civilization and Capitalism, 15th-18th Century*, the first part of which appeared in 1967, as well as in Sweezy and Baran's 1966, *Monopoly Capitalism*. But to some extent, it is obvious.

In a rational universe, clothing, food, shelter and transport would probably be matters of an excluded middle (clothes are either serviceable or they are not; food is either nutritious or it is not, and so on). Under capitalism, we have, instead, degrees of prestige, the highest of which is always prohibitively expensive. The top end of this particular ladder is a multi-variegated paradise. A world in which everyone is identical, but their possessions vary widely in shape, texture and affect is supposed to be vastly superior to one in which everyone is broadly unique, but whose possessions look and feel similar. Or to put it another way, the adventure of 'we' is exchanged for the socially approved production of envy in others.

We should note that capitalism in its modern form only became possible by continual improvements in the means of securitisation. The lockable factory building was amongst the first of these, without which the cotton gins and spinning jennies of the first Industrial Revolution would have been mere curiosities. Nowadays, every third person seems to be a mini-capitalist, for which we have to thank encrypted passwords and 2-factor authentication.

We should not, however, conclude from this that being a capitalist is in any way 'natural'. Capitalism is a game[48], and like all games, it is addictive: in a world where the moral solipsism on which it is premised pervades everything and infects all values, it is a game many people 'want' to keep playing – to the extent that we can hardly imagine a world without it.

The Securitisation of Society: Individuals, Nations and Beyond

For Marxists, modern capitalism began with the Industrial Revolution, and was the chief driver of that revolution. Individual entrepreneurs built factories, hired workers and made profits. Central to all this was the means of production, which the capitalists built and, in the nineteenth century, were gradually bringing to fruition. "Constant revolutionising of production," Marx says, "uninterrupted disturbance of all social conditions, everlasting uncertainty and agitation distinguish the bourgeois epoch from all earlier ones."[49]

Our own interpretation, which makes the means of securitisation primary, will naturally be different. What Max Weber called, 'The iron cage of capitalism' still begins with the Industrial Revolution, but, in addition to the means of production, the significant factors are, *inter alia*, factory

---

[48] Milton Friedman: "the social responsibility of business [is]… to increase its profits so long as it stays within *the rules of the game*" (New York Times 1970, italics added). Obviously, this cannot serve as a definition of capitalism (and Friedman did not intend it to), because capitalism can perfectly well exist outside the law. The mass production of heroin and fentanyl for recreational users and addicts is clearly a capitalist enterprise, and to make it a success, sometimes the business owners may have to kill those who stand in its way.

[49] Marx, K and Engels, E (1967), p83.

buildings, prisons, freight trains, the rise of an organised police force, strongboxes, machine guns and banks.[50] The railways are pivotal, and in order to appreciate the difference between history as we are presenting it, and history in the Marxian conception, one merely need ask: in what way can the steam train (or any other) be considered a part of the means of production? Perhaps as a necessary precondition? But that would not make it a part, rather a precursor. Or maybe the means of production can only be understood as a totality, within which some components are non-productive? Only, that seems to cast the net too wide. (Are window panes a part of the means of production? Are restaurants?) In fact, it is difficult to come up with a way of including many functionally central items without overextending the boundaries of the term 'means of production'.

Transportation made a big difference to the product of production. It meant it could be generated in unlimited quantities, and shipped anywhere, and its market need never dry up. So railways and merchant container ships became integral to capitalism. The ultimate expression of early modern capitalism - towards which it was always tending - was Fordism. In short, capitalism is characterised by an emphasis on the product of production in which the product of production becomes ideally infinite and thus capable of generating infinite wealth. It is the pursuit and securitisation by private individuals of significantly disproportional output on the basis of an increasingly frictionless mobility of supposed unlimited quantities of goods or money.

---

[50] In *Spaces of Global Capitalism*, David Harvey says, "Appropriating surpluses produced by others or seeking command over those natural conditions that permit the easy production of surpluses has been a long-standing human practice. The only interesting questions are: who gets to do the appropriating, how much surplus can be appropriated, and how does the surplus get used?" This misses the vital question: once appropriated, how is the surplus secured? The answer would be of interest to anyone who has ever studied, eg, the Brink's-Mat robbery.

Prior to the Industrial Revolution, the primary means of production was what we have called the non-human means of production: the natural growth of plants and animals, augmented at the second level by slaughtering, harvesting, milling, salting, smoking, cooking, and so on. But the land was always insecure. The Norman Forest Laws made poaching a far more serious offence than it had been under the Anglo-Saxons, nevertheless, poachers often enjoyed great success. Jacques Le Goff mentions "the silent guerrilla warfare of looting on the lord's lands, poaching in his forests, burning crops."[51] The 'Black Act' of 1723 made poaching punishable by hanging. And Michael Stockdale tells us that, "Since the Middle Ages the English have tried implementing, at one time or another, almost every law that could be imagined for the taking and harvesting of wildlife. The penalty for violations of these laws have ranged from a fine, prison, mutilation, transportation, to even death."[52]

The intrinsic insecurity of the land was partly solved by enclosing it, thus providing one of the pre-conditions of the Industrial Revolution. As Karl Polanyi says:

> "In retrospect, nothing could be clearer than the Western European trend of economic progress which aimed at eliminating an artificially maintained uniformity of agricultural technique, intermixed strips, and the primitive institution of the common. As to England, it is certain that the development of the woollen industry was an asset to the country, leading, as it did, to the establishment of the cotton industry – that vehicle of the Industrial Revolution."[53]

---

[51] Le Goff, Jacques (1964), p373.
[52] Stockdale, Michael (1993). Online at
https://seafwa.org/sites/default/files/journal-articles/STOCKDALE-732-739.pdf
[53] Polanyi (2024), p43.

The train and the factory building, perhaps the final expressions of the enclosures, radically foreclosed the opportunities for theft. Once the raw materials can be brought securely to a walled construction, their transformation into commodities can be undertaken in a relatively impregnable setting, which, once the workers leave, can be locked. Those commodities can then be securely transferred to wagons for distant markets. Warded locks had been around since Roman times, but the medieval period saw a huge advance, in the form of keys, and the beginning of the Industrial Revolution was marked by an explosion of new locksmithing technology: the Bramah lock in 1784, the 'double acting' lever tumbler lock in 1778, the Chubb detector lock in 1818. Improved building robustness, through the widespread use of cast iron, and a thoroughgoing securitisation of the public imagination using methods described by Foucault in *Discipline and Punish* served equally to underwrite the new era.

The factory was not restricted, as, for example, the medieval mill had been, to sourcing raw materials in the immediate locality; thanks again to the railways, such materials could be brought in from anywhere. To cap it all, the factory machines themselves could be reproduced to exact specifications and installed securely in any geographical location where there happened to be cheap labour. As endogenous growth theory discovered over a hundred years later, it was the *idea* of a factory that was important.

With this vastly improved securitisation of the means of production came a vast increase in the product of production, and thus, in capital, which could be secured in bank vaults and defended, if necessary, by personnel with guns. In the long run, we see the almost exponential growth of wealth, as both ends of the chain - the means of production and the product of production - are fully securitised. We are now in the age of modern capital, which henceforth proceeds according to its own logic – a logic by no means consistent with the paradigm encapsulated in (A) at the start of this chapter. In a word, capital seeks its own increase by any means possible. (A) is an expression of capital in this new, evolved sense, but modern gangsterism is a product of the acquisitive *spirit* of capitalism, so is modern war, so is colonialism: whatever achieves the transfer of wealth from one group of individuals to another.

Because capital is a thing whose only purpose is self-increase, and because it co-opts some human beings, rewarding a small subset of them beyond most people's wildest dreams, and, finally, because, in the end, it can only fulfil its purpose by converting everything outside it into its own body, colonialism, insofar as it involves the sourcing of raw materials for the production of commodities, is obviously an activity of capital at this stage.

Marx recognises all that, but assumes that there will be crises of overproduction which can only be overcome by "on the one hand, enforced destruction of the mass of productive forces; on the other by the conquest of new markets, and by the more thorough exploitation of the old ones. That is to say, by paving the way for more extensive and more destructive crises, and by diminishing the means whereby crises are prevented."[54]

In Marx's picture, on at least one historically influential interpretation, the wealth of the capitalist class and the wealth of the proletariat are inversely related, so that, given sufficient time, the egregious affluence of the former is mirrored by the absolute impoverishment of the latter.

There is no reason for things to turn out that way, and, of course, they have not. What has happened instead is that the capitalist class has attained the position Marx anticipated, but without ruining the rest of society. That has been possible because, utilising patents and intellectual property rights as a

---

[54] Marx, K and Engels, F, *The Communist Manifesto* (1967), p86.

controlling means of securitisation, it has ridden on the back of science, and thus generated wealth that dwarfs what was previously available. Large numbers of people have become relatively better off without significantly affecting the capitalists' aspiration to unlimited affluence.

It is not because capitalists 'want' the rest of the population to have a cut of the pie (which they might be reluctantly permitted as an indulgence, to preserve their quiescence, for example), but that, in the process of pursuing personal gain via the exploitation of science, they are also creating new funds. If hitherto, the wealth of a society, W, has consisted of 100 units, of which C takes 75 and P 25, it makes pragmatic sense, when W rises to 1000, for C to allow P 100 units if C now wants to take 900. As Daniel Susskind put it, "rather than get caught up in debates about how to slice up the existing pie, one could instead focus on making that pie far bigger in the future, increasing everyone's portions at the same time."[55]

'Allow' is obviously the wrong word, but it helps illustrate the point. What happens in reality is that C finds himself in competition with other C's, with whom he therefore cannot forge a fully united front against P. P recognises interests in common with other P's, with whom he unites – in conflictual circumstances, perhaps to go on strike or work to rule. C realises that his survival as such requires customers, and since the class of customers and the class of P's significantly overlaps, his survival depends on the P's having purchasing power. C realises that 'needs' are not necessarily fixed and biological, but can be created out of nothing, and so on.

The net effect of all this is that the class of P's *apparently* becomes co-opted. Whenever P buys a house or a car, he or she is, in one sense, being assimilated to capital, and will usually concur with its interests. Ultimately, the C's and the P's *seem to*

---

[55] Susskind, Daniel (2024), p92.

coalesce into a single class, whose only salient difference is that the former are significantly wealthier than the latter.

Even so, the situation is more complex than that, because a society characterised by capital is conditioned from top to toe by the modern means of securitisation. Members of that society will mostly own capital in the form of private property, but even if they don't, they will normally aspire to it. Here, even a tiny percentage of the total is a lot in absolute terms, and no one wants to relinquish their share, and virtually everyone wants to augment it. The scramble for position is fuelled by inflation, which produces a state of affairs in which standing still is often equivalent to a relative backsliding. The consequence is that, under modern capital, the means of securitisation has undergone an exponential advance, as everyone jostles for a better ranking, or tries to avert a depleted one. Ownership of private property is like a sea that rages continually back and forth as the vast majority of individuals try to acquire another little piece of it, and either supplement their existing share or stop it drifting away.

Only where the super-rich are is there tranquillity: those areas are relatively unassailable.

… But only relatively.

A society in which capital is the predominant force is thus saturated with securitisation devices: the lock and the key, barred windows, guards, gates, fences, razor-wire, as well as firearms, snares, surveillance devices, intruder alarms, and computer encryption. Notice that none of these things produces anything.

Likewise, the factory building is, in itself, inert. But nor is it there simply to keep off the rain.

The design of a building, as philosophers of power have long recognised, is often connected to its owners' aspirations to control subordinates and visitors. First of all, strong walls to keep most people out. Then, inside: regimented rows, restricted sightlines, limitations on movement, approved seating (or none), complementary lighting, the position of stairs and lifts, the size, number and placement of toilet facilities – all play a part in reinforcing the internal division of labour.

But the apparatus of securitisation is not simply about protecting machinery; it is also about ensuring the uninterrupted supply of productive human bodies. In everyday terms, and outside the factory walls, it becomes accommodation.

In early capitalism, as everyone learned at school, accommodation could be utterly basic: several families might share a single room, with sufficient amenities simply to keep them alive, no more. Indeed, Marxists have long argued that this was one of the supposed advantages (for capitalists themselves) of capitalism over slavery: it put the onus for providing accommodation on the workers, and thus relieved the proprietor class of a burden it could happily do without. Henceforth, the latter could concern itself solely with the apparatus of securitisation in its relation to non-sentient machinery.

But accommodation – even of the most basic kind – gave the workers a base, and something to improve upon.[56] As we mentioned earlier, vulgar nineteenth-century Marxism was predicated on the assumption that the workers owned virtually nothing, and that their condition would gradually worsen to the point where it would provoke them, as a matter of necessity, to rise up in revolution. The capitalists would be swept away, and a new world would beckon.

---

[56] So in Zola's 1885 *Germinal*: "At the Maheus' house, Number Sixteen in the second block, nothing stirred. Thick darkness filled the one and only first-floor room: it bore down like a crushing weight on the people sleeping there, whose presence could be felt rather than seen as they lay crowded together, their mouths open, stunned by exhaustion. Despite the bitter cold outside, the air was heavy with the warmth of the living, that stuffy heat to be found in even the best-kept bedrooms, with its reek of the human herd."

What happened instead was that the workers joined unions, and sometimes, when they came into conflict with capital, they would win concessions. Gradually, their living standards rose and the physical aspects of their accommodation improved. Its real nature as a species of securitisation was gradually forgotten. As was always inevitable, given the nature of capital, accommodation became commodified. Eventually, there were 'nice' houses in 'nice' areas. And capitalist society became an ever more blatantly 'indoor' society.[57]

Perhaps the best expression of the indoor society lies outside philosophy (texts such as Bachelard's *The Poetics of Space* are merely expressions of the pervasive illness) in a 1909 short story by the British author, EM Forster, called, 'The Machine Stops'. Set in the future, it depicts a humanity that mostly lives underground, though individuals can visit the Earth's surface using respirators, and they can also travel between continents in an airship. On the whole, each person dwells alone in a subterranean room furnished with an armchair and a bed, and connected to the rest of humanity by something rather like the internet.

Joris-Karl Huysmans's 1884 novel, *Against Nature*, deals with the same phenomenon, but from a different perspective. In the 21st century, the car is the quintessential expression of the 'indoor' society – it allows a person to remain in his or her own comfortable room across long distances – and thus it is not surprising that environmentally-inspired attempts to reduce car usage are so often met with the kind of anger that derives from fear. (This, despite the fact that road traffic injuries are the main of death for children and young adults aged 5-29, roughly 1.19

---

[57] Which may have been the case from the beginning. In the *Economic and Philosophical Manuscripts*, Marx writes: "The worker therefore only feels himself outside his work, and in his work feels outside himself. He feels at home when he is not working, and when he is working he does not feel at home." (1977), p66. See also Benjamin (1973), below.

million people die in car accidents annually, and 20-50 million are affected by non-fatal injuries.[58])

In his 1935, *Paris – the Capital of the Nineteenth Century*, Walter Benjamin traces the development of the indoor society to the reign of Louis-Philippe (1830-1848).

> "For the private citizen, for the first time, the living space became distinguished from the place of work. The former constituted itself as the interior. The office was its complement. The private citizen, who in the office took reality into account, required of the interior that it should support him in his illusions. The necessity was all the more pressing since he had no intention of adding social preoccupations to his business ones. In the creation of his private environment he suppressed them both. From this sprang the phantasmagoria of the interior. This represented the universe for the private citizen. In it he assembled the distant in space and time. His drawing-room was a box in the world theatre."

The history of the urge to get outdoors is also a history of attempts to escape capitalism (although, partly because it has so rarely recognised itself for what it is, not necessarily to overthrow capitalism). It might begin with Rousseau's 'natural man' and his insistence on the beauty of the 'state of nature'. It would include the Romantics, especially Blake, the early Wordsworth and Shelley. It would include fictional characters, such as Zarathustra in his mountain habitat; it would include the *Lebensreform*, the Agrarians, the *Wandervogel*, the Naturists, modern-day pagans, hippies, Beats, New Age Travellers and Deadheads. The list is far from exhaustive, of course. As Lucy Jones puts it, in *Losing Eden*, "Our behaviour has changed as the

---

[58] https://www.who.int/news-room/fact-sheets/detail/road-traffic-injuries

landscape has winnowed. Simply put, we've moved inside. We live in cubicles, cars and tower blocks, spending only one to five per cent of our time outdoors. We're used to surviving outside the rhythms of the natural world. Our need, opportunities and desire to interact with the rest of nature have dramatically decreased."[59]

As capitalism develops, it makes being indoors more and more entrancing – a process in which new technology plays by far the largest part - all the while engendering a culture conducive to neo-tribalism. The number of communal outdoor movements, such as those in the above list, declines. People's need for outdoors and community is paradoxically satisfied by a relocation to cities, where everyone becomes a *flâneur*, perpetually moving through an apparently limitless supply of physically real others without ever having to interact with them. In the 1950s, Guy Debord's *dérives* (drifts) through the Parisian streets were another name for the same thing. The *flâneur* is one satisfaction of the indoor society citizen's need to get out, to connect with the mass of humanity and even to love it, in a very abstract sense.

But ultimately, the indoor society has returned to The Machine Stops. 'Indoors' has now become 'cyberspace'. It consists of a virtual superhighway signed by posts, likes, comments and followers. In his 2024, *The Anxious Generation*, Jonathan Haidt argues convincingly that there has been a 'great rewiring' of childhood which began in roughly 2010 and was caused by smartphones. "As the MIT professor Sherry Turkle wrote in 2015 about life with smartphones, 'We are forever elsewhere.' This is a profound transformation of human consciousness and relationships, and it occurred, for American teens, between 2010 and 2015. This is the birth of the phone-

---

[59] Jones, Lucy (2020), p9.

based childhood. It marks the definitive end of the play-based childhood."[60]

The commodification of modern accommodation – implicit in its relation to capital – requires that nowadays, when we build, we tend to build outwards. Given a need to accommodate twenty families, the preference will nearly always be to build twenty houses than one high-rise. Houses, like cars, reinforce the class system: what they are (detached, semi-detached, terraced), where they are (countryside, town, cramped, abutting a main road), how they look (old, new, identikit, big, small) - all those things allow the observer to deduce the occupant's social class with a fair probability of success.

Yet houses reinforce the class system in another way: they bring the owner on to what, in Britain, is called 'the property ladder.' Once she obtains a mortgage, she will enter into a partnership with the bank or building society, in which her most fundamental material interests are again tied to the status quo.

By contrast, accommodation in a high-rise usually has to be rent or leasehold. Shared infrastructure requires a level of cooperation with other residents or a relationship with a landlord that may be more or less fractious. The status quo may well be viewed with some scepticism. In terms of social class, the status of high-rise residents is often impossible to gauge, certainly with the speed and success pertaining to house-dwellers. For that reason, and for sound ecological reasons, occupants of high-rise buildings may often be more radical than house owners. Obviously, only empirical research could establish that.

Nevertheless, accommodation as a species of securitisation is the basis for securitisation in other areas of social interaction, and is not dependent on the form or type of building. Social class generally can be understood as differentials in the securitisation

---

[60] Haidt, Jonathan (2024), p34.

of social space. As a poor person, there will be places I cannot go, or live, because I cannot afford them. The same will be true of the middle classes, but to a lesser degree. Only the super-rich will be able to 'access all areas'. As David Harvey noticed two decades ago[61], social class and geography are inextricable. We would add: with the world conceived as an interlocking system of zones (the smallest of which may be no more than a few square metres in size) of varying securitisation.

The home will be my literal physical 'address' which gives me access to a bank account and a job. I will keep my possessions there, and I will keep it locked when I am not present; I may even have it alarmed. When I leave it, I will take with me a variety of articles which will all be securitised, most typically a credit card and a phone. All my purchases and many of my social interactions will occur via these devices. When I enter and leave work, I will often have to sign in and out. If I work on a computer with an IP address, I will 'enter' and 'leave' a variety of securitised sites, some with 2-factor authentication. I will leave a digital trail that may or may not be monitored from afar. As I travel to and from work, I will be tracked by security cameras.[62]

In short, the society in which capital is the dominant force is one that is hyper-securitised. In this world, it is not surprising that our overriding way of relating to one another is via

---

[61] Harvey, David (2003). It is clear that, given the division of the world into securitised zones, the division of labour cannot be seen as the primary cause of social class: rather, the zoning and the division of labour work together. I am confined to the lower-quality zones as a result of my marginal position in the division of labour, which means that my experiences are geographically constricted, thus limiting my outlook. My children will be the inheritors of that, and thus likely to occupy marginal positions in the division of labour.

[62] This may have been anticipated by colonialism. Talking of the interrelation of maps, museums and censuses, Benedict Anderson writes: "The colonial state did not merely aspire to create, under its control, a human landscape of perfect visibility; the condition of this 'visibility' was that everyone, everything, had (as it were) a serial number." He compares this, via the Indonesian novelist, Pramoedya Ananta Toer, to Bentham's Panopticon. (1991), p188.

suspicion mixed with the hostility of our being rivals for a slightly bigger share in capital. We think and behave as if we live in a zero-sum game in which my gain is your equivalent loss. That may be because so much of the total of capital is under the dominion of so few people (who are themselves, in their own way, equally the victims of a common delusion).

The long-term effect of all this must be increased stress, and eventually, for some, mental ill health. For which there are, of course, readily available medicalised 'solutions', as well as soporifics such as alcohol and drugs. The result is that we mostly exist in a condition of what the Cambridge criminologist, Ben Crewe, has called 'sedative coping.'[63]

Having said all that, the fact that we nowadays exist as securitised subjects at the intersection of a fixed set of alphamerics - National Insurance numbers, house numbers, bank account numbers, birth dates, postcodes, etc. – has a dual aspect. On the one hand, it is oppressive, in that it breeds mistrust and even paranoia; on the other, it is reassuring, in that it seems to protect me. On the other hand, as in gangsterism, the 'protection' on offer is arguably protection against the operation extending the protection.

In this context, a division is often drawn between the 'old' system of capital in which people consumed goods they really needed and a 'new' system of capital, which arose in the first quarter of the twentieth century, in which people consumed goods whose desirability had been artificially generated by calculatedly emotive advertising, and which they 'needed' only in a rarefied sense. Adam Curtis's 2002 documentary series, *The Century of the Self*, singled out Edward Bernays (plus, perhaps, Sigmund Freud, whose protégé and nephew he was) as the principal architect of this move from 'old' to 'new'.

---

[63] Crewe, Ben (2024), p1080-1094.

Curtis connected this second phase in the development of capitalism to consumer individualism. Through a systematic series of high-profile advertisements, Bernays successfully persuaded people that they should not be content to look and behave like others, but should deploy consumer goods – particularly clothes - to express their 'individuality'. Once that idea caught on, capital almost literally gained a new lease of life.

Consumerist individualism might have emerged anyway. In any case, it pulls in opposing directions, mirroring the ways in which our securitisation as nodes within a system of different intersecting numbers functions as both a source of anxiety and a source of reassurance. On the one hand, it is a perceived *compensation* for the oppression that capitalism involves; on the other hand, it serves as a non-voluntary *symbolic expression* of that oppression. It is 'non-voluntary' insofar as, nowadays, there is no such thing as an opt-out from the system of culturally different markers between subjects: my decision not to have an individual style is *itself* the choice of an individual style.

In her 2018 examination of social media companies, Shoshana Zuboff claimed to find a third phase in the process of capitalist evolution, involving the crafted modification of human nature to produce individuals more disposed to purchase commodities on cue. The chief intellectual inspiration for this third phase was the behavioural psychologist, BF Skinner, particularly his 1948 utopian novel, *Walden Two* (which Curtis also mentions).

What we see, when we stand back and look at the whole picture, is an intensely securitised society whose members often live with malign psychological issues, who are sometimes addicted to chemicals, and whose chief consolations are emotionally charged commodities whose real value may be negligible. It is often claimed that human nature is not conducive to any kind of egalitarian world, but, under current conditions, how can we tell? Those opposed to such an assessment might well propose a modern version of Pascal's Wager: maybe we should have faith in each other: since we will all die anyway, what do we have to lose?

The securitisation of society as a collection of labelled individuals is consolidated by and through the nation. The nation is a securitised item of geography within which individuals themselves are securitised, and which facilitates the internal war of capital against capital. Territories have been modes of securitisation since the dawn of human history, and terrain claims significantly predated the rise of modern capital. Nevertheless, as Jared Diamond reminds us in *Guns, Germs and Steel*, "As recently as AD 1500, less than 20 percent of the world's area was marked off by boundaries into states run by bureaucrats and governed by laws. Today, all land except Antarctica's is so divided." His very next sentence should not surprise us: "Descendants of those societies that achieved centralised government and organised religion earliest ended up dominating the world."

Benedict Anderson's 1983 *Imagined Communities* goes some way to showing how that happened. He ties it to the slow decline of the "automatic legitimacy of sacral monarchy", beginning in the seventeenth century. The rise of print capitalism produced the novel and the newspaper, which produced the impression of a common linguistic and/or geographical community marked by simultaneity. Building on the hierarchical administrative areas of the old political framework, modern nationalism began first in the Americas and then spread afield through colonialism, the market and a linguistically homogenous intelligentsia.

Modern capital repurposed these imagined communities as means of securitisation for its citizens – guaranteeing them 'protection' - and devices for the plunder of distant geographical locations. Ultimately, as in so-called world-systems theory, the entire Earth was divided into a 'core', consisting of the most technologically advanced nations, and a 'periphery', consisting of nations created by, or redefined by,[64] the core in order to service it. But the division of the periphery into nations also allows the core to exert greater control: it can liaise and ally with peripheral elites, and it can regulate population movements; it can assign responsibility for to-do items on lists of demands; it can ascribe ownership of 'national' resources to potential collaborators - and so on. Giovanni Arrighi's distinction between 'territorial' and 'molecular' logic is relevant here[65]. Economic goods flow between nations in a molecular way, but productive human bodies are still (formally) assigned to nations on a territorial basis to prevent the unlimited flow of economic migrants. The fact that the two 'logics' pull in different directions was ultimately responsible for the collapse of the globalisation project of the early millennium: as Étienne Balibar pointed out at the time, borders run everywhere in the core territories, not just along geopolitical boundaries. The core nations are securitised internally by the likes of MI5 and the FBI (not to mention all of Althusser's Ideological and Repressive State Apparatuses[66]), and externally by the likes of MI6, the CIA and border patrols. The state, of course, is impossible to define in terms of the means of production. Both Hegel and Marx had difficulty in saying precisely what it was. Only when Max Weber came along was its nature finally clarified: it is 'a human community that (successfully) claims the monopoly of the legitimate use of physical force within a given territory.'[67] In other words, it is only properly comprehensible in terms of the means of securitisation.

Conventional Marxism, which sees history as driven by the means of production, and capitalism as its most recent motive

---

[64] Those nations created by the Sykes-Picot agreement in 1916 are examples of the former; India and Egypt might work as examples of the latter.

[65] Arrighi, Giovanni (1994).

[66] Althusser, Louis (1971).

[67] Weber, Marx (1991), p78.

force, likewise struggles to explain the existence of nations. In *The Communist Manifesto*, Marx seems to imply that they will imminently wither away. "In place of the old national and local seclusion and self-sufficiency, we have intercourse in every direction, universal interdependence of nations. And as in material, so in intellectual production."[68] Of course, that is to be expected if the means of production and capitalists are primary: the intrinsic nature of the former, and the interests of the latter, completely transcend 'national' boundaries: so much so that nations, as such, can reasonably be expected to melt away.[69]

But of course, they have not. Again, the priority of the means of securitisation explains why in a way that orthodox historical materialism cannot.[70]

So, to recap: what we now have is a world of highly securitised 'individuals', contained (or imprisoned, some might say) within the boundaries of individual nations, which are securitisation devices.

But we are not finished yet. There is one more tier to the cake: the tax havens.

Modern capital cannot subsist on nations and securitised individuals alone: it needs places to secure and hide its surplus.

---

[68] Marx, K and Engels, F (1967), p84.

[69] The same conviction that nation-states will wither in the face of unfettered capitalism is to be found as late as 2000 in Negri and Hardt's *Empire*. The idea there was that globalisation would eventually reduce nation-states to the status of mere transaction-recorders.

[70] Benedict Anderson (1991) sees nations as 'imagined communities', and Tom Nairn (2008) tends to agree, with the caveat that they often have an anti-colonial rationale. The limits of globalisation were brutally exposed in the second decade of the 21st century, beginning with Brexit in 2016 and continuing with the election of Donald Trump that same year. Both events arguably underlined the reality of nations as securitisation devices: their supporters seem to have wanted, among other things, an end to offshore outsourcing and immigration – ie, greater job and personal security. As against Anderson, there is no reason why communities, imagined or otherwise, should be exclusivist; as against Nairn, too many developing world nation-states were the creation of colonial powers and wracked by civil wars once those powers left: their mobilisation of cultural particularisms was probably a belated attempt to make the best of a bad situation.

The Crown Dependency of Jersey, the City of London, Zurich, Delaware, the Cayman Islands, Panama, the Marshall Islands, constitute a world in which Marx was right after all: national boundaries really have been eradicated, and capital now rules the world as a single, indivisible entity.

We can sum up by proposing one answer (there may be several) to the question Mark Fisher asked in *Capitalist Realism:* why is it so difficult to imagine a non-capitalist world? The answer lies in Marx's notion of the 'fetter', which we have already looked at. Modern capitalism has fettered the present state of affairs with a panoply of payoffs, as described above. In Britain, 53% of the population own their own home; in the USA, it is 66%, in France 63%, and in Germany (which has one of the lowest homeownership rates in Europe) 47%. Even in the developing world, the figure is not necessarily lower: in South Africa it is 68%, Benin 61%, Kenya 73%, Brazil 63%. Often, but not always, home ownership represents capital: in principle, it can be converted into money to command Productive Human Bodies. In any case, societies in which private property is endemic, and which are, in addition, highly securitised, can obviously be considered as fettered.

3. Ideology

The Classical Notion

There seems to be an ambiguity in Marx as to whether ideology is something that arises naturally, as an expression of the relations of production, or whether it is deliberately produced by the ruling classes to justify themselves to themselves and keep the subordinate classes down. Both conceptions appear in *The German Ideology,* which is the earliest version of the theory of historical materialism. The first is exemplified by the following passage:

> "Consciousness can never be anything else than conscious existence, and the existence of men is their actual life-process. If in all ideology men and their circumstances appear upside-down as in a camera obscura, this phenomenon arises just as much from their historical life-process as the inversion of objects on the retina does from their physical life-process… We do not set out from what men say, imagine, conceive, nor from men as narrated, thought of, imagined, conceived, in order to arrive at men in the flesh. We set out from real, active men, and on the basis of their real life-process we demonstrate the development of the ideological reflexes and echoes of this life-process. The phantoms formed in the human brain are also, necessarily, sublimates of their material life-process, which is empirically verifiable and bound to material premises. Morality, religion, metaphysics, all the rest of ideology and their corresponding forms of consciousness, thus no longer retain the semblance of independence."

The second is expressed here:

> "The ideas of the ruling class are in every epoch the ruling ideas, i.e. the class which is the ruling material force of society, is at the same time its ruling intellectual force. The class which has the means of material production at its disposal, has control at the same time over the means of mental production, so that thereby, generally speaking, the ideas of those who lack the means of mental production are subject to it. The ruling ideas are nothing more than the ideal expression of the dominant material relationships, the dominant material relationships grasped as ideas; hence of the relationships which make the one class the ruling one, therefore, the ideas of its dominance. The individuals composing the ruling class possess, among other things, consciousness, and therefore think. Insofar, therefore, as they rule as a class and determine the extent and compass of an epoch, it is self-evident that they do this in its whole range, hence among other things rule also as thinkers, as producers of ideas, and regulate the production and distribution of the ideas of their age: thus, their ideas are the ruling ideas of the epoch."

Both can be right only at the cost of raising awkward questions. If ideology arises naturally from the relations of production, how does that happen? If I were to trap a hundred people in a room and order them to produce food and clothes, should I expect them to start generating legitimating ideas? If ideology is a naturally emergent phenomenon, why do the ruling classes bother producing it? Do they produce it to bolster their authority, or because they genuinely think it is true? And how exactly do the intelligentsia get co-opted?

The issues are exacerbated by Marx's own example:

> "For instance, in an age and in a country where royal power, aristocracy, and bourgeoisie are contending for mastery and where, therefore, mastery is shared, the doctrine of the separation of powers proves to be the dominant idea and is expressed as an 'eternal law'."[71]

But if three classes are vying for supremacy, how does a compromise solution become the dominant idea, given that none of them assent to it? Or maybe they *do* assent to it? Does it bring an end to their conflict? If so why can't class conflicts always be resolved that way? And how is it then expressed as an 'eternal law'? Where, and by who?

In the 20th century, as the likelihood of Marxian-type working-class revolutions increasingly receded, the second understanding of ideology – that it was deliberately manufactured by the ruling class to maintain its authority – gained increasing traction. Lenin (and later György Lukács) saw ideology as a weapon wielded by the 'bourgeoisie' against the proletariat, in response to which the proletariat should deploy its own ideology. [72] The Frankfurt school began analysing music, theatre, and art as a means of understanding why so many workers had sided with fascism. More or less simultaneously, Antonio Gramsci developed a theory of 'cultural hegemony',

---

[71] This passage reads as if Marx thinks the separation of powers is the separation of the literal powers of the three contending classes, instead of what it is normally taken to mean; the separation of executive, legislature and judiciary.

[72] Lenin, VI (1999), p28-29. Eg, "Why, the reader will ask, does the spontaneous movement, the movement along the line of least resistance, lead to the dominion of bourgeois ideology? For the simple reason that bourgeois ideology is far older in origin than socialist ideology, that it is more fully developed, and that it has at its disposal immeasurably more means of dissemination."

according to which the ruling classes control society through intellectual attraction:

> "There does not exist any independent class of intellectuals, but every social group has its own stratum of intellectuals, or tends to form one; however, the intellectuals of the historically (and concretely) progressive class, in the given conditions, exercise such a power of attraction that, in the last analysis, they end up by subjugating the intellectuals of the other social groups; they thereby create a system of solidarity between all the intellectuals, with bonds of a psychological nature (vanity, etc.) and often of a caste character (technico-juridicial, corporate, etc.). This phenomenon manifests itself 'spontaneously' in the historical periods in which the given social group is really progressive – ie, really causes the whole of society to move forward."[73]

The move towards a concern with ideology became so pronounced that by the late twentieth century, it was relatively rare for Marxists to focus principally on economic questions. The most prominent among them were cultural critics like Fredric Jameson, Slavoj Žižek, Pierre Macherey and Terry Eagleton.

Made in Stockholm

Reading some contemporary accounts of ideology, one could be forgiven for thinking that it is sagaciously produced by a committee of the ruling classes sitting around a table to produce a formally agreed set of half-truths designed to keep the

---

[73] Gramsci, Antonio (1971), p60.

subaltern classes in place. We encounter claims like, "capitalism wants you to believe...", "capitalism deceives us into thinking...", and "capitalism is hostile to..." Capitalism becomes a homunculus with needs, desires and antipathies, and we are left with a strong whiff of the old, outlandish conspiracy theory whose main architects were the Illuminati, the Freemasons, and/or 'the Jews'.

In Gramsci's day, that sort of thing might have been just about plausible: the world was not flooded with text in the way it is today, and the mass media, owned then, as now, by capitalists, had more intellectual 'empty space' within which to make its pro-capitalist views and arguments heard.

But even then, it was flawed. The modern intellectual community is much more than merely journalists, and capitalism rarely exists as a 'thing' that needs to be defended against its enemies. Even when it does, it still consists of individual capitalists who, more often than not, are at each other's throats. So, for example, in our own day, some of the more minor capitalists have combined to denounce Amazon's 'exploitative business practices' – essentially its consistent capitalism. And, as Mark Fisher pointed out, and as we all know today, anti-capitalism presents capitalism with a rich set of commercial opportunities.

Similar in intent, but equally flawed, is the Althusserian notion (which goes back to Adorno and Horkheimer) of 'interpellation' where social-institutional phenomena produce compliant individual subjectivities to order. To some extent, how they do so draws on generally acknowledged truths (children are enculturated by parents, teachers, etc.), but it provides no way of accounting for the very real fact of dissent; nor does it explain how the interpellating social phenomena themselves are produced. It seems therefore to be vulnerable to Marx's criticism from another context: "This doctrine must, therefore, divide society into two parts, one of which is superior to society."[74]

In any case, it is difficult to see why capitalism needs a legitimating ideology at all. It has an increasingly effective means of securitisation, and it is flexible enough to give people much of what they want should they become troublesome.

A better way of explaining where ideology comes from lies in a population's need to justify itself morally and intellectually to itself – *in order to live a relatively unreflective, and therefore relatively contented life* (which – since thinking is difficult, and sometimes unpleasant - has always been the goal of the vast majority of humankind).

Imagine I am kidnapped by a gang of thieves and forced to work with them. If I have hitherto been conscientious and law-abiding, I will probably find this psychologically strenuous. If there is no possibility of escape, I have two options: I can either torment myself on a continuous basis, which may lead to my self-destruction, or I can modify my outlook by (a) telling myself that the criminals' behaviour is defensible, and (b) preferring all and only those moral, intellectual and cultural ideas that help me excuse my own behaviour to myself. Some of my fellow thieves will already have undergone this same process, and they may help me adjust.

The point is probably obvious. Imagine a population under a particularly unjust economic system. The means of securitisation possessed by the presiding faction means that there is little or no possibility of escape. I may not go so far as to believe that the rulers' behaviour is defensible (since my situation is not as bleak as in the thieves story), nevertheless, I may sometimes find myself in a situation in which my daily work makes me technically their collaborator, and I need to cope

---

[74] *Theses on Feuerbach* III. At
https://www.marxists.org/archive/marx/works/1845/theses/theses.htm.

with that. I will prefer the moral, intellectual and cultural ideas that help me do so.

Obviously, everyone in this hypothetical society – owners as well as workers – will be in the same situation, and compelled to weave similar self-justifications. Ideology, on this understanding, is *a kind of generalised Stockholm Syndrome,* and is principally produced by the subaltern classes, since they have the most need for mental adjustment. It has to conceive the established system as essentially benign (despite its occasionally obvious aberrations). Ultimately, the ruling classes seize upon it, and, by way of bolstering their own power, re-broadcast it, suitably embellished, in the media. But they do not primarily produce it, nor do they need it: they have other and better means of securitisation. Nevertheless, it helps clear up several mysteries that tormented Marxists in the first third of the twentieth century: why are the working classes so apparently eager to sign up for wars? Why do they so often support Fascism? The answer may be that they are fighting for something that they themselves have produced: the nation – not as it really is, but as it appears in ideology.

As just mentioned, however, in the society story – unlike the thieves story – the abductee does not have to go so far as to justify the rulers' behaviour, since his predicament is not so straitened. There exists, therefore, some leeway for turning some of the ideas he has accepted (and which now form the intellectual landscape of that age) against his perceived oppressors. He will, of course, be obliged by the seeming contradiction to engage in the hard business of thinking, but that is a price he will have to pay.[75]

---

[75] There may be some mileage in the idea that the captive's outlook is conditioned not just by the things that restrict him, but by the illusory outlets the system provides by way of recompense. There are, for example, good reasons for thinking that modern consciousness is strongly conditioned by the car, which is neither a part of the means of production nor the means of securitisation (although it can, with a lot of work, be assimilated to both/either). It represents an illusory freedom,

Ideology Today

According to the Slovenian philosopher, Slavoj Žižek, ideology is too big a phenomenon to characterise,[76] but, with respect, we can do better than that. An uncharacterizable concept is not a concept at all.

An ideology would seem to have two parts: an apologetic element, in which the society that produces it is depicted as harmonious, and a deeper, intellectual component that generates the optimal mindset for tranquil conformity with the system. It seems likely that, as regards its particulars, the latter is drawn from the dominant worldview at that time and place (eg, Christianity in medieval Europe, or Islam in Ottoman Anatolia), and that it does not exhaust it.

That is not the conventional view of ideology. In the conventional view, Christianity and Islam are themselves ideologies. So, it might be asked: on this new model, if Christianity and Islam are not in themselves ideologies, then what are they, and where did they come from? The answer is: we can be agnostic about that. Hegel, above all, persuaded us to expect a philosophical response, but actually those sorts of problems are best left to historians.

In his 1962 *Structural Transformation of the Public Sphere*, Jürgen Habermas argued that the same cultural phenomenon might possess ideological and non-ideological aspects. The coffee houses of the Enlightenment were run on utopian ideals, such as equality and fraternity, which were eventually degraded and ultimately extinguished as those institutions evolved to

---

and is nearly always advertised as such: the freedom of the open road, of self-expression, of speed, of travel. It is a consolation which conceals its nature as such, and appeals so strongly because of its contrast with what it is compensated for. It can also be understood as a not-very-safe-at-all safety valve.

[76] Žižek, Slavoj (1989).

become increasingly elitist. Nevertheless, they held a utopian promise that persisted into future ages, and which could not – and cannot – be so co-opted.

In general, however, the apologetic part of an ideology depicts a world in which the means of securitisation has succeeded for everyone's benefit, and a fundamental harmony reigns between the different social groups. The picture looks something like this: yes, all of those groups have their faults, and individuals within them may exhibit them to a greater or lesser extent, but each of the faults is excusable. The rulers may occasionally be thoughtless and apparently cruel, but underneath, they are well-intentioned, and much of their apparent cruelty comes from not knowing all the facts. The lower classes may occasionally go hungry, but that is the exception, and sometimes it is their own fault; on the whole, they possess an earthy, instinctual wisdom, they enjoy hard but rewarding lives, and they possess a good sense of humour. In the ideological representation, even criminals are either driven to extremes by force of circumstance, or they are lovable, childish rogues who see crime as a kind of play. Everyone in the society has their place, which need not have been ordained by God, but which is certainly long-established, and to some extent, natural (although not natural enough to make it shatterproof: everyone is lucky to have it). There are very few real outsiders in the ideology, except those who can soon be brought inside the fold, or who live far away, and who can therefore, if necessary, be permanently excluded or eliminated. Nations, which might seem to require a condition of mutual antagonism as a condition of their existence – being populated by supposed genuine outsiders – can be reconciled to each other on the understanding that they constitute an amicable 'community of nations' in which everyone stays happily within his or her borders unless invited to move for morally justifiable reasons.

The beliefs underlying the Hindu caste system probably constitute the paradigmatic example of an ideology: the Brahmins, Kshatriyas, Vaisyas, Sudras and Pariahs exist in an underlying harmony, and each group has its rightful place, function and character. Even the Pariahs are assimilable – not in this life, but in the next. The apologetic component, depicting harmony between the different castes, is provided by their origin in different parts of God's body, and by their complementary 'colours'. The philosophical part is provided by the ideas of karma and samsara.

In many ways, apologetic ideology looks like what it is: an advert for the society, produced by itself for itself. In England, it is first exemplified in *The Canterbury Tales*, where all types of individuals and classes come together, united by a common purpose.

But it is also significantly represented in the visual arts. In pre-capitalist societies, ideology does not usually function as a set of doctrines, but much more as a collection of images for the illiterate: pictures, carvings, sculptures, in which different classes of people are shown in appropriate relations, or with suitable respect, and which may sometimes display a kind of subversive humour, albeit not too extreme. Theatre may fulfil the same function, and it can be tragic to the extent that it shows the severity of fate, the inscrutability of the gods, or the moral inadequacy of different eras, countries, or out-of-favour historical figures, but rarely if it reflects badly on the current regime.

Virtually everyone within the society will accept the ideology for reasons we have already outlined: they are trapped, and the ideology helps them come to terms with the otherwise uncomfortable fact that they have accepted, embraced, or sometimes even actively collaborated in, their entrapment. For that reason, it is important that the ideology always makes some allowance for harmless dissent. Dissenters who find themselves

81

reflected as such in the ideology will not be seen a threat, or as an example to others. Nowadays, ideology is often violently opposed to immigrants, because any addition to the system can only be for the worse.

The ideology can rarely appear in its entirety, all at once, because it is so implausible. It has to appear in snapshots, and it is the cumulative effect that is important. Each individual snapshot is innocuous in isolation from the others. They impress themselves on particular subjectivities not by way of anything resembling an argument, but in the way a relentless series of repetitions might. If anyone was to be presented with the whole harmonious picture, and asked, is society like that? of course they would say no. But that is entirely the point: they will never be asked.

The actual society, the reality behind the ideology, is always more or less dysfunctional. Virtually nothing is as good as it is presented as being, and sometimes it is egregiously worse. A good idea of the mismatch can be appreciated by looking at the way women were depicted in adverts throughout the 1950s: always perfectly dressed, fully made up, and, of course, delighted with their ironing boards, vacuum cleaners and soap powders.

However, it is possible to make a deeper point about the way nostalgia is evoked by past ideologies and bolted onto present-day ones. Ninety-nine per cent of the past has disappeared and is irretrievable: a historian might be able to discover, say, that a certain 'Alfred Jones' lived in his own house at the beginning of the twentieth century; he may even be able to discover a few facts about Alfred Jones. But precisely what Alfred Jones did on 23 March 1903, 24 March 1906, and so on, is almost certainly lost forever. Alfred Jones himself no longer has much meaning, except as the man who once occupied the historian's house, and perhaps as someone's great-grandfather. What remains of 1901 and 1903, in the minds of most people, are evocative remnants of its ideology. We see Queen Victoria and Edward VIII in their dignity; we see men in suits and hats, women in long dresses; we see clean pavements, well-defined public monuments, horses and carriages, motor buses, a certain lost 'orderliness'. Non-white people are usually missing, although they would have been there in the reality. The 1901-1903 ideology survives as a vague impression of 'our' past harmony as a society, a harmony that was supposedly even greater then than it is now, and which lives within, and nurtures, the present-day ideology.

Functionally speaking, ideology usually plays a facilitating role: it oils the cogs of what would otherwise be a very friction-heavy machine. An unjust society without ideology is a society that is radically at odds with itself – the questionability of the rulers' behaviour is not mitigated by any palliating ideas consistent with a (perhaps reluctant) acceptance of it - and it is probably inclined to implode. In such a society, technical and scientific innovations are much less likely to occur, because fractiousness encourages short-termism. What we end up with is a long period of successive revolutions disguising an underlying historical stagnation, or even a collapse.

But no society *needs* ideology. It is one more means of securitisation, and not necessarily the most effective. The masses can be kept in place by mounted soldiers, with guns if need be.

In any case, ideology works differently in multi-party democratic societies, where, ominously (it might seem), there is significant scope for criticism of the ruling powers.

But the system in which those powers are embedded rarely comes under sustained attack (though it can be criticised). We have already said that ideology is significantly represented in the visual arts, often more as a collection of images than a set of doctrines. That remains true throughout history, up to and including our own time. So, in present-day Britain, for example, TV soaps such as *Coronation Street, EastEnders* and *Emmerdale* depict society in microcosm, and while the characters exhibit

83

degrees of moral rectitude, the community itself rarely faces an existential crisis, and to the extent that it does, it always pulls together at the eleventh hour. Comedy shows and the news showcase parts of society, but again, the fundamental unity of the whole is rarely questioned. As Benedict Anderson noticed, the glue here is provided (as it could not be in previous societies) by simultaneity and geography: *these* events – real or fictional – are taking place in a *here and now* that I share with other members of the same imagined community.

However, multi-party democracies are fragile, and the fact that much of their apologetic ideological apparatus has to allow for disruptive voices means that they need an extra level in which social harmony is unquestioningly presented as the natural and only state of affairs. This requirement is satisfied by the advertising industry, where, in addition to advertising specific products, adverts also endorse the society for which they have been produced. So, meals feature ideal families in ideal homes; cars feature ideal drivers on ideal roads in ideal landscapes; clothes feature ideal humans in ideal locations; furniture features ideal couples in ideal stores with ideal sales assistants. If we are outdoors, the sun is always shining; if we are indoors, everything is clean, cosy and well-ordered. Everyone is happy. The purchase of the product is the characters' icing on the cake, but theirs was an ideal world well before that, and the good news is, it is also our world. Bearing all this in mind, the destabilising potential of Culture Jamming may have been underestimated; particularly phenomena like Subvertising, Artivism and Billboard Hacking.

In any case, readers may notice similarities here to Roland Barthes's analysis of modern 'myths' in his 1957, *Mythologies*. Examples of Barthesian myths include: the face of Garbo, plastic, ornamental cookery and toys. Barthes thought that myths consist of the meanings added to signs in order to make the ruling ideas of the age – the ideology, to put it in Marxian terms

– appear natural (which it is not), rather than arbitrary or imposed (which it is). Myths are thus second-order signifiers. Myth generally is "a metalanguage, because it is a second language, in which one speaks about the first."[77]

The chief problem with Barthes's account is that he sees a meaning being *attached* to an image atomistically, rigidly and unproblematically. But the truth is that meanings always *supervene* on images: any one image is open to a potentially infinite number of interpretations, each or all of which could qualify as *the* 'meaning'. As a consumer, I will always be unable to interpret a single image unambiguously, but I will always be susceptible to successive presentations of happy faces enjoying flawless commodities in a perfect world. That susceptibility does not have to issue in cognitive mental content, much less any propositional sentence about the meaning of the images I have seen: it is sufficient that I recognise the world in the advert as one to which I would like to belong, and could well already belong. In other words, it is always *the world behind* the commodity that is decisive, and it impresses itself on me non-rationally.

But even here, there must be a shared set of assumptions on which the ideology is based. I am better able to bear my entrapment if certain things are true, and others not worth considering. Here we come to the second part of ideology: the deeper, intellectual component that generates the optimal mindset for tranquil conformity with the system.

The three exemplars of that component for pre-capitalist societies were probably (1) an eternal sanction for local social relations, (b) moral absolutism and (c) a belief that this life was not the only one.

What constitutes the intellectual component of ideology in the capitalist age is an open question. For orthodox Marxism it

[77] Barthes, Roland (1972), p114.

has usually been religion, morality and nation. In his 1844, *Contribution to the Critique of Hegel's Philosophy of Right,* Marx famously described religion as 'the opium of the people', while morality, as we learn in his 1875, *The Critique of the Gotha Programme* is an attempt to "pervert … the Party's realism [with] ideological nonsense."

The Marxist idea is that, as a worker, I will find the horrors of industrial capitalism easier to bear if I think (a) that I will be compensated in an afterlife (religion), (b) that I will stand a better chance of getting into heaven if I am meek and forgiving (morality), and (c) that Britons never, never, never will be slaves (nation).

Marxists have therefore tended to be atheists (not always – the liberation theologians of South and Central America were, and are, exceptions), and relativists about morality. Their position has been that, to the extent that there is any correct standard of moral behaviour, only the Communist society will reveal it. Its current manifestations are simply sentimental shackles on revolutionary action.

Marxists have also been internationalists, but nations are the odd one out in their list of three. Under capitalism, religion and morality can be utilised to foster deference to the establishment. But nations are a hindrance to commerce, so capitalists are allegedly even more opposed to them than are communists. As Marx puts it in *The Communist Manifesto:* under capitalism, "national one-sidedness and narrow-mindedness become more and more impossible."

In what follows, we shall argue that the ideological pillars on which modern capitalism rests are very different from – and in two cases the flat opposite of - those identified by classical Marxism. They are materialism, moral relativism, and nationalism. Of these, moral relativism defuses what is by far the greatest threat to any existing order perceived to be unjust, so that, arguably, the other two pillars underpin it rather than being entirely significant in themselves.

Materialism eliminates Kant's 'three postulates of the moral life', God, immortality and free will. If we are simply our bodies, which must die, and if radical social improvement in our lifetimes, and that of the next generation, is highly improbable, we might as well reconcile ourselves to our circumstances and make the best of them (which needn't be an entirely selfish aspiration).

Equally, if morality is simply a cultural-subjective matter, there can be no definitive evaluation of any system as unfair: who am I (and who is anyone) to say that capitalism fosters injustice?

And finally, my incarceration in a nation – from which I may, incidentally, derive some comfort, as 'institutionalised' inmates sometimes do – restricts my view of global reality, and may persuade me that my own worldview is universal, that everyone, everywhere in the world is just like me and my close friends (so that I may feel repulsed by the discovery that people in other countries think differently); in addition to which it may lend credence to moral relativism by making different 'peoples' evolve along different paths.

Finally, in the interests of fairness, it should be pointed out that because we are saying that materialism and moral relativism are ideological phenomena – ie, that they are conducive to an active or passive support for the present system – that is not to say that they are not true. The question of whether a belief leads to a subjective reconciliation with a particular worldview, and the question of whether it is true, are different concerns.

But let us look at each of the three in detail.

1. Materialism

Materialism is the ideology of capital, as even the most cursory look at modern history will confirm: capitalism and materialism achieved dominance together. Under late capital, its triumph is virtually complete. If the power of capital is reflected in the power of its ideology, then nothing attests to that power as unequivocally as the fact that many anti-capitalist movements – including Marxism – are avowedly materialist.

This is not always obvious. Indeed, some thinkers have claimed that it is dualism, not materialism (which is a form of monism) that is integral to capitalism's ideology. Always central to this position is a withering presentation of René Descartes as a kind of philosophical arch-villain, and his Cogito ("I think therefore I am") as concealing a malign political agenda. Herbert Marcuse thought the Cogito led to a world of absurdity; for Fredric Jameson, it was the metaphysical prefiguration of the bourgeois ego; Judith Butler thought it ignored the social and performative aspects of subjectivity and gender; Jacques Derrida thought it was a site where the possibility of madness is present, and so on.

The latest proponent of such a position is the degrowth philosopher, Jason Hickel. Hickel claims that the pre-capitalist world was largely animist in its approach to nature, but that capitalism, riding on the back of Descartes, endorsed a mind-body dualism which facilitated the view that only humans mattered, and that nature was a lifeless 'thing' waiting to be exploited.

> "Descartes's theory of matter came to be known as mechanical philosophy. It was an explicit attempt to disenchant the world – a direct attack on the remaining principles of animist philosophy. And from the 1630s, these ideas came to dominate science … During the

Enlightenment, dualist thought became mainstream for the first time in history. It gave sanction to the enclosure and privatisation of common land, as land was rendered but a thing to be possessed. And it was enclosure, in turn, that enabled dualism's rise to cultural dominance: only once commoners were alienated from the land and severed from forest ecosystems could they be convinced to imagine themselves as fundamentally separate from the rest of the living world, and to see other beings as objects."[78]

But there are serious problems with this. Firstly, it runs several things together: 'dualism' is presented as shorthand for Descartes's own philosophy, which under the term 'mechanical philosophy' is conflated with science and with the Enlightenment. But science was never Cartesian: until the twentieth century, the mind was largely unexplored territory; scientists - consistently with the central principles of their enterprise – tended to be agnostic about it. Nor was the Enlightenment constituted by Cogito-cheerleaders. Voltaire thought Descartes was simply mistaken; John Locke, Adam Smith, Jean d'Alembert and David Hume were all empiricists who had little time for his rationalism; Denis Diderot called the Cogito 'a fantasy beyond the retina', Jean-Jacques Rousseau thought it neglected emotion and sentiment, Immanuel Kant considered it a mere function of thought, not a thing, and so on.

But even if pre-capitalist societies had, as Hickel claims, been characterised by a significant degree of animism (a claim which is, in itself, controversial), animism is arguably dualist, insofar as it implies a distinction between appearance and reality. There may well be tree, wind and river spirits, but they are not immediately visible. I may still need a shaman to access them,

[78] Hickel, Jason (2020), p71.

because the shaman can perceive things that I cannot, in ways that are disbarred to me.

Yet there is a sense in which Hickel is right. Science depends not only on an appearance-reality dualism and a true-false dualism. but on a subject-object dualism. In order to investigate nature, I have to factor out my own subjectivity, and simply regard the world as it supposedly is 'in itself'. But I cannot do this if I cannot distinguish what pertains to the subject from what, for the purposes of the enterprise, is external to it.

Nevertheless, this has given us enormous benefits: it has enabled us to cure diseases, prolong lifespans, improve travel, communications, hygiene, and so on. It has enabled us to see that astronomy and modern chemistry are full of facts, and astrology and alchemy are full of nonsense. Whether it has ever been used to 'sanction the enclosure and privatisation of common land' (and much less whether Cartesian dualism has ever been put to work for that purpose) is doubtful.

In fact, materialism, not Cartesian dualism, is science's starting point. It deploys materialism in its historically early stages as a working hypothesis, simply because materialism promises to bring all the empirical phenomena within its purview. Cartesian dualism would not work, because Descartes's immaterial mind is a thing about which nothing can be said, and we have no idea how we might investigate it (Phenomenology had a stab, but not until the twentieth century). At best, we can say what it is not, and science has no time for necessarily impregnable black boxes.

The convergence of capitalism and science in materialism is coincidental. Materialism works for modern capital firstly because it implies short-termism. If I think my life will end when my body dies, I may as well cooperate with the existing state of affairs, especially if everyone else is. The purpose of life becomes enjoyment and comfort, and is best achieved by accumulating goods conducive to that. Naturally, those goods will have been commodified. We ourselves become yet another instance of property: we 'own' ourselves. The 'Good Life' becomes one of gradually expanding ownership, at the end of which retirement allows for the uninterrupted enjoyment of all one has accumulated. Death, when it arrives, is always tragic.

The second way in which materialism works for modern capitalism is that it tends to deny free will. As the American philosopher, Alex Rosenberg, put it, "If the brain is nothing but a complex physical object whose states are as much governed by physical laws as any other physical object, then what goes on in our heads is as fixed and determined by prior events as what goes on when one domino topples another in a long row of them."[79] Obviously, if I have no free will, I cannot be blamed if I choose to accept capitalism, or even if I choose to fully collaborate with it. Indeed, no one in the system can be blamed for anything. Why, for example, should anyone be held accountable for the 2008 global financial crash? Or for climate change? Or even for corporate corruption?

Materialism in capitalist societies works in partnership with psychology, presented as a science. Materialism is the philosophical arm of capitalism; psychology – which takes materialism as a tentative and provisional (in principle - but in practice, dogmatically established) 'working hypothesis' - is its therapeutic arm, but also its intimate collaborator. In *Modern Man in Search of a Soul*, Carl Jung comments:

> "To think otherwise than our contemporaries think is somehow illegitimate and disturbing; it is even indecent, morbid or blasphemous, and therefore socially dangerous for the individual. He is stupidly swimming against the social current. Just as formerly the assumption was unquestionable that everything

---

[79] Rosenberg, Alex (2000), p9.

that exists takes its rise from the creative will of a God who is spirit, so the nineteenth century discovered the equally unquestionable truth that everything arises from material causes."[80]

Adam Curtis's 2002 documentary series, *The Century of the Self,* convincingly charts psychology's long history of service to consumerism from Freud onwards. Wittgenstein's judgement at the end of the *Philosophical Investigations* remains relevant: "In psychology there are experimental methods and conceptual confusion … The existence of the experimental method makes us think we have the means of solving the problems which trouble us, though problems and method pass each other by."[81] The same almost certainly applies to sociology.

As capitalism's therapeutic arm, psychology is always on hand to redress the brain's balance. It can do this, as Freud did, by innocuous, non-invasive means, but nowadays it often involves chemicals. In Britain, 20% of the adult population now takes at least one brand of psychiatric drugs.[82] In *Capitalist Realism*, Mark Fisher passionately appealed to the reader to seek the causes of mental illness in public-social, as opposed to subjective-psychological phenomena. In his recent *Sedated: How Modern Capitalism Created Our Mental Health Crisis*, the anthropologist James Davies issues the same call, reinforced with stronger evidence. "Psychiatric labels," he writes (in an analysis that echoes Wittgenstein's), "do not correspond to known biological pathologies that treatments can then target and 'cure'. They are rather socially constructed labels ascribed to collections of feelings and behaviours deemed disordered or pathological by the psychiatric committees who make up the

---

[80] Jung, Carl (1933), p202-3.
[81] Wittgenstein, Ludwig (1958), p232.
[82] Cf. eg. https://www.gov.uk/government/publications/prescribed-medicines-review-report/prescribed-medicines-review-summary

DSM [*The Diagnostic and Statistical Manual of Mental Disorders*]."[83] It seems intuitively probable, given that over 20% of adolescents suffer mental health problems,[84] that teenage rebellion – and in fact, any kind of rebellion against the system at all – is increasingly self-presenting as a low-level psychiatric disorder. Part of this must have to do with the capitalist-created 'indoor/cyberspace society' that took off, as we suggested above (following Jonathan Haidt), in roughly 2010. Haidt again:

> "I refer to the period from 2010 to 2015 as the Great Rewiring of Childhood. Social patterns, role models, emotions, physical activity, and even sleep patterns were fundamentally recast, for adolescents, over the course of just five years... Children born in the late 1990s were the first generation in history who went through puberty in the virtual world. It's as though we sent Gen Z to grow up on Mars when we gave them smartphones in the early 2010s, in the largest uncontrolled experiment humanity has ever performed on its own children."[85]

Of course – as is almost too obvious to be worth saying – all this creates significant profits for pharmaceutical companies, many of which are actively pushing dubious diagnoses dressed up as sound methodology and good practice.

Materialism fosters the importance of 'looks', of how my body appears to me, and others, and how I perceive the latter's evaluations. So, in addition to a parasitic pharmaceutic industry, we have a parasitic diet industry, a parasitic nutritionist

[83] Davies, James (2021), p11.
[84] https://www.mentalhealth.org.uk/explore-mental-health/statistics/children-young-people-statistics
[85] Haidt, Jonathan (2024), p35, 44.

industry, a parasitic cosmetics industry (which may employ surgical procedures), and so on.

Arguably, under developed capitalism, there are three arenas in which my 'looks' present: (1) to myself, in the mirror; (2) to other people, in real time and geography, as when I go outside, for example, to shop, drive, eat; (3) to what might be called the hyper-public arena, the realm in which I appear in photographs and on social media. The three are not mutually exclusive, of course.

The first and third combine to create a fictional version of me which is consciously or unconsciously wish-fulfilling. The second is civil society, where the 'me' who inhabits objectively public spaces is produced as a kind of weak after-projection of (1) and (3). The self is a series of reflections and insertions into social settings where what appears subjectively authentic is, in fact, alienated. And I suffer the psychological consequences of that.

One has to turn to pre-capitalist societies to recover a worldview that significantly differs from the materialist. Often there, the human person was more than a body; accretion of wealth was a familial thing, and one entered the equivalent of retirement within the context of the extended family, which might involve a significant degree of individual material divestment. This is exemplified, for example, in the Hindu Ashrams, the stages of life: of the four – student, householder, retiree, and holy man – it is the second that will be the most materially well-endowed.

Materialism is essentially the intellectual *weltanschauung* of the late 19th century; we know enough now to know that it is at least questionable: we have Leonard Susskind's holographic theory of the universe, we have Schrödinger's cat, we have parallel worlds, we a fine-tuned universe, we have dark energy and dark matter, and so on. The universe is bigger, stranger and more replete with possibilities than any 19th-century materialist could conceivably have imagined.

2. *Moral Relativism*

Moral relativism is the ethical ideology of capital, as even the most cursory look at modern history will confirm: capitalism and moral relativism achieved dominance together. Under late capital, its triumph is virtually complete. If the power of capital is reflected in the power of its ideology, then nothing attests to that power as unequivocally as the fact that many anti-capitalist movements – including Marxism – are avowedly champions of moral relativism.

On the face of it, this is odd, because clearly the most cogent arguments against injustice are moral arguments; yet if moral judgements have no truth-value - if they resemble judgements of aesthetic or gastronomic taste - then they cannot prevail against modern capital. The latter is just one economic system amongst many, none of which bear coherent scrutiny by morality. But that is precisely the point.

3. *Nationalism*

As we saw above, the harmonious community is the principal object of ideology, and in modern times that community is conceived as a nation. Because it is also conceived as one member of a community of nations, the ideology has to accept that things may be different elsewhere, hence the validity of moral relativism. The nation is a taken-for-granted reality even for people who feel no allegiance to its most explicit presentation in patriotism. Their allegiance is to the community, not to its symbolic accoutrements.

But there is another sense in which the nation pervades consciousness: that in which it is assumed as a given in most people's mode of relating to the world. For example, as a citizen of Country X, if I feel aggrieved enough to take action against an injustice in my own country, the same injustice in another nation will not necessarily provoke me to take the same action. I may feel it is 'none of my business', and/ or that it is for the citizens of that other nation to organise their own affairs. In many cases, for all practical purposes, those nations do not exist. Women's rights in the UK are rightly a matter of intimate concern to many UK citizens; but when women in Iran are killed for not wearing a headscarf, that is less intimately my business. Organisations like Amnesty International have tried hard to make human rights a 'borderless' concern, but most people still think in terms of different countries: mine first, the others later, and sometimes (to avoid treading on cultural landmines), not at all. 'Nationalism', in the sense we are talking about here, has nothing to do with jingoism, and everything to do with an ideological limitation of the moral imagination.

For traditional Marxism, nationalism is a cluster of ideas that must, in the long term, buckle under the free market. Pressurised by capitalist globalisation, the nation itself is destined to atrophy and eventually die. Of course, so far that has not happened, although, for some commentators, it briefly seemed to re-emerge as a possibility as recently as the early years of the twenty-first century.

In fact, nation-states are the pre-condition of modern capital: capital cannot survive without them, and far from withering away, they are destined to persist for its duration. As Benedict Anderson showed, capital invented them for a good reason, then it exported them. "Nationalism has proved an uncomfortable anomaly for Marxist theory," he says, "and precisely for that reason, has been largely elided, rather than confronted."[86] In the sixteenth century, when modern capitalism

---

[86] Anderson, Benedict (1991), p3.

began, the nation-state was comparatively rare. Nowadays, it is everywhere, and its borders are often the creation of colonisers.

As was noted above, Anderson located the birth of the modern nation-state in 'print capitalism', particularly the invention of the newspaper and the novel. Each helped bring about an imagined community of persons linked by place and simultaneity.

But the newspaper and the novel pull in different directions. Both tell stories, but in the newspaper, villains are never wholly absent, and are usually front and centre. Obviously, there are villains outside the national borders, but their most useful representatives are within; being more proximate, they elicit greater fear and indignation, and they sell more newspapers.

The novel, at least in its baldly commercial form, can profit by working with the newspaper: it is then populated by cardboard villains. In its more developed form, it questions and explores the moral issues the newspaper takes for granted. Both enterprises, newspaper and novel, are premised on the notion of insiders and outsiders – although the line that divides them may be contested and subject to revision – and both help consolidate the nation.[87]

All nations resemble prisons to a certain extent, and they contribute to producing the 'generalised Stockholm syndrome' we spoke of above. As a citizen of any nation, I am owned by that nation from birth. So I am 'British', 'German', 'Thai' or 'Russian'. Even where the freedom to travel abroad is guaranteed by law, a person can usually only travel to other nations as a guest. If I outstay my welcome in any of them, I will generally be ejected by force. And while I am there, I will be excluded from the 'real life' of the country, either legally, or by

---

[87] Nowadays, we tend to think of newspapers aligning with political parties, but historically, it may be that political parties grew out of the political prejudices of newspapers. The first English newspapers were the Oxford Gazette (1665), and the Daily Courant (1702). The political party can probably be traced to Edmund Burke's 1770, *Thoughts on the Cause of the Present Discontents*.

language, or by prejudice, or by my own unfamiliarity and lack of local expertise – or by all four.

But some nations are more prison-like than others, depending partly on when, in history, they entered the swelling system of world capital (those established later tend, on the whole, to be more oppressive), the competence or honesty of their rulers, climate, the resources available for exploitation by developed industries, and, obviously, where any particular occupant sits on the social ladder.

Our nation enculturates (or commodifies us) to make us into reasonably standard 'citizens' who resemble each other more than we resemble foreigners. And through its engagement in international relations, as relayed through the media, it subtly encourages us to feel allegiances and antipathies to other nations. It aggrandises the ideology produced by its own subaltern classes and re-transmits it as a hotchpotch of military pomp, sport, and special occasions, accompanied by historically endorsed, emotionally charged symbols. When we come of age, we will be expected to work for capital; or, if we are enterprising, we can get it to work for us, by starting a business (but always on national terms).

The enculturation process is never perfect, but, under normal circumstances, it is aided by our self-commodification: longstanding, deep-seated conventions regarding what to wear, how to deport ourselves, how to address others, even how to laugh, sit and stand, are things we impose on ourselves, and which exist in fine gradations, but always within a narrow, nationally-reserved band of the spectrum of global possibilities. More pervasive are intellectual and moral fashions, which bring the inbuilt delusion of autonomy.

Sometimes, in rare circumstances, our commodification as national subjects and culturally constructed persons will be insufficient to prevent a society breaking down. The ties that bind us together may loosen suddenly for reasons beyond the rulers' ability to handle, and the victims may be shocked into revolt. There will be a revolution. Yet since it only takes place in one or two nations, it can be contained.

What would a world without nations look like? We are institutionalised enough to regard that question with fear. Yet there was a time when they didn't exist. Obviously, their removal now would not be a reversion to those times.

4. The Lumpenproletariat

The term 'lumpenproletariat', invented by Marx and Engels for polemical purposes in the mid-1840s, defies integration into their theory of historical materialism. It appears to undergo a change in meaning in about 1850, although the term itself is so indeterminate to begin with, it is difficult to tell. Often translated into English as 'the dangerous classes', it is taken by the majority of commentators to refer to a class outside and beneath the working classes, one characterised by impoverishment and cynical opportunism.

Does this class have revolutionary potential? Both Marx and Engels are unambiguously of the view that it does not. Modern commentators have been increasingly inclined to disagree. They usually argue like this:

A. The lumpenproletariat is constituted by those who have fallen out of the proletariat for a cluster of different reasons. It represents an extra level of impecuniousness.

B. Nowadays, we understand the reasons someone might 'fall out of' the proletariat much better than Marx did. Such reasons would include unemployment, disability, racial prejudice, and so on.

In the most recent major analysis of the phenomenon, *The Dangerous Class: The Concept of the Lumpenproletariat* (2020), Clyde W Barrow defines the lumpenproletariat in something like the above manner, in terms of its position outside capitalist relations of production. It is a displaced component of what would, in better circumstances, have been the proletariat, and is produced by a relative surplus population – 'surplus', that is, to the requirements of an effectively functioning capitalist

100

economy - whose connection to the working proletariat is fluid and constantly shifting. While the working proletariat has a precarious relation to employment, the lumpenproletariat is, on the whole, excluded from it by virtue of deep-seated factors such as inaptitude, age, disability, entrenched temperament (including criminal and recalcitrant temperaments), and prolonged homelessness. Individuals belonging to those categories develop social identities out of kilter with the distributive positions of the labour market/ social relations of production. Members of the working proletariat can, of course, find themselves cast down into the lumpenproletariat. For Barrow, the lumpenproletariat has a Marxian revolutionary potential.

This reading of the term as designating a 'lowest of the low', a class related to the proletariat just as pariahs are related to labourers in the Hindu caste system, has a long history, and includes, as Barrow reminds us, Frantz Fanon's *The Wretched of the Earth*, as well as the Black Panthers. In his 1975 book, *Marx*, David McLellan interprets the term to mean, "the drop-outs of society who had no stake in the development of society and so no historical role to play – except occasionally to sell their services to the bourgeoisie."[88] Michel Foucault thought the lumpenproletariat were part of the proletariat, and had been falsely distinguished from them by the bourgeoisie as a kind of divide-and-rule tactic intended to "separate the delinquents from all the lower classes that they came from and with which they remained linked."[89]

But (A), above, is contentious from the start. Both Marx and Engels discuss the unemployed, in *Capital* and elsewhere, under the heading 'The Industrial Reserve Army'. There is no

---

[88] McLellan , David (1975), p45. He thinks – not without justification - that Marcuse comes close replacing the proletariat with the lumpenproletariat.
[89] Foucault, Michel, *Surveiller et Punir* (Paris: Gallimard, 1975), 291. Quoted in Bourdin, Jean-Paul, *Marx and the Lumpenproletariat* (Actuel Marx, No 54(2), 39-55). https://shs.cairn.info/journal-actuel-marx-2013-2-page-39?lang=en.

suggestion that they identify it in any way with the lumpenproletariat. The same could be said of the disabled[90], and racial minorities. In *The Communist Manifesto*, Marx describes the lumpenproletariat as part of the 'old society' (*der alten Gesellschaft*), and later, it includes 'ruined and adventurous offshoots of the bourgeoisie.' Its status as a discarded substratum of the proletariat, in the sense of being its indigent waste product, finally loses all credibility in Marx's *The Class Struggles in France 1848 to 1850*, to which we shall turn in a moment.

'Lump' is first used by Marx in 1845, in *The German Ideology*, to refer to the plebeians of ancient Rome, and also to castigate Max Stirner's 'self-professed radical constituency of the Lumpen' (a reference to the 'ragamuffin' (*Lump*) in *The Ego and Its Own*[91]).

After *The German Ideology*, it appears in a more developed form in *The Communist Manifesto*:

> "The lumpenproletariat, the social scum, that passively rotting mass thrown off by the lowest layers of the old society, may, here and there, be swept into the movement by a proletarian revolution; its conditions of life, however, prepare it far more for the part of a bribed tool of reactionary intrigue."[92]

---

[90] Cf. eg, Bengtsson, Staffan (2017), 'Out of the frame: disability and the body in the writings of Karl Marx', which never feels the need to refer to the lumpenproletariat.

[91] Eg, "On this depends whether you are to be an owner [*Eigner*] or a ragamuffin [*Lump*]! The egoist is owner, the socialist a ragamuffin." (1995), p277. 'Ragamuffin', David Leopold's preferred translation may seem quaint, but it may preserve some of the sense. According to The Merriam-Webster dictionary, 'the *muffin* part of *ragamuffin* may have its origin in either of two Anglo-Norman words for a devil or a scoundrel.' See Draper, below, on the possibility of 'lump' meaning something like 'knave'.

[92] Marx and Engels (1967), p92.

This reference to 'the old society', already mentioned, chimes with Engels's claim in his 1850, *The Peasant War in Germany*, that the lumpenproletariat comprised "ruined members of the middle-class and that mass of the city population which possessed no citizenship rights".[93]

On the other hand, in the same text, Engels twice apparently calls it a "low-grade proletariat", which would go some way towards confirming that the lumpenproletariat is deposited out of the proletariat:

> "...The numerous beginnings of the lumpenproletariat which can be found even in the lowest stages of development of city life. This *low-grade proletariat* is..."

> "[In the sixteenth century, the lumpenproletariat] retained a considerable foundation of peasant nature, and had not developed that degree of venality and degradation which characterise the modern civilised *low-grade proletariat.*"[94]

However, in both cases, 'low-grade proletariat' is a stylistic innovation by Engels's 1926 English translator, Moissaye J Olgin (probably to avoid too much repetition): it does not appear as such in the German. The German reads 'lumpenproletariat' in both instances.[95]

To sum up so far, we have a class that is:

(1) Constituted by 'the lowest layers of *the old society*';

---

[93] Engels, Friedrich (1926), p14.

[94] Ibid. p15.

[95] Respectively, "den zahlreichen Anfangen des Lumpenproletariats, die sich selbst auf den untergeordneten Stufen der städtischen Entwicklung vorfinden. Das Lumpenproletariat ist ..." and "und noch lange nicht die Käuflichkeit und Verkommenheit des heutigen zivilisierten Lumpenproletariats entwickelt hatte." (*Der deutsche Bauernkrieg* p18)

(2) Old enough to have been around since Roman times;

(3) Composed of 'ruined and adventurous offshoots of the bourgeoisie/ the middle classes';

(4) In 'a condition of life' that chiefly predisposes it to become 'a bribed tool of reactionary intrigue'.

This does not look like a super-indigent proletariat. Arguably, in the word, 'lumpenproletariat', we are not dealing with a compound noun such as can be dismantled and understood in terms of its two components (Lumpen + Proletariat), but a proper noun - something more like a name. It may be best translated into English by something like 'low life', which also, deceptively, invites interpretation in terms of its two components, but which also escapes comprehension as such. Note that in Marx and Engels's usage, 'lumpenproletariat' always comes loaded with moral contempt - just like 'low life'.

An intensification of this semantic complexity occurs in Part 1 of *The Class Struggles in France 1848 to 1850*, where Marx writes:

> "Since the finance aristocracy made the laws, was at the head of the administration of the state, had command of all the organised public authorities, dominated public opinion through the actual state of affairs and through the press, the same prostitution, the same shameless cheating, the same mania to get rich was repeated in every sphere, from the court to the Café Borgne, to get rich not by production, but by pocketing the already available wealth of others, Clashing every moment with the bourgeois laws themselves, an unbridled assertion of unhealthy and dissolute appetites manifested itself, particularly at the top of bourgeois society – lusts wherein wealth derived from gambling naturally seeks its satisfaction, where

pleasure becomes *crapuleux*, where money, filth, and blood commingle. The finance aristocracy, in its mode of acquisition as well as in its pleasures, is nothing but the rebirth of the lumpenproletariat at the heights of bourgeois society."[96]

Then, two years later, in *The Eighteenth Brumaire of Louis Bonaparte*, Marx wrote:

"On the pretext of founding a benevolent society, the lumpenproletariat of Paris had been organized into secret sections, each section led by Bonapartist agents, with a Bonapartist general at the head of the whole. Alongside decayed roués with dubious means of subsistence and of dubious origin, alongside ruined and adventurous offshoots of the bourgeoisie, were vagabonds, discharged soldiers, discharged jailbirds, escaped galley slaves, swindlers, mountebanks, lazzaroni, pickpockets, tricksters, gamblers, *maquereaux*, brothel keepers, porters, literati, organ grinders, ragpickers, knife grinders, tinkers, beggars — in short, the whole indefinite, disintegrated mass, thrown hither and thither, which the French call *la bohème;* from this kindred element Bonaparte formed the core of the Society of December 10. A 'benevolent society' - insofar as, like Bonaparte, all its members felt the need of benefiting themselves at the expense of the labouring nation. This Bonaparte, who constitutes himself chief of the lumpenproletariat, who here alone rediscovers in mass form the interests which he personally pursues, who recognises in this scum, offal,

[96]

https://www.marxists.org/archive/marx/works/download/pdf/Class_Struggles_in_France.pdf.

refuse of all classes the only class upon which he can base himself unconditionally, is the real Bonaparte, the Bonaparte sans phrase."[97]

What do these two texts – for all their brevity, among the longest Marx ever wrote on the topic of the lumpenproletariat – tell us? In *The Class Struggles in France,* the finance aristocracy – one of the wealthiest groups of social individuals - is 'the rebirth of the lumpenproletariat at the heights of bourgeois society'; it is 'at the head of the administration of the state, had command of all the organised public authorities'; and in the *Eighteenth Brumaire,* Louis Napoleon – the last monarch of France - has 'constituted himself chief of the lumpenproletariat.'

These are not people who have been excluded from employment by virtue of inaptitude. What they share with the lumpenproletariat conceived as 'vagabonds, discharged soldiers, discharged jailbirds, escaped galley slaves', etc. is a definite *moral* character. Engels puts his finger on it later when, in his 1870 preface to the second edition of *The Peasant War in Germany,* he calls them "an absolutely venal, an absolutely brazen crew."

It will immediately be objected that this is a misreading of Marx: in the two passages cited, the finance aristocracy and Louis Napoleon are 'lumpenproletarian' only in a metaphorical or honorary sense: the former are the lumpenproletariat 'reborn [in a new sphere]' and Louis Napoleon 'constitutes *himself*' its

---

[97] https://www.marxists.org/archive/marx/works/download/pdf/18th-Brumaire.pdf. Walter Benjamin tells us: "It should be noticed that Napoleon III himself began his rise in a milieu that is related to the one described above [ie, in the Marx passage cited here]. As we know, one of the tools of his presidential period was the Society of the Tenth of December, whose cadres, according to Marx, had been supplied by 'the whole indefinite, disintegrated mass, thrown hither and thither, which the French call *la bohème.'* During his emperorship Napoleon continued his conspiratory customs. Surprising proclamations and mystery-mongering, sudden sallies and impenetrable irony were part of the raison d'état of the Second Empire" (1973), p12.

head. In both cases, we may legitimately doubt whether their inclusion is meant to be taken literally. What Marx is saying is that the finance aristocracy and Louis Napoleon *strongly resemble* the lumpenproletariat, nothing more.[98]

But two questions then arise: (1) in what does this resemblance consist? and (2) at what point does strong resemblance shade into identity?

As regards (1), the resemblance is obviously a moral one: the finance aristocracy is full of 'unhealthy and dissolute appetites', it is engaged in 'shameless cheating', 'prostitution', 'pocketing the already available wealth of others'; it is a place where 'money, filth, and blood commingle'. If the lumpenproletariat is essentially the most dispossessed class, there can be no question of a resemblance of material position within the economic system. Moral likeness is all we have, a fact which would gain support from Hal Draper's 1972 claim that the true root of 'lumpenproletariat' is 'lump' (knave, rogue) not 'lumpen' (ragged).[99]

As regards (2), unless we have a prior essential definition of the lumpenproletariat – which we do not - upon which immorality might supervene as an accidental feature, we should assume that the moral resemblance here is strong enough to count as identity.[100]

---

[98] At the beginning of his long essay, 'The Paris of the Second Empire in Baudelaire', Walter Benjamin notes that Louis Napoleon came from the same milieu as the one Marx identified in his review of Chenu's *Les conspirateurs* in 1850, and that "during his emperorship Napoleon continued his conspiratorial customs." (1973), p12.

[99] Draper, Hal (1972).

[100] In this context, it is worth mentioning Antonio Gramsci's identification of the lumpenproletariat   with the *morti di fame* ("Lumpenproletariat – called in Italy by the picturesque name of *'morti di fame'*" (1971, p203). "There exist two distinct strata of *morti di fame:* the day labourers and the petty intellectuals. The essential characteristic of the day labourers is *not their economic situation but their intellectual and moral condition...* The petit-bourgeois *morti di fame* came originally from the rural bourgeoisie" (1971, p273. Italics mine).

The fear of the lumpenproletariat seems to have reached a pitch in the France described in Marx's essay on Louis Napoleon. In *Discipline and Punish*, Foucault mentions a widely experienced "'great fear' of a people who were believed to be criminal and seditious as a whole … a barbaric, immoral and outlaw class which, from the empire to the July monarchy, haunted the discourse of legislators, philanthropists and investigators into working-class life."[101]

The Fourierists had noticed this before Marx, and like Marx, they insisted on the identity of indigent criminals and bourgeois criminals. "This criminality of need or of repression masks, by the attention paid to it and the disapprobation surrounding it, another criminality that is sometimes its cause and always its extension. This is the delinquency from above."[102]

Modern authors have recognised the same thing. Beginning with the Bulgarian Marxist, Dimitar Blagoev, in 1906, followed up by Béla Kun in 1920, and continuing with György Lukács and Arthur Koestler in the 1940s, the term 'lumpenbourgeoisie' made its way irresistibly into sociological literature. Andre Gunder Frank's 1972, *Lumpenbourgeoisie and Lumpendevelopment: Dependency, Class and Politics in Latin America* is generally considered to have established it. The term is often, but not always, used in the context of post-colonial studies. Nevertheless, notwithstanding sociology's claim to scientific status, it cannot slough off its moral-normative character.

In short, not only is 'lumpenproletariat', for Marx, a moral category, but it is *clearly and unambiguously* a moral category: nowhere in his writings is there any real attempt to give it a technical meaning. Whenever the lumpenproletariat is mentioned, it is always with righteous abhorrence.

We are free, of course, to ignore Marx: maybe there really *is* a category which the term can be made to pick out. If so, perhaps

---

[101] Foucault, Michel (2020), p275.
[102] Ibid., p287.

we can avoid the incongruousness of hosting an egregiously evaluative term in what claims to be a scientific theory; maybe we can iron out the difficulties, and 'lumpenproletariat' can be assigned a role in that theory.

Maybe. The more interesting question, however, is: what is such an overtly moral category doing in Marx anyway? A Derridan analysis might conceive it as a 'supplement' in the theory's margins, haunting, and even defining, the putative centre. Put more prosaically, maybe it is an instance of the way history can sometimes reveal that seemingly peripheral phenomena are really not so peripheral after all.

A much better analysis would show that, for all its claims to scientific objectivity, morality has always been embedded in the theory of historical materialism. Consider the following two scenarios, involving a machine for making some commodity, X.

In the first scenario, a slave (it must be a slave in order to discount wages as a factor) cuts strips of processed clay into discreet blocks as part of a brick-making process. In the second scenario, exactly the same job is done by a non-sentient robot. Now, does the slave belong to the means of production, or to the relations of production? Marxism would have to answer: the latter: the relations. And yet it would have to consider the robot a part of the means. So, what is the difference between the slave and the robot? Well, there is no difference in *function*. The only difference is a moral one: the slave counts as a *person* (with all the inherent value that implies), the robot does not. So moral phenomena seem to be implicit in the theory of historical materialism, after all. And since that is true here, at the most basic level, we may reasonably assume that it is true throughout.

In any case, the strength of Marx's aversion to the lumpenproletariat seems to attest to something real. It exists in a highly disturbing way - and yet it cannot be accommodated within the theory. Marx's tone when he visits the topic, and his infrequency in doing so, might even be interpreted as a deliberate attempt to keep it at arm's length. It represents a radically disquieting alterity.

Its dual moral-normative and descriptive-scientific character in some ways mirrors the same confusion within Marxism generally. If the theory of historical materialism is true, then it is an interconnected web of *facts*. It can neither entail the desirability of a particular course of action, nor the preferability of Communism. To the extent that it demonstrates the inevitability of revolution, it nullifies the need to commit to it. Why bother, if it going to happen anyway?

The Lumpenproletariat and the Means of Securitisation

Taking into account all the jumbled signals here, the most burning question about the lumpenproletariat may be: how real is it? Is it real at all? Here, we find ourselves confronting one of the issues that has distinguished right- from left-wing politics in modern discourse. The right insists that criminality is a primordial phenomenon; the left sees it as chiefly the product of adverse social conditions. Except at the extremes, neither suggests that the other is completely mistaken.

In Chapter 2, we distinguished two forms of the means of securitisation: defensive and proactive. The defensive is designed to safeguard an already acquired surplus against those who would carry it off or despoil it; the proactive arises as a development of the defensive, as soon as it becomes clear that certain of the tools used to defend any one group's surplus – eg, spears, knives and slingshots - can also be used to carry off or despoil someone else's.

What if, originally, the means of defensive securitisation actually *created* the criminal class, as a kind of self-fulfilling prophecy? What if, in securing their goods, the first securers put ideas of theft into others' minds, ideas they would not otherwise have entertained, and which they then became disposed (either because of a prolonged period of material hardship, or because they felt tempted by the thought of forbidden fruit) to act upon?

That would mean thieves arose as a reaction to the securitiser's behaviour, rather as Foucault claimed. What we would really have, underneath, is a class of excluded individuals who simply want to survive, or who are mischievous, and who get labelled as criminals for purely pragmatic, polemical reasons.

Obviously, this is an originary myth, which is not to say it cannot be 'true' in its way. Nevertheless, it does not seem very plausible. The first thieves were probably not other human beings, but wild animals, and it seems likely that, in terms of theft, the class of animals and the class of rival hunter-gatherers were never entirely separate. Humans too are animals.

But even apart from those considerations, it seems improbable. What seems more likely: (a) that the means of defensive securitisation was invented at a time when there was no real prospect of theft, or (b) that it was invented after bitter experience had proven the need for it? Added to which, the primordial thieves and the primordial securitisers were probably one and the same individuals fulfilling different roles at different times.

For all of those reasons, we need to acknowledge that the class of thieves is real. Securitisation is not a defence against some figment of anyone's imagination, but against a real category of individuals. The lumpenproletariat really does exist.

To say it is real, however, is not to say that it can be precisely delineated. In fact, it cannot. Although the class of thieves is real, in securitising his goods, the securitiser must conceive an abstract/ thought-experimental thief. He or she must consider all the possibilities open to that thief, and take those possibilities into account. In the business of effective securitisation, he must envision that thief to be utterly determined, infinitely resourceful, incorrigibly malign, and part of an overwhelming mass of similar individuals. He must, in other words, imagine "an absolutely venal, an absolutely brazen crew." Thus, the lumpenproletariat is born; part reality, part fantasy – and no one can really say how much of each. It is an "indefinite, disintegrated mass."

Because it is both real and (socially) imagined, and because the imagined component is produced out of the means of defensive securitisation, the lumpenproletariat remains relatively nebulous from age to age. Its indistinctness is related to the difficulty of identifying the precise markers of social class generally, but especially of defining capitalism, which we looked at above.

But while the lumpenproletariat is difficult to pin down, we should not underestimate its power to disrupt: there really is "an absolutely venal, an absolutely brazen crew" out there: Marx's rather quaint list of "porters, literati, organ grinders, ragpickers," etc. can easily be updated to include sex traffickers, drug barons, blackmailers, online fraudsters, ivory poachers, child pornographers, etc; and, as he recognised, since it exists at both ends of the social scale we also have tax evaders, modern slavers, money launderers, inside traders, state sponsors of terrorism, dictators and their coteries, high-ranking war criminals, and so on. To some extent, the lumpenproletariat and the means of securitisation are two parts of the same whole: when the product of production, and the wealth it represents, is significant, the means of securitisation is used, in its most advanced form, chiefly by lumpenproletarians to keep other lumpenproletarians out.

The area staked out by the lumpenproletariat and the means of securitisation constitutes a cultural field which is highly congenial to capitalism, as it was to every regime that preceded it. It is the cultural field in which we all live, and which defines us. Today, the insatiability of the lumpenproletariat drives the evolution of the means of securitisation, just as the means of securitisation sustains the spectral power of the lumpenproletariat, which haunts society in every age far more effectively than the proletariat ever haunted Marx's age.

The lumpenproletariat makes active use of the means of securitisation at all times, chiefly as a way of protecting itself against itself. Because the lumpenproletariat can never possess a unifying class consciousness of the sort that would allow it to delimit itself against other players in the division of labour; for all practical purposes, there are no other players. The individual lumpenproletarian is permanently at war with other lumpenproletarians, and that endeavour takes up nearly all of his time and energy.

The Lumpenproletariat and the Middle Classes

The lumpenproletariat may be described as that class of persons who are socially inclined to subsist by systematically taking the bulk of their money - or goods that can be sold for money - from others in a way that is deliberately hidden from public scrutiny; and whose act of taking is so hidden on the grounds that it would otherwise be widely and strongly censured (and possibly, circumstances permitting, severely punished). As a class of individuals (rather than a true social class) it frequently overlaps with capitalism, especially where capitalism is markedly successful; so we can talk about 'lumpenproletarian capitalism'. [103]

Where do the middle classes fit into all this? Marx identifies the capitalist class with the bourgeoisie, but how plausible is

---

[103] According to our definition, above, capitalism is 'the private pursuit of unlimited monetary wealth by means, *at least to begin with*, of the scalable production of commodities'. Lumpenproletarian capitalists would be those who have successfully survived the earliest stages of competition, who have established a relatively secure base, and who have increasingly turned to extra-legal means of financial accumulation as a means of achieving unlimited monetary wealth. Not every successful capitalist will necessarily fit this description.

that, really? The term 'bourgeoisie' – for which we may, for the purposes of this discussion, substitute its English equivalent, 'middle-class' (though the two are not wholly identical) – is not made up chiefly of capitalists: it is made up of doctors, lawyers, administrators, teachers, architects, surveyors, and so on, some of whom may be antithetical to capitalism.[104] Karl Marx, Friedrich Engels, Vladimir Lenin and Leon Trotsky were all middle class, so were Pierre-Joseph Proudhon and Mikhail Bakunin, so were Rosa Luxemburg and Karl Liebknecht, so was Errico Malatesta, so were Georgi Plekhanov and Nikolai Bukharin and Leonid Kantorovich, so was György Lukács, so was Frida Kahlo, so were Fidel Castro and Che Guevara, so was Louis Althusser, so were Sylvia Pankhurst, George Orwell and Sylvia Townsend Warner, so were Simone de Beauvoir and Jean-Paul Sartre, so was Frantz Fanon, so was Michel Foucault, so were Gilles Deleuze and Félix Guattari, so were the entire Frankfurt School. In our own day, Jeremy Corbyn, Tariq Ali, Gayatri Chakravorty Spivak, Amia Srinivasan, Slavoj Žižek and Greta Thunberg are middle class.[105] The vast majority of Marxists in university departments of sociology, political science, history, and so on, are indisputably middle-class.[106] In

---

[104] In his 1975, *Marx*, David McLellan says: "How many classes [for Marx] are there? There is the beginning of an answer in *Capital*, Volume III, where Marx stated that, in terms of identity of revenues and sources of revenue, there were three great social classes – wage labourers, capitalists, and landowners; but the manuscript broke off just as Marx was putting the crucial question as to why doctors, lawyers, etc. were not separate classes" (p44).

[105] Leo Tolstoy, Pytor Kropotkin, Anna Filosofova, Bertrand Russell and Tony Benn were all aristocrats; Joseph Stalin and Mao Zedong were peasants. One might ask: What if the middle classes decided to throw a party for the proletariat, and the proletariat didn't come?

[106] Britain is, and probably always has been, a pathological class-conscious nation. Public intellectuals on both right and left are often at pains to assert their working-class 'origins', or conceal their middle-class ones. One can earn three times the average national wage, live in a huge house, and, providing either of one's parents was working class, one can always claim to be, oneself, 'really' working-class. According to a recent study by Oxford University, "Six out of ten people in Britain today consider themselves working class because they believe

the France of May 1968, it was middle-class students who began and ended the protests (the workers having been bought off by the Grenelle agreements). Of course, that is not to say that there are no capitalists in the middle-classes, but they are a small minority.

The flip side is that the middle-classes are overwhelmingly private property owners, thus allied to capitalism by way of maintaining a status quo in which property values do not deteriorate and private property is not abolished. Which coincides – as far as it goes - with the agenda of capitalism.

Even so, that is not nearly enough to establish the interchangeability of 'capitalist' and 'bourgeois'. Although capitalism clearly depends on private property, the converse is untrue: we can imagine a nation of subsistence farmers in which all citizens own their own land and grow their own food, but where no one commands anyone else's productive human body, or makes a profit.

The truth is that the middle-classes are contingently, but not necessarily, linked to capitalism, and that is one reason so many middle-class individuals can be avowed anti-capitalists without significant fear of contradiction. (For example, a 20-year-old child of middle-class parents may own no property to speak of, and may have no intention of changing her position in that respect.)

Private property is a consequence of an effective means of securitisation. Although capitalists benefit from the means of securitisation, so do others, and some people will securitise a portion of the available stock as a bulwark *against* the radical unpredictability of the capitalist lumpenproletariat, as *in itself* a means of securitisation. In terms of motives this would be the

___

their family background determines class, rather than occupation or whether they went to university. Just under half (47%) of those in 'middle class' jobs (classified as managerial or professional) said they were working class."
https://www.ox.ac.uk/news/2016-06-30-most-people-britain-today-regard-themselves-working-class.

opposite of a collaboration with capitalism, although otherwise, it would generally serve its interests.

Indeed, we may go further: the identification of the capitalist class with the bourgeoisie is an ideological construction, and is one of the ways in which Marxist analysis was infected by ideology from its inception. The middle-classes, for all their defects, are generally educated, restrained and useful, although, like all classes in society, since they exist (as we all do) within the cultural field defined, in different directions, by the means of securitisation and the lumpenproletariat – a field characterised by a default mutual hostility and suspicion - they can also use those advantages for detrimental ends. The Marxian and left-wing ideological attempt to make 'capitalism' coterminous with 'the middle-classes' has the effect of concealing the former's partly lumpenproletarian character, and gives it an unmerited air of respectability.

In fact, all the empirical evidence suggests that the middle-classes have significant revolutionary potential, however much orthodox Marxism suggests the flat opposite. The English, French and American Revolutions were led by the middle-classes, as was the *Risorgimento*, and, although, in Marxist eyes, those were 'bourgeois revolutions' for bourgeois ends, they turned out internally better than the Russian, Chinese and Cambodian revolutions. (Added to which, the idea of a successful bourgeois revolution 'for bourgeois ends' implies a group of people able to foresee and install a bespoke future to order).

But how can the most apparently conservative class exhibit (at least occasionally) the most radical behaviour, to the point of supporting or even fomenting revolutionary change?

The answer may lie in a concept originally defined in the writings of Alvin Toffler, but given a Marxist twist by, amongst others, Bernard Paulré, Yann Moulier-Boutang and the Italian *operaisti*, Antonio Negri. Following Toffler and Paulré, Moulier-

Boutang discerned a 'third' phase of capitalism, which he called cognitive capitalism. "By cognitive capitalism," he wrote, "we mean a mode of accumulation in which the object of accumulation consists mainly of knowledge, which becomes the basic source of value, as well as the principal location of the process of valorisation."[107] His point is that, in this third phase, the proletariat is supplanted as a subversive force by a 'cognitariat'.[108]

The precise character of the 'cognitariat' differs from author to author, but all agree that these are workers who produce commodities in which a significant degree of expertise is involved, and more than the general term 'skilled worker' designates. To put it another way, we are talking about workers who produce – individually, but perhaps more often as part of a team - custom-built or highly specific products, either as ends in themselves or as machines (real or virtual) to achieve complex and difficult ends. It is likely that the 'cognitariat' exhibits a significant degree of overlap with the middle classes. In many ways, it overlaps with Karl Mannheim's 'free-floating intelligentsia' *(Freischwebende Intelligenz)*, whose indeterminate position in society allows it to transcend political ideologies, to achieve new insights and to offer constructive criticism to progressive movements.[109]

Criticism of the notion of a 'cognitariat' has revolved around the issue of just how extensive it actually is, whether it is essentially a developed world phenomenon (global production generally being still overwhelmingly dependent on unskilled 'proletarian' labour (something like Negri's 'mass worker'));

---

[107] Moulier-Boutang (2012) p57. This of course follows Robert Lucas and Paul Romer's insight in the 1980s, that human capital and ideas have a significant part to play in economics.

[108] A term whose origins are obscure, but which may go back ultimately to Toffler, although Moulier-Boutang attributes it to a 2001 interview with the Italian Marxist, Franco Berardi.

[109] Mannheim, Karl (1936).

whether, in other words, there really are any grounds for identifying a knowledge-suffused 'cognitarian' 'third phase' of capitalism.

The correct response to that is probably: there may well be no 'third phase' of the sort Moulier-Boutang and others claim to discern, but that is only because the 'cognitariat' was integral to capitalism from its very beginning, and modern capitalism was always inconceivable without it. Equally, as EP Thompson showed in 1963, the working class always had a marked cultural-intellectual element: in Britain in the early nineteenth century, the many Jacobin-inspired associations, The London Corresponding Society, and early Methodism were clearly 'cognitarian' in character. Many of the earliest capitalists – James Watt, John Roebuck, Richard Trevithick, Eli Whitney, Elijah McCoy, to name just a few - were inventors and arguably 'cognitarians', which suggests that the present-day divorce between the more intellectual 'cognitarian' and the less innovative, more mercantile capitalist occurred at some point during the first Industrial Revolution.

In any case, the 'cognitariat' today straddles the working- and the middle-class as they have traditionally been conceived, but probably exhibits a bias towards the latter. It would exist on a spectrum, from shop-floor skilled labourers to Research & Development officers in large multinationals, and entirely encompass the category of professional securitisers in society, which is probably more extensive than it looks.

The reason it does not self-identify as a social group almost certainly has something to do with the social division of knowledge as described, for example, by Hayek in 1945.[110] The vast majority of cognitarians may be quietists, indifferentists and self-satisfied reactionaries, but somewhere amongst them are the radicals and the revolutionaries. In some ways, the latter

---

[110] 'The Use of Knowledge in Society' in *The American Economic Review*.

may be thought of as possessing a 'collective will' of the sort described by Ernesto Laclau and Chantal Mouffe in 2001,[111] only tenuously related to the social class of which it appears to be an expression.[112]

In any case, the middle classes and the capitalist lumpenproletariat constitute an unhappy symbiosis, in which a section of the former – often led by the (for now) propertyless young – perpetually threatens to break off and topple the system. Of course, that never happens. The young are always brought into the system as they grow older and make compromises (or at least, they have so far). The middle-classes can be – and often are – characterised by a degree of self-loathing and/or guilt, middle-class intellectuals frequently being eager to publicly distance themselves from supposed 'middle-class attitudes'.

Arguably, much political theory, including Marxism, has hitherto been too atomistic. It has considered politics as occurring within an area that, for Hegel, constituted 'civil society', where individual egos meet to conduct their affairs, and which is distinct from the family, the arena of private affairs. Marx accepted Hegel's use of the term and the division it sought to establish. Yet as long ago as 1795, Sophie de Grouchy observed that, rightly understood, history is the history of families rather than "a few men".[113]

---

[111] Laclau, Ernesto and Mouffe, Chantal, *Hegemony and Socialist Strategy: Towards a Radical Democratic Politics* (Verso 2001).

[112] Another solution to this problem may lie in Erik Olin Wright's notion of 'contradictory class locations'. According to Wright, the 'middle class' is not actually a single class at all, but a conglomerate of different classes with different interests. Some members are closer to the owning class than others, and may command higher wages as a result of scarce technical expertise. Others may be undervalued and consciously feel themselves to be so. The recent COVID epidemic highlighted the need for 'key workers', some of whom were cognitarians, but whose pay was low in relation to many other middle-class, less essential jobs. Of course, when the crisis ended, so did the related issue.

[113] https://plato.stanford.edu/entries/sophie-de-grouchy/

The meaning of 'civil society' has undergone several shifts in its history, but in any case, Hegel's attempted redefinition is instructive in more ways than he intended. In the early nineteenth century, his 'civil society' would have been all male; the family would have been the domestic realm of (private) men, women and children – although, of course, ruled by men. This assumption is preserved in Marx, along (probably) with its attendant valuation. In *The Communist Manifesto*, 'the bourgeois family' comes under sustained attack, but it is not clear how far what Marx says about it is, or is not, an attack on the family *per se*. To what extent does it resemble Plato's rejection of the family in *The Republic*, for example?

And yet, the family is deeply and irreducibly political. By 'family', we mean a group of people related either by consanguinity or by a socially endorsed bond. At its minimum, it will consist of two people: either a couple, or a parent and her/his child. To the extent that it can achieve stability in a world ruled by lumpenproletarian capitalism and predicated on the means of securitisation, that stability will, ideally at least, be grounded in private property. So, as we have already suggested, its acquisition of private property should not be taken to imply sympathy with capitalism, much less collaboration: such a move is a defence against capitalism's vagaries. Taken far enough, it will tend to make the acquirers middle class, but even so, it may still inspire no loyalty to the dominant economic system.[114]

In sum, the economic activity of the capitalist-lumpenproletarian class is principally *horizontal*, and its interminable goal is to achieve the elimination of intra-class competition. Sometimes, individual participants seek victory by

---

[114] Beyond the alleged failings of the bourgeois family, and the failings of particular families, the family has an important role to play in socialising – and socialism. As Harper Lee put it in *To Kill a Mockingbird*, "You can choose your friends but you can't choose your family." The family can train us to get along with people we would not necessarily choose to spend time with, and whose views we might disapprove of.

strategies of undercutting, designed to lure customers from the competition, and which result in short-term gains for other social classes. In that case, those classes have been co-opted for a period. The capitalist-lumpenproletariat class is dynamic, but also rootless. It possesses no loyalty to persons, places or traditions. Its sole aim is to make a profit. It possesses property in the form of factories, warehouses, office blocks, etc., which it sees primarily in terms of liquidity: it has no intrinsic attachment to it as bricks-and-mortar. When circumstances change, it will happily sell up and move.

The economic activity of the middle classes, by contrast, is principally *vertical*; it is a rooted phenomenon designed to persist over time. The middle classes use property as a securitisation anchor designed to withstand the caprices of the future, and they frequently use it to safeguard their families. Property is not just an acquisition, it is a potential bequest to biological children and grandchildren. While it has obvious liquidity value, its unique value as a particular material instantiation is rarely insignificant. The middle-classes are essentially cautious and conformist. In general, they feel loyalties to particular persons, and (perhaps less often, but still significantly) to places and traditions.

As we have already argued, they may develop a socially radical outlook (like the Robespierres and Marxes and Lenins of that class). Some of the reasons for that may already be apparent, but the most interesting reason may be that new parents always find themselves behind an equivalent of John Rawls's 'veil of ignorance', as described in his 1971, *A Theory of Justice*.

In Rawls's thought experiment, a random collection of pre-societal individuals is asked to decide the principles that should govern a society into which they will soon be inserted. They do not know what place they will occupy in that society in terms of social class, gender or ethnicity. Rawls's claim is that they would choose to maximise justice in order to minimise their chances of ending up in destitution.

A new parent (P) is in a similar situation. She does not know what sort of person her child (C) will grow up to be, or how the world will change in the eighteen years it takes C to reach adulthood. However C turns out, a just and equitable world is more likely to accommodate C than an unjust and arbitrary one, so – assuming P is rational – P has an interest in helping bring about such a thing; and since C will obviously be part of that world, and since social justice is a difficult thing to achieve, C needs to be encouraged to follow suit.

In summary, what we have is two classes – the lumpenproletariat capitalist class and the middle class – both of which are predicated on property: the former for kleptocratic purposes, the latter as a bulwark against the rapacious forays of the former. The arena where they materially rub up against each other to do battle is politics in the formal, conventional sense: public offices, entitlements, privileged positions, decision-making powers, status. The ultimate prizes are presidencies, prime ministerships, chancellorships, director-generalships, and so on. These pass continually to and fro between the two classes, and take on a more or less felonious hue, depending on which class is in the ascendancy.

The whole of society can thus be pictured as a closed, live battlefield with bullet-proof pods inserted into the earth. The earth and the enclosing walls represent the legal and moral framework which more or less constrains everyone's movement. The pods are property-possessions, and they penetrate the soil more or less deeply, depending on how substantial they are. Because the battlefield is sealed, it is safer at the edges, so the pods representing the most substantial property-holdings are to be found there. The least substantial, most shallowly rooted, lie towards the middle. At the very centre are those who do not possess pods at all, the victims of hostile fire from all sides, who do not usually last long. The pods house the middle- and working classes, except at the four corners, where they are deep and large, and house the super-rich (including what Yanis Varoufakis calls the 'Technofeudalists'[115]). The super-rich, while in no way tied to the middle classes, have copied their strategy of property-holding – only on a far more monumental scale - as a means of securitisation against the volatility of lumpenproletarian capitalism, of which they themselves are the most successful representatives. They are the really significant combatants on this battlefield, and they are engaged in a war of each against all. Their own pods are construed chiefly as liquidity, and thus permit a significant degree of mobility. There are 'peacekeepers' on the battlefield – the political and administrative classes – but they are at least partly corrupt, and, as a whole, can be relied upon to keep the battle going. Finally, there is a literal underground, comprising tunnels, where the middle and working classes can travel limited distances in undignified, but relative, safety.[116]

---

[115] Varoufakis argues that capitalism has come to an end and 'been replaced by something much worse', ie, 'technofeudalism.' Technofeudalist companies like Amazon and Apple have established virtual fiefdoms on which capitalists have to appear, and for which they pay rent. Rent was the hallmark of feudal system, so we are seeing a return to that, in modern technological form (hence the name). This ignores the fact that, to appear on, eg, Amazon, capitalists are probably paying something more like tax than rent, and that, on those grounds, capitalists have been living in fiefdoms since long before the internet (in the form of nationally determined income tax on company profits). Secondly, one might wonder whether the technofeudalists are really calling the shots, or whether they are the vassals. What might happen if Amazon decided to ban, say, Heinz on a whim of Jeff Bezos? Heinz's lawyers would likely stir up the media, and Parliament, and public opinion. Antitrust laws would be invoked.

[116] The reader might notice that this conforms to Foucault's notion of power as a 'capillary' phenomenon with multiple nodes; or Deleuze and Guattari's 'rhizome'.

A Lumpenproletarian Human Nature?

When Saint Augustine claimed that human beings were 'froward' – perverse in their desire to commit wrongdoing - and Thomas Hobbes described them as essentially self-centred, and, more recently, John Gray said, "humans are weapon-making animals with an unquenchable fondness for killing"[117] they were all expressing an observational truth. The mystery is that, given the wretchedness of the prevailing conditions, there should be any good in human beings at all.

Yet perhaps there is some unpacking to be done. One thing most people agree about humans is that they are social animals, vulnerable to collective pressure, desirous of the admiration and respect of those around them. In the *Republic*, Plato noticed that communal disapproval is a powerful brake on ruthless egoism. The story of the Gyges Ring tells of a peasant who unexpectedly comes into possession of a ring that confers invisibility on its wearer. Thus armed, he sneaks into the royal palace, kills the king, marries the queen, and becomes the new ruler. The intended moral is that only the possibility of being seen and censured stops people from behaving unjustly.

But there is more to be said. The story also suggests that what people primarily want is *public* power; not private power, and not wealth. They want to be *seen* to be a roaring success. After all, the ring has already given the peasant private power: probably far more than any king. And, in the long term, he can probably obtain more wealth than any king.

That contention probably finds its best philosophical expression in the writings of Friedrich Nietzsche. Nietzsche presents the will to power as the most basic of all human drives, and an explanation for the character and course of human history. "Where I found the living, there I found the will to

---

[117] Gray, John (2002), chapter 3.

power; even in the will of servants I found the will to be master."[118] The idea that humans are universally possessed of such a will, which of course has to be restrained if society is to function effectively, is behind many political theories concerning the necessity of strong central government. To some extent, Nietzsche's central claim is thought to be knowable by intuition: ponder your own motives, examine your own behaviour, and, if you are honest, you will find them all explained by your own will to power.

Which looks damning for any social theory whose ideal is a harmonious, egalitarian society.

Only, it may not be as self-evidently true as it might appear. What if we claim, instead, that human beings are not motivated by a will to power, but only by a will to recognition; that all they want is to be recognised as having worth by other humans, but that, in society as it has existed for millennia, human disconnection has been so entrenched that the will to recognition has always overreached itself? I can make others acknowledge my existence and value by simply fulfilling my everyday business in a way conducive to others' well-being, but mostly, in society as it stands, that won't get me very far. If I want recognition, I need power.

This is arguably the point behind Hegel's 'master and slave dialectic' in the *Phenomenology:* the master has power, but taken to extremes, his exercise of it results in the annihilation of the slave. What the master really wants is recognition, which he can only obtain by means of a mutual acknowledgement. In other words, the will to recognition is the reality underlying the felt will to power.[119]

---

[118] Nietzsche, Friedrich, *Thus Spake Zarathustra*, p93.
https://www.nothuman.net/images/files/discussion/1/9994c4af16851fe2bc691b8896cf6694.pdf
[119] Even in Alexandre Kojève's pessimistic reading of the story, the slave gains the possibility of recognition by the master through labour.

Whatever the truth, the will to recognition and the will to power clearly occupy different positions on the same spectrum. Common sense, however, might suggest that most people would prefer recognition to power. Power, after all – leaving aside political power, with which Nietzsche wasn't really concerned, and which usually comes with considerable material benefits (but also many drawbacks) – is accompanied by burdens: above all, it has to be maintained, and that requires inputs that, in the long term, I may not be able to sustain. And it is stressful. And it is usually a sham: it is a social construction that all too often requires the support of social institutions.

Hegel's story may reveal more of the truth than appears. Power can only be achieved and maintained by means of securitisation, and securitisation brings separation. The master achieves recognition as an abstract person, a *ruler* whose reality as such could be filled by any number of concrete individuals, within a palace-fortress; what he wants is recognition as a *real person*. Meanwhile, those outside the fortress – those who have been securitised *against* – want something of what the ruler has. They want *power*, which, since they do not possess it, they conceive in one-sided, ideal terms, as a kind of hyper-recognition devoid of burdensome responsibilities. Their mutual dissatisfaction can be resolved in communism.

Marx abandoned the idea that humans had a fixed nature, an 'essence', after completing the *Economic and Philosophical Manuscripts* in 1844. Thereafter, he seems to have believed that the way human beings related to one another was determined by historical circumstances, in particular the level of development of the means of production. Arguably - though it is never explicit in Marx - this position ties human failings to the phenomenon of scarcity: humans behave badly because there are not enough essential resources to go around. Once we overcome that problem, humans will no longer feel the need to steal or murder, because there will be nothing to steal or murder for: everyone will have sufficient - or more.

As claims go, it is a weak one, but it may underlie much communist thinking. Its difficulties arise from the fact that the well-off are often those whose behaviour is worst: the overcoming of scarcity seldom seems to improve them. Of course, it is possible to object that the overcoming of scarcity for a few specific individuals, at a time when scarcity still affects the mass of people as a whole, is not the same as the permanent overcoming of scarcity for everyone.

But that raises the question: scarcity of what? Two balanced meals a day, and a place to live? 'From each according to his abilities, to each according to his needs' does not get us very far unless we can specify what human needs are. Until then, it is certainly not obvious that, in some future society characterised by an over-abundance of material goods, humans will cease to be selfish and destructive.[120]

Consistent with Marx post-1844, orthodox Marxists are generally not keen on the idea that some view of human nature underlies their hopes:[121] they prefer to cloud the issue with pedagogic or economic explanations (a tendency highlighted by Carl Schmitt in his 1922, *Political Theology*). The many Socialist societies of the 20th century – and we should not forget that, at one point, Marxist governments covered a third of the world – failed to improve human nature, and, arguably, the Marxian prejudice against 'essentialism' did not help. If there is no human nature, then what entitles us to think that future persons will respond to having all their needs fulfilled with a greater inclination to cooperate with others? Marxists have answers to that question, of course, but none are very convincing.

---

[120] James, Oliver (2007): "Two-thirds of Britons believe that they cannot afford to buy everything they need, which shows how widespread the confusion has become between wants and needs." p52.
[121] Cf. Eg, Kamenka, Eugene (1962), Ollman, Bertell (1971), Mészáros, István (1970).

The notion of mental illness is relevant here, partly because, to some degree, it too is a social construction; it requires the majority population to constitute a 'mentally well' norm against which it can be defined.[122] Nevertheless, it nearly always has a real element; a material background or cause: in trauma, malconditioning, chemical imbalance, life circumstances, etc.

But what if we redefine mental illness so that, under just about every social system that has ever existed, including our own, it constitutes the overwhelming 'norm', and that true mental health is the tiny exception – if it exists at all? Practically speaking, as a means of addressing the problem, that might be counter-productive, but there is nothing self-contradictory about it. After all, most eras have been characterised by war and violence, so large numbers of persons have probably always been traumatised, directly or indirectly, as a matter of course; nowadays, many people are on long-term medication, and function within a society that is, in crucial respects, irrational in terms of the goods it prioritises. Under such conditions – and the list of features just provided is obviously not exhaustive – can we really say that we know for certain that human nature, as it manifests itself in our society, manifests itself authentically (which is to say, as it would under ideal parameters)? that it is therefore intrinsically selfish and destructive? Probably not.

The word 'insane' has dropped out of polite vocabulary, so we rarely hear society described as such anymore. However, it used to be relatively common. Statements such as Nietzsche's - "In individuals, insanity is rare; but in groups, parties, nations and epochs, it is the rule"[123] – and John Lennon's "I think our

---

[122] See Chaney, Sarah (2022), the blurb of which reads: "Before the nineteenth century, the term normal was rarely ever associated with human behaviour. Normal was a term used in maths: people weren't normal - triangles were. But from the 1830s, this branch of science really took off across Europe and North America, with a proliferation of IQ tests, sex studies, a census of hallucinations - even a UK beauty map."
[123] An English translation, but that is beside the point.

society is run by insane people for insane objectives" captured important truths. The entire issue was probably best addressed by the Fromm, in *The Sane Society*.

> "What is so deceptive about the state of mind of the members of a society is the 'consensual validation' of their concepts. It is naively assumed that the fact that the majority of people share certain ideas or feelings proves the validity of these ideas and feelings. Nothing is further from the truth. Consensual validation as such has no bearing whatsoever on reason or mental health... The fact that millions of people share the same vices does not make these vices virtues, the fact that they share so many errors does not make the errors to be truths, and the fact that millions of people share the same forms of mental pathology does not make these people sane."[124]

Commenting on this, Herbert Marcuse wrote:

> "As a tentative definition of a 'sick society' we can say that a society is sick when its basic institutions and relations, its structure, are such that they do not permit the use of available intellectual and material resources for the optimal development and satisfaction of individual needs. The larger the discrepancy between the potential and the actual human conditions, the greater the need for what I term 'surplus-repression', that is, repression necessitated not by the growth and preservation of civilisation but by the vested interest in maintaining an established society. Such surplus-repression introduces (over and above, or rather,

---

[124] Fromm, Erich (1956), p14-15.

underneath the social conflicts) new strains and stresses in the individuals."[125]

The mere fact that, by and large, we have stopped talking about society as 'insane', in a way that was common just fifty years ago, suggests that something has made us much more accepting of our condition (and/or perhaps unable to recognise it for what it is). We are living in an 'age of the fetter', such as was outlined earlier, and there are good reasons we now live in a correspondingly fettered condition.

As to when that fetter began to appear obvious, it is difficult to say: a plausible timeline might include the advent of Mrs Thatcher in Britain, Ronald Reagan in the USA, the fall of the Berlin Wall – which could, and probably should, have provoked a worldwide 're-evaluation of all values' – the creation of neoliberalism, and the rise of social media to lock us into what Shoshana Zuboff calls 'instrumentarianism', the manipulation of our behaviour for the purposes of modification, prediction, monetisation and control, and what Jonathan Haidt describes as mental 'rewiring'.

And yet, although humans can undoubtedly appear 'froward', recent research has revealed a significantly sunnier picture. In 2011, the American economists Samuel Bowles and Herbert Gintis summarised the new empirical landscape:

"Biological classics such as Konrad Lorenz's (1963) *On Aggression* and Richard Dawkins's (1976) *The Selfish Gene* have now been joined by works whose titles signal the shift in attention: *Good Natured* by Frans de Waal (1997), *Mother Nature* by Sarah Blaffer Hrdy (2000), *The Moral Animal* by Robert Wright (1995), *Origin of Virtue* by Matt Ridley (1998), *Unto Others* by Elliot Sober and

---

[125] Marcuse, H (1972), p251.

David Sloan Wilson (1998), *Altruistically Inclined?* by Alexander Field (2004), *The Genial Gene: Deconstructing Darwinian Selfishness* by Joan Roughgarden and *Moral Origins: Social Selection and the Evolution of Virtue, Altruism and Shame* by Christopher Boehm (2011). These recent works are reminiscent of Pytor Kropotkin's *Mutual Aid* a century earlier, a book that had advocated a kinder, gentler view of the evolutionary process in opposition to the then popular dog-eat-dog Social Darwinist claims about what natural selection entails for human behaviour."[126]

As the Oxford University Professor of Economics, Paul Collier, recently put it:

> "Remarkable recent advances in evolutionary social psychology confirm that humans are an unusually pro-social mammal. We have evolved to learn from each other, accumulating communal collective minds which guide our actions. We live in communities-of-place whose collective minds guide our children; we spend most of our day in communities-of-work whose collective minds guide new recruits. Within each, we come together for common purposes unattainable by individuals."[127]

And Kate Raworth:

> "*Homo sapiens*, it turns out, is the most cooperative species on the planet, outperforming ants, hyenas, and even the naked mole-rat when it comes to living alongside those who are beyond our next of kin. In

---

[126] Bowles, S and Gintis (2011), p6-7.
[127] Collier, Paul (2024), p7.

short, along with our propensity to trade, we are also drawn to give, share and reciprocate."[128]

And given the fact that, for all our present stupidity, destructiveness and cruelty, there is still significant good in the world, it does not seem unreasonable to suggest that, under much kinder conditions, we ourselves, as a species, might be much kinder.

Perhaps the best candidate for a communist view of human nature is to be found (as Bowles and Gintis proposed) in Peter Kropotkin's 1902, *Mutual Aid,* subtitled 'A Factor of Evolution'. Kropotkin was a geographer and administrator who agreed with Darwin's theory of natural selection, but who thought Darwin had been overly influenced by Thomas Malthus. Malthus had produced plausible arguments to demonstrate that population must outstrip food supply, and, applied to natural selection, that might suggest intra-species competition is always inevitable. Kropotkin argued that, while Malthus's theory found apparent confirmation in England (a small country where overcrowding was a problem) and also in the Galapagos Islands (where the climate was conducive to Malthusian-type progression), it did not hold true in more expansive regions, such as Russia. A more global overview, Kropotkin thought, would show that 'mutual aid' is as much an outcome of natural selection as is competition. The surprise is that modern research has increasingly confirmed his assessment.

In his 2019, *The Future of Anarchism*, Hugh Small defends Kropotkin against his denigrators. Kropotkin did not, for example, use the term 'altruism', although he is often accused of conceiving human nature in such terms; nor did he believe in 'the perfectibility of humankind'.

---

[128] Raworth, Kate (2017), p104.

"What Kropotkin wanted to do in *Mutual Aid* was to undercut Darwin's claim that natural selection used competition between members of one species to ensure that only the fittest would survive. On the contrary, Kropotkin's evidence showed that natural selection more often favours traits that reduce competition. The type of behaviour he studied was that in which a species evolves to act in harmony in a way that benefits all equally. Creating quadrupeds that herd together, or birds that form flocks, or fish that shoal is a more effective way for natural selection to ensure individual survival than evolving more armour or better individual evasion skills. It is, as he was at pains to point out, not self-sacrifice because all benefit equally."[129]

Using evolutionary psychology, Small charts a line that runs directly from *Mutual Aid* to modern optimistic assessments of human nature. He begins with the Greenland Ice Sheet Project in 1988, which completely altered our understanding of what Africa was like in the run-up to the biological emergence *Homo sapiens*. In short, we now have a good idea why we are so cooperative, and it has to do with the fact that our earliest environment was so capriciously hostile that we could only survive by working together. Natural selection was forced to 'work overtime' to cope, and, as part of the same process, that gave us big brains.

In many ways, *Mutual Aid* is a book whose time has come, contrary to all expectations. It used to be categorised as Social Darwinism – part of an outdated corpus that would include, inter alia, Herbert Spencer, Francis Galton and the Eugenicists (and Darwin himself, if *The Descent of Man* is to count) – but that

---

[129] Small, Hugh (2019), p16.

has turned out to be premature. Kropotkin presents a plausible view of human nature which commands wide acceptance amongst contemporary experts: humans tend to overproduce and seek recognition for their efforts in what is effectively charitable distribution of the surplus. Small fills in the details from modern scientific studies. One of the surprising results of his analysis is that he finds a firm ally for Kropotkin in Adam Smith, whose modern association with laissez-faire capitalism he describes as "a very successful repetition-induced illusory truth."[130]

In short, Hobbes's notion that prehistoric life was 'solitary, poor, nasty, brutish, and short' is about as far from the truth as it is possible to get. Gray's view that we are "weapon-making animals with an unquenchable fondness for killing" has an evidential basis, but it exaggerates the problem. The likelier truth is that, when we emerged from the evolutionary womb of 'pulsed climate variability', about 1.7 million years ago, we were overqualified for our new, easier environment, and, in our failure to readjust in time, we drove several species to extinction. But nature also furnished us with massive cognitive capacity and a predisposition to cooperate, such as ought to enable us to eliminate that sort of blunder.

Of course, 'that sort of blunder' does continue to happen. Nowadays, we usually kill, steal and lie because there is a potentially infinite quantity of money to be had, and we are products of a hyper-securitised world in which the viciousness of those at the top is replicated throughout the lower levels. But we should not be shy of imagining a world in which those incentives no longer obtain. To the extent that we permit ourselves such an indulgence, we have the evidence on our side.

---

[130] Ibid. p83.

The Proletariat - and its Descendants?

In 2009, *The Economist* claimed that over half the world's population now belongs to the middle class. But that is probably an overestimate. In Britain, 40% of people consider themselves middle-class. The figure is 46% for the USA and 74% for France. China is now 52%, India 32% and Brazil 55%. Nevertheless, it is growing everywhere. Which might suggest that it is winning its war with the lumpenproletarian-capitalist class.

Only, this is a war in which victory would suit neither side. The lumpenproletarian-capitalists shield the middle classes from some of the brutalities of their lifestyle (for example, how many middle-class people who eat inexpensive meat and buy cheap clothes are fully comfortable with factory farms and sweatshops?) In return, the middle classes provide the lumpenproletariat-capitalist class with a stable social system in which banking makes sense and money does not suddenly lose its value. And of course, the two social categories overlap in places.

The obvious question - the one some readers might think has been most glaringly overlooked so far - is, what about the proletariat? What role does it have to play in all this?

There has never been a mainly working-class motivated revolution, and perhaps there never will be one. Had such a thing been possible, it would probably have occurred in England sometime in the middle of the nineteenth century. By the time Max Horkheimer penned 'The Impotence of the German Working Class' in 1927, it was probably already too late for such a thing. Thereafter, it was only possible to proceed, as György Lukács wanted to do, on the basis of an 'actual' and an 'ascribed' proletarian consciousness – the latter the property of well-meaning intellectuals, mostly middle-class, as Lukács himself was.

On the other hand, that is only half of the story. Although the working classes have not fronted a revolution, their achievements have been significant, and may include most of the civil liberties we still take for granted. As David Graeber put it:

"We now largely think of [the real origins of the modern social welfare state] - when we think of them at all - as having been created by benevolent democratic elites. Nothing could be further from the truth. In Europe, most of the key institutions of what later became the welfare state - everything from social insurance and pensions to public libraries and public health clinics - were not originally created by governments at all, but by trade unions, neighbourhood associations, cooperatives, and working-class parties and organizations of one sort or another. Many of these were engaged in a self-conscious revolutionary project of 'building a new society in the shell of the old', of gradually creating Socialist institutions from below. For some it was combined with the aim of eventually seizing control of the government through parliamentary means, for others, it was a project in itself. One must remember that during the late nineteenth century, even the direct heirs of Marx's Communist Party had largely abandoned the idea of seizing control of the government by force, since this no longer seemed necessary; in a Europe at peace and witnessing rapid technological progress, they felt that it should be possible to create a social revolution through peaceful, electoral means."[131]

---

[131] Graeber, David (2016), p153.

In Britain, as Hugh Small points out (drawing on Colin Ward's 2004 *Anarchism: A Very Short Introduction):*

> "The NHS was not a new system of health care. It was a state takeover of 'the vast network of friendly societies and mutual aid organisations that had sprung up through working-class self-help in the 19th century'. Herbert Morrison, the minister in charge of the nationalisation programme, favoured leaving these organisations in the care of municipalities, but was overruled by the Health Ministry. The contributions that working-class families had paid to their friendly society had not been taxed, but when the state took over, according to [Colin] Ward, the revenue became 'the plaything of central government financial policy'."[132]

In the developed world, the workers' mastery of pre-figurative politics receded with the demise of heavy industry and large-scale manufacturing, the simultaneous rise of outsourcing, and the discovery of cheaper labour in countries with few human rights protections; with the triumph of neoliberalism, in other words. The power of the working classes is tied to unionism, and unionism seems to be in long-term decline. In Britain, it reached its peak in 1979, when 13.2 million workers belonged to trade unions; by 2022, the figure was 6.2 million.[133]

But that may not be the end of the story. In his 2019, *The Socialist Manifesto,* Bhaskar Sunkara, New York editor of *Jacobin*

---

[132] Small, Hugh (2019), p126. I would have used the primary source here but in 2022, Oxford University Press replaced Ward's 2004 text with a new edition penned by a different author.
[133] https://lordslibrary.parliament.uk/trade-unions-members-and-relations-with-the-government/

magazine, warns against discounting the working classes, but acknowledges that, "Today, you might find pockets of organised, class-conscious working class people across the advanced capitalist world, but these are the exceptions, not the rule. The twenty-first-century working-class is fragmented."[134] He re-describes the term to include members of the middle-classes and the cognitariat. "The traditional workplace should still be central to our vision. That means putting special emphasis on workers in growing sectors, such as education and health care, as well as those working in supply and logistics."[135]

In his 2011, *The Precariat: The New Dangerous Class* (2021), Guy Standing identifies a new working class, made up of those on fragile or fluid work contracts over which they have limited control, which he calls the 'precariat', a portmanteau of 'proletariat and 'precarious'.

> "The global precariat is not yet a class in the Marxian sense, being internally divided and only united in fears and insecurities. But it is a class in the making, approaching a consciousness of common vulnerability. It consists not just of everybody in insecure jobs – though many are temps, part-timers, in call centres or in outsourced arrangements. The precariat consists of those who feel their lives and identities are made up of disjointed bits, in which they cannot construct a desirable narrative or build a career, combining forms of work and labour, play and leisure in a sustainable way."[136]

---

[134] Bhaskar, Sunkara (2019), p224.
[135] Ibid. p225.
[136] Standing, Guy, 'Who will be a voice for the emerging precariat?' in *The Guardian* 1 June 2011.
https://www.theguardian.com/commentisfree/2011/jun/01/voice-for-emerging-precariat

It is a 'dangerous' class for the left as well as the right because "Chronically insecure people easily lose their altruism, tolerance and respect for non-conformity. If they have no alternative on offer, they can be led to attribute their plight to strangers in their midst."[137] As many commentators have noticed, the Precariat probably overlaps with the NEET ('Not in Education, Employment, or Training'), a phenomenon global enough to have equivalent terms in other languages (eg, 'freeter' in Japan, 'ni-ni' in Spain and South America), and be recognised as a worldwide phenomenon. In 2023, according to the International Labour Organisation, one-fifth of people worldwide between the ages of fifteen and twenty-four were considered NEETs. Their revolutionary potential is difficult to assess, but there is a significant section of that class that consciously rejects conventional materialism: the N-po generation in South Korea, Tang Ping in China, the Satoris in Japan, the Big Quitters in America, and so on. On an optimistic assessment, they may be dreaming of an alternative social arrangement.[138]

Idealising the Lumpenproletariat

Clyde W Barrow's attempt to salvage (and arguably, sanitise) the lumpenproletariat in order to assign it a place in the Marxian schema is only the latest in a long series of similar attempts – mostly unaware of themselves as such – to give that class a canonical status. Even were those attempts not connected to Marx, they could only be modern. In general, the rise of criminals and vagabonds as picaresque anti-heroes coincides

---

[137] Ibid.
[138] One of the better cultural expressions of this phenomenon may be Hanna Jameson's 2023 novel, *Are You Happy Now*, about what happens when, one day, young people across the world decide simply to sit down and never get up again. The phenomenon is probably connected to Jeffrey Arnett's year-2000 theory of 'emerging adulthood', although of course that does not explain it.

with the triumph of modern securitisation. Nowadays, most of us no longer knowingly encounter real criminals.

There is a parallel here to the way in which, in the late nineteenth century, wild animals started to appear as children's toys: as Western populations became increasingly urbanised, they lost contact with nature. What had hitherto appeared threatening and even grotesque, gradually became both pitiable and endearing as the natural world receded into the distance. The teddy bear did not become a popular toy until the early 1900s: hitherto, bears were considered to be little more than monsters.

Nowadays, as a result of a parallel process, the criminal can be a perversely admirable figure, as in the novels of Elmore Leonard or the films of Quentin Tarantino and Guy Ritchie. The situation differs from that involving wild animals, insofar as, unlike natural laws, human laws can be more or less just. Hereward the Wake and Robin Hood have entered folklore as 'good' criminals, and Gandhi and Martin Luther King were both officially classed as criminals at one point. But obviously, the fact that laws are made, for example, by 'bourgeois' states does not suffice to give all criminals the benefit of the doubt.

We pointed out earlier that the lumpenproletariat is part reality, part fantasy, in proportions that can never be precisely determined. From roughly the French Revolution onwards, western culture – and thus, eventually, global culture – became fixated on a category of persons supposed to combine the qualities of brazen criminal and relatable folk hero. As Foucault puts it in his discussion of the mid-19th century murderer and poet, Pierre François Lacenaire, "What was being celebrated was the symbolic figure of an illegality kept within the bounds of delinquency and transformed into discourse – that is to say, made doubly inoffensive; the bourgeoisie had invented for itself a new pleasure, which it has still far from outgrown."[139]

The criminal as closet socialist hero has a long history, and may achieve its highest philosophical expression in Stirner's *The Ego and Its Own* – even though it is completely implausible there.[140] The Krays were nothing like the loveable folk-heroes of the 1990 movie, nor were any of the Great Train Robbers anything like Buster in the 1988 film of the same name. It is possible to create Don Corleones, Chili Palmers and Edward 'Eddie' Hornimans mainly by underplaying, sanitising or omitting the truly nasty bits.

This hotchpotch pseudo-class of 'loveable' (often psychopathic) rogues has been the pretext for persistent attempts to give the lumpenproletariat a socialist aura. The underlying idea is that if (as sometimes appears plausible) the individual lumpenproletarian is *forced* into acute criminality by virtue of being poor, anti-bourgeois and an outsider, it may be that the criminality is a mere 'accident' of the bigger phenomenon in which exclusion, pent-up energy and antipathy to middle-class values are 'essential'. The 'accident' can be overlooked, the more so as it will evaporate in any future, more equitable society. Thus, we have a long, depressing history of leftists cosying up to Brownshirt-types, from Mikhail Bakunin's sycophantic devotion to the cold-blooded murderer, Sergey Nechayev, to Jean-Paul Sartre's lionisation of the literary paedophile Jean Genet, and beyond, in which genuine progressives try hard to excuse venality by appeal to a cocktail of 'virtues' supposed to be compensating.

It is only a short step from this relatively pathetic gesture, in which a generous degree of criminality is tolerated and compensated for by being an *accidental* fraction of the whole, to

---

[139] Foucault, Michel (2020), p284.
[140] I argued methodically for this position in the penultimate chapter of my *21st Century Philosophy* (2012).

the rather stronger gesture in which criminality completely disappears, on the grounds that an accident cannot be considered constitutive. In this latter universe, any level of criminality is justifiable, so long as it serves the purposes of a (properly conceived) revolution. Albert Camus had much to say in denunciation of this in *The Rebel*, but it undoubtedly keeps one, mistaken notion of the lumpenproletariat alive, as a class with progressive potential within the legitimate purview of 'praxis'. We are now within a realm where terrorism can be condoned and even encouraged: the realm of the Red Brigades, *Gruppo XXII Ottobre* and the *Rote Armee Fraktion*, amongst others.

Conclusion to Part 1

In the first part of this book we have argued that the means of securitisation, not the means of production, is the key to understanding the scope and limits of social organisation and historical change. Ideology is one way – but not the most significant: bullets and prison bars always trump seductive ideas - in which the subaltern classes are kept in place, and they, themselves, produce it as a kind of generalised Stockholm Syndrome. It achieves its highest modern form in advertising, but intellectually, it is bolstered by a threefold allegiance to materialism, nationalism and moral relativism. No radical communist social critique can ever be 'scientific' in the sense of being value-free: on the contrary, if it is to be effective, it has to be grounded in moral principles, whether it admits it or not. The lumpenproletariat is central to understanding the nature of capitalism, because it knows no moral or legal boundaries: instantiated (eventually) in effective capitalism, it enables it to realise its essence, the accumulation of potentially infinite wealth. The working classes have helped build a world in which capitalists are theoretically constrained by civil liberties and the rule of law, but their ability to complete or even sustain this project was fatally undermined by the triumph of neoliberalism sometime in the last quarter of the twentieth century. Nowadays, the chief players in the social-economic battlefield are the lumpenproletarian capitalists and the middle classes, who are, to some extent, locked in what looks like a very reluctant symbiosis. However, appearances are deceptive, and some people of all classes have always seen past the ersatz collaboration to the vastly better world that might, with rightly directed effort, lie ahead.

In Part 2, we will consider the options.

PART TWO

1. Reflections on the Road to Communism

Sam Freedman begins his 2024 book, *Failed State*, by observing: "A common problem with books like this one is that they spend a lot of time focusing on problems and have a thin chapter at the end with a few anaemic suggestions for improvements."[141] He might equally have been talking about nearly every capitalist-critical book ever written. If we are to avoid falling into the same trap, we must begin by outlining goals. Once we have done that, we will discuss ways and means of achieving them.

What is Communism?

Marx and Engels's *The Communist Manifesto* provides a ten-point programme designed to realise its aims.

1. Abolition of property in land and application of all rents of land to public purposes.
2. A heavy progressive or graduated income tax.
3. Abolition of all rights of inheritance.
4. Confiscation of the property of all emigrants and rebels.
5. Centralisation of credit in the hands of the state, by means of a national bank with State capital and an exclusive monopoly.
6. Centralisation of the means of communication and transport in the hands of the State.
7. Extension of factories and instruments of production owned by the State; the bringing into cultivation of waste-

---

[141] Freedman, Sam (2024) p17.

lands, and the improvement of the soil generally in accordance with a common plan.

8. Equal liability of all to work. Establishment of industrial armies, especially for agriculture.

9. Combination of agriculture with manufacturing industries; gradual abolition of all the distinction between town and country by a more equable distribution of the populace over the country.

10. Free education for all children in public schools. Abolition of children's factory labour in its present form. Combination of education with industrial production, &c, &c.[142]

It is difficult not to notice the ominous tenor here, and Marx admits that it is 'despotic' (although, with astonishingly breezy optimism, he thinks it will lead to the gradual disappearance of class distinctions). Nowadays, article 6, 'centralisation of the means of communication' could easily be achieved by routing everyone's phone through GCHQ. And what if the state decides you are a 'rebel' (article 4)? Since it controls all credit (article 5), it could easily starve you to death. The abolition of *all* rights of inheritance (article 3) looks draconian: what about items of sentimental value?

Some things are conspicuous by their absence. There is no mention of liberty, equality and fraternity, much less of anything resembling human rights. There are no explicit measures to alleviate women's oppression. Given how volatile post-revolutionary states of affairs always are, and that the *Manifesto* provides no protective reassurances for marginal groups, and that its characterisation of the victorious class ('the State, ie, the proletariat organised as a ruling class') is risibly vague, it is difficult to see why it should not simply lead to

---

[142] Marx, K and Engels, F (1967), p104-105.

Stalin's Russia or Mao's China, or even Pol Pot's Cambodia. It may be halfway there already.

Fast forward a long way: the 2025 'draft programme' of the Communist Party of Great Britain contains a section entitled 'immediate demands', featuring over one hundred bullet-pointed articles of intention. It is difficult to say how long that package would take to implement, or even how long the CPGB would stay in power, since it wants 'annual elections' and a 'single-chamber parliament with proportional representation'. It also wants, intriguingly, 'provision of low interest rates for small businesses.'[143]

The difficulty of creating anything like a ten-point programme such as Marx and Engels attempted should not be underestimated. Bhaskar Sunkara's *The Socialist Manifesto*, already mentioned, ends with a fifteen-article list, but which turns out, on closer examination, to be purely concerned with morale-boosting, and vague (it includes elements such as 'history matters', 'we need to democratise our political institutions' and 'we need socialists'). The seventh chapter of Yanis Varoufakis's *Technofeudalism* contains a subsection entitled, 'Democratised companies' which gives a plausible account of how a post-capitalist society might work,[144] but which does not constitute a list of reforms designed to get us there.

In any case, there is a disingenuousness at the heart of *The Communist Manifesto:* its authors decry utopianism, but actually, manifestos are simply utopias-by-other-means: both are essentially social wish-lists. Utopias depict a world in which those wishes have already been fulfilled; manifestos assume one in which such fulfilment is possible. Which is the more appealing? It is a matter of personal preference. Which is more honest? Probably utopianism.

[143] https://communistparty.co.uk/draft-programme/3-immediate-demands/
[144] Varoufakis, Yanis (2023), p194f.

However, because we need to know what we mean when we talk about the 'road to Communism', it is necessary to attempt something like Marx and Engels did.

We should be bold. We should concede that, as in the *Manifesto*, the following ten are meant to be *preparatory measures* designed to establish communism in the longer term – but also that we think they have a much better chance of succeeding than Marx and Engels's.

1. Limitarianism': an upper cap on wealth. This is roughly equivalent to Marx's Article 2, though its principal theorist, the Dutch-Belgian philosopher, Ingrid Robeyns, points out that it need not be achieved by means of income tax. She suggests a 'political limit' above which a person should not be legally allowed more, and an 'ethical limit', keeping more than which would not be illegal, but only immoral. Alongside these, she propounds a 'riches line': "the level at which additional money cannot increase your standard of living." She says ten million per person would be her rough upper *political* limit ("above which a fortune starts to become utterly wasteful"), and one million her *ethical* limit ("It doesn't matter whether this is in euros, dollars or pounds; we should focus on the general principle and remember that we are discussing an order of magnitude, not the precise figure.")[145] Robeyns argues that when political measures are introduced that directly reduce the income of the poor, they are usually fairly quickly observable (in, eg, increased homelessness), but direct measures to increase the wealth of the rich tend to have the

---

[145] Robeyns, Ingrid (2024) p15. Robeyns is regularly accused of 'envy'. Those of her opponents who adopt this line of attack presumably have difficulty explaining why she does not feel envious of a family of four whose combined assets total thirty-nine million pounds (when most people who are inclined to envy probably would), and why her envy only kicks in at forty million pounds and a penny. She points out that she has many supporters among the super-rich themselves.

same effect far more gradually, and thus much less noticeably. Wealth takes longer to be sucked upwards from the bottom, and this slow-motion visibility provokes fewer awkward questions. The United Nations points out that "between 2014 and 2019, the pace of poverty reduction slowed to 0.6 percentage points per year, which is the slowest rate seen in the past three decades"[146], while a 2023 report by Oxfam showed that "the richest one percent captured fifty-four percent of new global wealth over the past decade."[147] For Robeyns, there is a direct connection: she quotes the American senator, Elizabeth Warren: 'Wealth does not trickle down, it trickles up.' With the introduction of Limitarianism, capitalism as we defined it above – 'an inadvertent economic system premised on the private pursuit of unlimited monetary wealth etc.' - would technically have been abolished, since it would no longer be possible to accumulate unlimited wealth. Limitarianism would need to be bolstered by a robust tax avoidance investigative agency, and eye-watering fines for convicted offenders.

2.   A comprehensive overhaul of social media. When it first appeared, the internet was probably the greatest potential advance in democratic governance since the invention of voting, and, at its inception in the 1990s, it was widely recognised as such. As Chiara Scuro recently put it, "It is the only thing in the world that allows human beings to coordinate at scale." As is now obvious, not only did it fail to fulfil that promise, but it became a breeding ground for disinformation, prejudice and assorted toxicities. The conventional view today is that the original assessments

---

[146] https://www.un.org/en/global-issues/ending-poverty
[147] https://www.oxfam.org/en/press-releases/richest-1-bag-nearly-twice-much-wealth-rest-world-put-together-over-past-two-years

were badly mistaken, so we must accept the new reality and try to make the most of it.

But that is defeatist. As everyone knows, what happened is that the internet was settled by capitalism and monetised. Users were brought on board for the purposes of data harvesting, and the collected information about them was sold to advertisers. Since that was the plan, it did not matter how users were recruited, or how they presented themselves online. They were allowed to adopt false names, accompany those names with incognito avatars, create multiple accounts, and voice opinions that they would never have dared express in person (and may not even have held). The entire setup worked as a charter for bullies, braggarts, mudslingers, racketeers, recidivists, slicksters and trolls. The biggest losers were women, minorities and adolescents.

The only way of restoring the whole thing to what it was meant to be is to go back to basics. Social media should be reconstructed as quickly as possible so that people can only contribute comments under their real names accompanied, where necessary, by their faces.

Some people will object, however, that this is an infringement of civil liberties: everyone has the right to anonymity. Which is true, but only up to a point.

(a) Rights are never absolute. The right to freedom of movement does not apply, for example, to convicted murderers; the (moral) right to freedom of speech does not apply to those who intend to shout fire in a crowded theatre; similarly, the right to express an opinion in a public forum does not apply to those who can only express it under assurances of complete anonymity; to those who refuse, on principle, to express it as *their own* opinion. 'Sock puppets', as they used to be called, are members of no community whatsoever. In a world in which they prevail, everyone is forced to follow suit: they create an environment in which authenticity looks to be loaded with danger. Why would they exist, otherwise?

(b) Clive Jones's 'right to anonymity' is not secured, eg, by calling himself 'WizardLord' and providing a picture of a dragon as his avatar. The social media company and the state security services will still know exactly who he is, and his pseudo-name will not afford him the least protection should they decide to come for him. The only potential losers are his fellow citizens, and thus society as a whole.

When Twitter became X, it was repurposed on the basis of so-called free speech fundamentalism. When Donald Trump became president, Facebook, Instagram and other social media providers – sensing the way the wind was blowing - rolled back their anti-hate-speech programs. Because they ignored the root problem, which is that anyone can appear under any name on social media, nothing changed. When a bigot is defeated by reasoned arguments, he or she simply sets up camp elsewhere, under another false name. His priority is to hang on to his equally bigoted friends.

The fact is that free speech is one of the most fundamental and precious of all human rights, and 'free speech fundamentalism' is not far from being a reasonable position. The caveat is that make-believe people do not possess that right, any more than Harry Potter, Jack Reacher or Frodo Baggins do. It belongs only to real people *as* real people. At the time of writing of this book, Facebook is just over twenty years old; Twitter/ X and Instagram are even younger. What can be built in two decades can be dismantled and rebuilt in the same time or less. We will all be the beneficiaries.

This switch to a new model of social media may be imminent anyway: 'web3' has been the focus of increasing interest in recent years. Premised on the blockchain, it has the potential to demolish 'technofeudalism', and rebuild social media on Ethereum-based transparent interactions. There are many sceptics, but according to Chris Dixon in his 2024, *Read Write Own*, that may be because new technologies arrive in one of two ways: 'inside out' or 'outside in'. Inside-out technologies emerge fully developed from inside Big Tech, and their potential is obvious from the start. By contrast:

> "Outside-in technologies are much harder to see coming, and they're routinely underestimated. Their builders work out of garages, basements, dorm rooms, and other unconventional spaces, outside official hours. They tinker after work, during breaks, and on weekends. They're motivated by a distinct philosophy and culture that can look strange to the outside world. Other people don't get them. The outsiders launch products half-baked, without clear uses. Most onlookers dismiss their technologies as toylike, weird, unserious, expensive, or even dangerous."[148]

Dixon points out that the internet is still in its infancy, and that Moore's Law suggests that its potential for development is still considerable. Meanwhile, blockchain technology has three distinct advantages over the

---

[148] Dixon, Chris (2024), p52.

monopolistic fiefdoms of web2: it is democratic, it is transparent, and it is far less whimsical.

> "Traditional computers can't make commitments like these ...Applications built on programmable blockchains like Ethereum inherit the platform's security guarantees. This means apps - social networks, marketplaces, games, and more - can also make strong commitments about their future behaviour."[149]

3. State appropriation of the biggest sectors of the retail industry. The profits would go to fund social welfare projects designed to raise the poorest, most disadvantaged members of society to a position of parity with the majority. In practice, superstores may be creative, up to a point, but they do not primarily produce goods. Rather, they are parasitic on manufacturers. And people would buy manufactured goods anyway. At present, supermarkets can, and sometimes do, operate virtual cartels to manipulate prices at the expense of human and animal welfare. Under the new system, they could keep their present chain character (in which, in the UK, for example, Waitrose differs from Lidl). Not all shops would come under state control, but the smaller ones could be encouraged to join in return for benefits. State control of retail would allow the gradual modification of consumers' diets, so that obesity and addiction can be eliminated.

4. A significant increase in scientific Research and Development (R&D). The setting of long-term industrial goals of innovation, aimed at the repair of environmental damage and the escalation of human flourishing. Scientists

---

[149] Ibid. p66-67.

to be paid a wage befitting their contribution to society. Prestigious rewards for genuine achievement. A thorough revision of Intellectual Property Law, especially patents, to ensure that the best scientific ideas receive the fullest cumulative elaboration. A clampdown on 'patent thickets', 'patent trolls' and 'patent hoarders.'[150]

5. The transformation of all existing towns and cities, as far as possible into biophilic 15-minute cities or biophilic 30-minute territories.

Carlos Moreno, the originator of 15-minute cities and 30-minute territories (although the underlying idea goes back to the American-Canadian activist, Jane Jacobs), summarises his two central ideas thus:

> "The 15-minute city represents an urban model in which the essential needs of residents are accessible on foot or by bicycle within a short perimeter in high density areas. Similarly, the 30-minute territory extends this concept to less densely populated areas where commutes can take a little longer."[151]

---

[150] N. Stephan Kinsella's 2008 philosophical work, *Against Intellectual Property* ineffectively tries to show that intellectual property rights "necessarily involve an infringement of other individual property rights, ie, one's right to use one's property as one sees fit" (p58). "The problem with IP rights," he insists, "is that objects protected by IP rights are not scarce" (p31) – which is simply false: original, time- and work-saving ideas that accelerate human progress are *incredibly* scarce. More: if I can spend ten years writing a book, only to have someone else print it in bulk and sell it for a huge profit, common sense would suggest that I should be entitled to some of the return. But Kinsella thinks not. "IP law trespasses against or 'takes' the property of tangible property owners by transferring partial ownership to authors and inventors" (p36). Throughout, there is a confusion between ideas, which are purely abstract objects, and their realisation in the empirical world.

[151] Moreno, Carlos (2024), p14. 15-minute cities are currently the nemesis of a paranoid and infantile right, on the grounds of a grotesque conspiracy theory that

'The essential needs of residents' typically include food outlets, workplaces, gyms, shops, medical centres, social hubs and public transport stops. To complement this: a comprehensive programme of works designed to replace private with public transport, conceived as a first step towards reclaiming the outdoors.

The notion of the biophilic city, which complements Moreno's thinking, was developed by the University of Virginia professor, Timothy Beatley, and is based on Edward O Wilson's 'biophilia hypothesis', ie, that human beings are hardwired to affectively connect with the natural world for reasons of health and wellbeing.[152] Beatley sums up the biophilic city thus:

> "A biophilic city is a city abundant with nature, a city that looks for opportunities to repair and restore and creatively insert nature wherever it can. It is an outdoor city, a physically active city, in which residents spend time enjoying the biological magic and wonder around them. In biophilic cities, residents care about nature and work on its behalf locally and globally."[153]

6. Doughnut Economics, named after the eponymous 2017 work by Kate Raworth. "What if we started economics not with its long-established theories," she asks, "but with humanity's long-term goals, and then sought out the economic thinking that would help us achieve them? ... I tried to draw a picture of those goals and, ridiculous though

---

connects the World Economic Forum, King Charles III, Oxfordshire County Council, climate concerns and the 2020 COVID lockdown.
[152] Wilson, Edward O (1984).
[153] Beatley, Timothy (2010), p12.

it sounds, it came out looking like a doughnut... Below the inner ring - the social foundation - lie critical human deprivations such as hunger and illiteracy. Beyond the outer ring – the ecological ceiling – lies critical planetary degradation such as climate change and biodiversity loss. Between these two rings is the Doughnut itself, the space in which we can meet the needs of all within the means of the planet."[154]

7. The creation of a number of independently adjudicated, fully transparent awards for journalistic investigative excellence, modelled on the Paul Foot awards. Control of the press handed to senior journalists who have been publicly recognised by receipt of such awards. Expropriation of all billionaire, non-dom and foreign media owners.

8. State ownership of the 'commons': electricity, water, healthcare, transport, etc. so that essential services can be fully integrated and run on a not-for-profit basis. Better remuneration for key workers.

9. The provision of full human rights as itemised in the United Nations 1948 Universal Declaration. But also: animals, including 'livestock', to be treated with the compassion that their level of sentience and capacity for suffering deserves. Rigorous legislation to enforce that.

10. An education system geared towards fostering rational thinking, critical appraisal and independence of mind, with a centralised inspection system to protect standards. Primary and secondary education to include an awareness

---

[154] Raworth, Kate (2017), p10.

and evaluation of local, national and global affairs. The distinction between vocational and academic studies to be effaced by a common emphasis on innovation. A move from a corrupt CV-tocracy to a true meritocracy based on moral goodness, practical aptitude and intellectual capacity. The newly liberated press would assist in this, since it would not be hamstrung by its owners' apathy and/or malignity. But critical assessment of the media generally would be part of every young person's education.

Measures 1 (Limitarianism), 2 (overhaul of social media), 4 (increase in R&D), 6 (Doughnut Economics), 7 (press control handed to qualified journalists), and 9 (provision of full human rights) are mutually supportive. We will examine the question of economic growth in the next section, but in his 2020, *How Innovation Works*, Matt Ridley makes a compelling case for the notion that innovation (defined as "turning ideas into practical, reliable and affordable reality"[155], to be distinguished from 'invention'), is the key to eliminating global poverty and saving the planet.

---

[155] Ridley, Matt (2020), p29. The words in brackets in the preceding paragraph are my own inferences from Ridley, and do not (as far as I know) represent his own views. Ridley is usually regarded as a moderate right-wing thinker; in any case, his book on innovation is probably the best in its field right now. Its nearest competitor, Vaclav Smil's 2023 *Invention and Innovation* is much less searching, and does not mention Ridley at all, even to refute him (despite the fact that *How Innovation Works* appeared at least two years previously). For a writer whose Wikipedia page states that 'he reads 60 to 110 non-technical books a year', this is a surprising omission. Smil tends to treat innovation as a top-down concern, as suggested in his 2020, *Numbers Don't Lie*, in which he declares it wrong 'to genuflect at the altar of innovation on two counts': [firstly] "It ignores those big, fundamental quests that have failed after spending huge sums on research. And [secondly] it has little to say about why we so often stick to an inferior practice even when we know there's a superior course of action" (p133). Ridley has convincing responses to both those concerns, however.

But innovation, he contends, is stifled by big firms[156] (which is why we need Limitarianism: because, after passing a certain secure level of success, a business tends to switch focus from innovation to securitisation and exploitation of its gains and the enrichment of shareholders), and sometimes even by governments (which is a second reason we need Limitarianism: because billionaires often want to control governments). He agrees with Chris Dixon (see above) that innovation is usually a bottom-up phenomenon (which is why social media needs overhauling – because that is one place where good ideas originate), and that it can only flourish in an environment of genuine political freedom (which is why we need full human rights, and why journalists need greater freedom to investigate abuses of power):

> "The main ingredient in the secret sauce that leads to innovation is freedom. Freedom to exchange, experiment, imagine, invest and fail; freedom from expropriation or restriction by chiefs, priests and thieves; freedom on the part of consumers to reward the innovations they like and reject the ones they do not. Liberals have argued since at least the eighteenth century that freedom leads to prosperity, but I would argue that they have never persuasively found the mechanism, the drive chain, by which one causes the other. Innovation, the infinite improbability drive, is that drive chain, that missing link... Innovative societies are free societies, where people are free to express their wishes and seek the satisfaction of those wishes, and where creative minds are free to

---

[156] In his 2024 *The Unaccountability Machine*, Dan Davies plausibly explains why. Big firms are more likely to build 'accountability sinks' into their structures because managers, on the whole, do not find having their decisions questioned 'humiliating and unpleasant.'

experiment to find ways to supply those requests so long as they do not harm others. I do not mean freedom in some extreme libertarian, lawless sense, just the general idea that if something has not been specifically prohibited, then the assumption should be that it must be allowed: a surprisingly rare phenomenon today in a world where governments try to dictate what you can do as well as what you cannot."[157]

Growth, Degrowth or Growth Agnosticism?

It is important to establish the context for all this. 'Doughnut economics' requires the setting of long-term goals, and this demands a consideration of the problem of economic growth. Growth is the increase in the inflation-adjusted system of the production, distribution and consumption of goods and services in a financial year, calculated as the geometric rate of growth of Gross Domestic Product (GDP) per capita. In the present system, many economists believe that GDP has to grow at 3% per year for citizens in a developed economy to maintain their standard of living.

The problem is that this is an exponential progression, and a growing economy needs to use energy and resources taken ultimately from the planet. And, of course, we are living in an age of climate emergency. We may be able to deal with that emergency if we act quickly enough, but for many thinkers, that urgently necessitates a global policy of 'degrowth'. As Andrew Sayer puts it, in his *Why We Can't Afford the Rich:*

"We can't afford to perpetuate a system predicated on inequality and endless compound growth. The dream of 'green growth', with capitalism delivering

---

[157] Ridley, Matt (2020), 359-60.

sustainability, is like selling guns to promote peace. We need an economy that can function on the basis of enough rather than insatiable acquisitiveness."[158]

The degrowth movement began in the late 1960s, when it was arguably driven by the so-called precautionary principle. It then fell into relative obscurity until the twenty-first century, when the increasing undeniability of climate damage earned it a significant comeback. In the English-speaking world, it is nowadays associated with Jason Hickel, Matthias Schmelzer, Andrea Vetter, Aaron Vansintjan and Kohei Saito, amongst others. There are different versions of degrowth, some of them explicitly communist, but all prioritise concern for the environment. Hickel is probably representative in this regard:

> "Let me emphasise that degrowth is not about reducing GDP. GDP is not a dial we can turn. Of course, slowing down unnecessary production and decommodifying public services is likely to cause GDP to grow more slowly, or stop growing, or even decline. And if so, that's OK. Under normal circumstances, this might trigger a recession. But a recession is what happens when a growth-dependent economy stops growing. It is chaotic and disastrous. What I'm calling for here is something completely different. It is about shifting to a different kind of economy altogether: an economy that doesn't require growth in the first place. To get there, we need to rethink everything from the debt system to the banking system, to liberate people, businesses, states and even innovation itself from the stuffy constraints of the growth imperative, freeing us to focus on higher goals. As we take practical steps in this

---

[158] Sayer, Andrew (2015), p341.

direction, exciting new possibilities come into view. We can create an economy that is organised around human flourishing instead of around endless capital accumulation; in other words, a post-capitalist economy. An economy that's fairer, more just, and more caring."[159]

Kohei Saito's degrowth is based on a close reading of Marx, in particular the new collected works of Marx and Engels, which contains much of their previously unpublished work, some of it connected with Marx's notion of 'metabolism', which is one way in which environmental concerns were framed in the nineteenth century. Saito proposes five 'pillars' to degrowth, all of them present in the writings of Marx, which he summarises thus:

> "Marx called for a shift in production to emphasize use-value and reduce both production associated with the creation of surplus value and the work hours that go with such production. He also called for the abolition of the division of labour that robs workers of their creativity. At the same time, he called for the increased democratisation of the labour process. Workers would make decisions about production democratically. It doesn't matter that this kind of decision-making process will take more time. Moreover, there will be a sharp increase in the social value assigned to essential work that's needed by society and low in environmental impact."[160]

Growth agnosticism, by contrast, is a position most familiarly associated with Kate Raworth, the inventor of Doughnut Economics, and is no less concerned with

---

[159] Hickel, Jason (2020), p30.
[160] Saito, Kohei (2025), p207-28.

environmental issues. Raworth thinks there is a problem with traditional conceptions of economic growth. Asked to draw a picture of its long-term path, she says, most economists will produce a graph of GDP against time whose leading tip climbs exponentially then hangs mid-air. The obvious question, 'what happens next?' is left unanswered, but the implication is that growth will be infinite.[161] What the conventional representation hides, she thinks, is that the upward curve must eventually turn into an S. "Early economists acknowledged what most of their successors have since ignored: that economic growth must eventually reach a limit."[162]

Given that both degrowthers and growth agnostics are urgently concerned to safeguard the environment, and that both see those who prioritise growth as the problem (and 'green growth' as a pernicious delusion), it might come as a surprise to learn that some economists have put forward persuasive arguments in favour of economic growth of precisely the exponential kind. For Daniel Susskind, the problem is not with growth, but with the growth-promoting technologies we have chosen to develop and adopt in society. Those same technologies have been "not only growth-promoting, but also climate-destroying, inequality-creating, work-threatening, politics undermining and community-disrupting."[163] Susskind subscribes to the notion of 'directed technological change', associated with the economist John Hicks since the 1930s, but recently given influential support by Daron Acemoglu. The evolution of technology of a certain kind is not inevitable: we have real choices. "The incentives that drive people to develop some technologies and abandon others are not fixed features of life that must be accepted as natural facts of the world over which

[161] Raworth, Kate (2017), p247.
[162] Raworth, Kate (2017), p251.
[163] Susskind, Daniel (2024), p96.

we have no control. On the contrary, these incentives can be constructed and maintained by us through the taxes and subsidies we set, the laws and regulations we pass, and the social norms we cultivate. And we can alter or replace those incentives if we wish."[164]

For a variety of reasons, including those just mentioned, degrowth, for Susskind, "is partly mistaken as a diagnosis, entirely mistaken as a solution, and if taken seriously would be a catastrophe."[165] Multiple studies show a strong correlation between economic growth and human flourishing. Degrowth economists would not necessarily deny that this has been true to date, but would claim that the two things – intertwined until now - are in the process of diverging, and will do so with increasing starkness as the Anthropocene extinction gathers pace. We now have enough of what we need in terms of goods and services. We need to degrow and focus on redistribution.

Susskind believes that this shows a faulty grasp of economic history, and in particular, of the development of growth theory. He points out that the notion of 'growth' only took hold of conventional politics in the middle of the twentieth century, after World War Two made the issue of Gross National Product unavoidable, since it was strongly linked to a country's potential for weapons-production. British and American manufacturing was radically diverted from the production of goods like cars and toys to the production of armaments. When peace returned, the changeover had to be reversed, and post-haste, because conscripts were being demobbed in huge numbers. Full employment became a priority, and that required increased production, which eventually turned into an obsession with growth.

So, the history of serious growth theory is not that old, and does not really go back to Marx. For Susskind, it unfolded in

---

[164] Ibid. p210-211.
[165] Ibid. p248.

three significant phases, each representing a significant corrective to the previous one. The first emerged in the 1930s and 40s with the work of Roy Harrod and Evsey Domar. The 'Harrod-Domar' model said that growth was wholly dependent on the level of a country's investment in physical capital: factories, dams, mines, machinery, etc. This model eventually fell foul of empirical reality: it became increasingly clear that an increase in material resources did not necessarily produce growth. Nevertheless, politicians and economists continued to act as if the theory was correct, even after its shortcomings became a matter of common knowledge.[166]

The second stage emerged in the 1950s, with the work of Robert Solow and Trevor Swan. The 'Solow-Swan' model showed that more investment in material capital – the Harrod-Domar trajectory - was a matter of diminishing returns. In fact, growth could only really be achieved by technological advances.

> "Having set down these ideas, Solow then turned to real-world data for confirmation he was on the right track. What he uncovered was striking. In the US economy from 1909 to 1949 the four decades before his famous papers were published - output per person had roughly doubled. And yet, Solow discovered, only a small proportion of that growth, about 12.5 per cent, could be accounted for by the use of more capital or the hiring of more workers. Other economists noted the same phenomenon. The implication was that the vast majority of that economic growth - the remaining 87.5 per cent, nicknamed the 'Solow residual' - must have been caused by something besides increased investment or hiring. And Solow argued that this 'something' must be technological progress: that, in

[166] Ibid. p30.

short, US growth did not come from using more resources, but from using those resources more productively."[167]

The next stage came in the late 1980s with another two economists: Robert Lucas and Paul Romer. Solow-Swan had left a problem: technological progress fired growth, yes, but where did technological progress come from? Robert Lucas located the solution in *human capital,* the idea that humans were constantly learning new skills, and that it was these – not the number of workers, or the physical capital – that were the decisive factor in growth. Paul Romer completed the investigation that Lucas began when he realised it was *ideas* that were the decisive factor in growth. Ideas are 'non-rival': they can be used over and over again without leaving fewer for others.

Put simply, Susskind believes that the degrowth movement is premised on the Harrod-Domar model, and fails to consider anything since.[168] It is because of Lucas-Romer in particular that 'green growth' is far from the impossibility they claim.

> "Solar energy is the most striking case of this technological progress. It began in the 1970s as a tool of last resort, an expensive source of energy reserved for only the most extreme situations: isolated lighthouses, outer space, cooling medicine in remote places. But today solar panels have become commonplace, carpeting rooftops and filling up deserts and fields. Technological progress drove a precipitous fall in the cost of solar modules, with prices collapsing from over $100 per watt in 1976 to less than half a dollar per watt by 2019, and their use increased dramatically as a result

---

[167] Ibid. p34.
[168] The evidence for that claim is strong: neither Hickel (2020) nor Saito (2025) nor Raworth (2017) discuss Solow-Swan or Lucas-Romer.

... In practice, this means that just a couple of decades ago solar energy was more than twenty times as expensive as energy from fossil fuels, but today it is cheaper: fossil fuel energy costs somewhere between $50 and $150 per 100 kWh (kilowatt hours), while solar energy only costs around $40 to $54 per 100 kWh."

Susskind does not draw the conclusion explicitly, but the implication is that had degrowth begun in earnest when the movement advocating it first emerged - in the 1970s – then solar panels would still be prohibitively expensive. The same might be said, by extension of other technologies, including those yet to come.

Ridley makes the same point:

"Much 'growth' is actually shrinkage. Largely unnoticed, there is a burgeoning trend today that the main engine of economic growth is not from using more resources, but from using innovation to do more with less: more food from less land and less water; more miles for less fuel; more communication for less electricity; more buildings for less steel; more transistors for less silicon; more correspondence for less paper; more socks for less money; more parties for less time worked ... In the ten years from 2008, America's economy grew by 15 per cent but its energy use fell by 2 per cent. This is not because the American economy is generating fewer products: it's producing more. It is not because there is more recycling, though there is. It's because of economies and efficiencies created by innovation. It will always be possible to raise living standards further by lowering the amount of a resource that is used to produce a given output. Growth is therefore indefinitely 'sustainable'."[169]

Ridley identifies 'innovationism' as the chief, and perhaps the only reason humankind has made material progress in the last hundred and fifty years.[170] Susskind essentially agrees: he thinks that an abandonment of growth would be a shocking betrayal of the world's poorest people.

> "Without growth, we do not stand a chance of achieving even our most basic goals, ones that I would hope the degrowthers share as well - eradicating poverty, providing good healthcare, supporting decent education and so on. And that is to say nothing of the grander goals that I hope humankind will explore in the future, from creating a world of material abundance for everyone to becoming an interplanetary species and setting out to seriously explore the stars."[171]

But degrowth is unworthy of the political Left for other reasons.

> "This discussion reveals one of the degrowth movement's most frustrating characteristics: its lack of imagination. To some extent, this is an unexpected weakness. Traditionally, the Left - the political home of

---

[169] Ridley, Matt (2020), p268-9. I indicated in the introduction to this book that, as I use the word 'science', it should generally be understood to mean STEM. Ridley makes the important point that 'science', in the restricted sense of the word, does not always, or even usually, stand 'upstream' of technology and innovation (an assumption that he calls 'the linear model'). "It is just as often the case that invention is the parent of science: techniques and processes are developed that work, but understanding of them comes later" (p282).
[170] Ibid. p4.
[171] Susskind, Daniel (2024), p163-64.

degrowth - has been a source of enormous intellectual creativity, making it the first stop for those seeking radical proposals for rebuilding society, blueprints for possible utopias... The prospect of making things go vastly better is one it has marched for, stirred up revolutions for, died for - yet today a fight to reimagine the future is what the degrowth movement seems keen to avoid."[172]

Susskind advocates a 'dashboard approach' to growth: it should be one among many of the ways in which we measure human flourishing. The important thing is to prioritise technological progress, encourage the production of new ideas, and not dogmatically reject growth. Ultimately, his approach seems similar to Raworth's. At one point, he recommends 'a nautical metaphor' as a good way of thinking about the future:

"Picture the economy as a boat bobbing about on the open water, with policymakers at the helm. They can raise the sails to speed up, or lower them to slow down, as before, but they can also steer their craft wherever they please on the sea. Just as a sailor can change both their speed and direction of travel, we can in principle shape both the quantity and the quality of growth."[173]

While Raworth says:

"A skilled kite surfer rides her surfboard across the rolling waves while catching the wind in her kite, and she must continually adjust - bending, dipping, and twisting her body - to maintain that dynamic interplay of the wind and the waves. That is just how GDP

---

[172] Ibid. p164-65.
[173] Ibid, p208.

should come to move in the twenty-first century, with the value of products and services sold each year bobbing and dipping in response to the constantly evolving economy."[174]

'Green decoupling' – the decoupling of economic growth from environmental concerns, and the vigorous prioritisation of the latter – is arguably a red herring. What is really required is the decoupling of capitalism from science, again for the purposes of boosting the latter. Yet it is easy to see how the degrowth movement arrived at its conclusions: the defining feature of capitalism - the 'private pursuit of unlimited monetary wealth' – suggests a curve that strongly resembles the exponential growth curve, and might even be mistaken for it. Nevertheless, it is capitalism that we need to overturn, not growth.

Capitalist Realism: Is There No Alternative?

Is it *really* easier to imagine the end of the world than to envisage the end of capitalism? It only seems so because capitalism presents itself as the whole of social reality.

Under normal conditions, that only becomes obvious when, for the sake of argument, capitalism is hypothetically conceived as one system among others, and its apologists state the time-worn arguments in its favour. Chief among those begins from Adam Smith's claim that capitalism is premised on *competition*, and that competition in production gives consumers *choice*.

The next step in this defence states that, since choice implies *freedom*, capitalism also generates, as a kind of bonus, a system conducive to *civil liberties and democratic government*.

---

[174] Raworth, Kate (2017), p284.

The third, and final, step of the apologetic is that, in order to find out what will appeal to consumers, capitalists need to keep an open mind in trialling different products, thus, as another bonus, we get *a system conducive to scientific experimentation*.

The conclusion barely needs to be made explicit. A capitalist society is necessarily *democratic, rational and scientific*, and humanity's best hope for the future.

Almost nothing in this narrative withstands scrutiny. Capitalism is an endeavour in which an individual, the capitalist, attempts to make a profit from the sale of commodities, usually, in the end, produced by others. Astonishingly – since past discussion has so immured us in the polar opposite conviction that it takes a moment to recognise the fact – the word 'capitalism' nowhere implies the existence of competition. To paraphrase David Hume, "Examine capitalism in all lights, and see if you can find that matter of fact, or real existence, which you call competition. Competition entirely escapes you, as long as you consider the object."

Evidence for this can be found in the term 'free market'. Although 'free market' is often used as a synonym for capitalism, it is equally common to encounter the expression 'free market capitalism', which should, if the two terms have equivalent meaning, be tautologous (ie, = 'capitalist capitalism'). However, 'free market capitalism' is not normally used as if the first two words are redundant, and that strongly suggests what we have already said: that there must be varieties of *non*-free market capitalism, hence that the term 'capitalism', in itself, does not imply competition.

Indeed, as we have said throughout, it would be better for the individual capitalist if competition was impossible: he would then have a captive market. And capitalism *can* exist without competition: it is rare, but possible, to have a capitalist enterprise that attracts no competitors – because no one knows where the capitalist in question sources his raw materials, for example, or because a capitalist system has been allowed to run unchecked, and quickly degenerated, under its own internal logic, into gangsterism and a handful of plutocratic monopolists, as in Vladimir Putin's Russia.

We do not need to rely solely on reason here, because we now have convincing empirical evidence that not only does capitalism fail to produce liberty, democracy and science, but that it actually emboldens their opposites. In 1992, a group of the world's top free-markets theorists helped introduce capitalism to Boris Yeltsin's Russia with the expectation, as Naomi Klein put it, that "if the optimal conditions for profit making were created, the country would rebuild itself, no planning required."[175] To say the result was a dismal failure would be an understatement; it was catastrophic.

But of course, a single experiment may not be decisive, so the same thing was tried again, by an equally well-qualified coterie of ideologues, in Iraq, after the fall of Saddam Hussein in 2003. The result confirmed the original 1992 findings: that, just as we have argued, capitalism is unrelated to democracy, science or human rights. One might as well try to build a skyscraper by shaking a jar full of rocks.

We do not normally notice the failures of capitalism, because when it implodes – as it frequently does – the terminology undergoes a revision: the chief players are not 'capitalists' but 'oligarchs'. But the word 'oligarch' originally meant a member of a numerically small government called an oligarchy.[176] Boris Berezovsky, Mikhail Khodorkovsky and Vladimir Vinogradov were not government officials; they recognisably did what capitalists routinely do: they 'invested' money in businesses in order to extract a profit. They succeeded as capitalists but, of

---

[175] Klein, Naomi (2008), p224. Yegor Gaidar, the then Russian Prime Minister, had already set the ball rolling.

[176] 'Plutocracy' would be better here, but still inaccurate, because its members do not belong to the government.

course, they also drove many people into penury. Their British equivalents would include Sir Philip Green, Lady Michelle Mone and Lord Ben Houchen. American 'oligarchs' would include Donald Trump, Elon Musk, Sam Bankman-Fried and Bernie Madoff. Because civil society is stronger in the UK and the US, the 'oligarchs' can do less relative damage, but of course, 'oligarchs' are always on the lookout for opportunities to cash in at the expense of the majority. Such opportunities arise most frequently when society runs into an emergency for which the government is poorly prepared (as happened in the UK with Personal Protective Equipment during the COVID outbreak), or when a government appeals to capitalists for partnership, without foreclosing the possibility of its own exploitation (as happened with many Private Finance Initiatives during John Major's then Tony's Blair's tenure as Prime Minister[177]), or when it trusts capitalists to help determine the strength of economic regulation (as caused the 2008 global financial crisis).

Capitalism as a competitive system must always end by soiling its own bed, simply because the bigger will always consume the smaller, and, by that procedure, will become even bigger and stronger. At best, competition characterises one stage in its limited life cycle.

In practice, of course, the possibility of easy money will always attract challengers, just as carrion attracts rival scavengers, so, as a rule, competition *does* arise – but crucially, *as an intrusion from without*; in the form (from its own point of view) of an unavoidable evil. Because there is nothing intrinsically competitive in the business of scavenging.

But the word 'competition' itself is not unproblematic. It conceals a multitude of possibilities, and, in itself, is neither good nor bad. The Olympic Games is a 'competition', so is a chess tournament, so are lots of activities at village fetes and

---

[177] Cf. eg, Monbiot, George (2000).

agricultural shows, but so is pistols at dawn, so is bear-baiting, so is warfare, so may be survival in a death camp[178], so were gladiators in circuses, so is nature's 'red in tooth and claw' survival-of-the-fittest.

Free and fair competition is a small subcategory of competition, and difficult to achieve when the participants do not voluntarily agree to abide by the rules. But if my goal is to make a profit, why would I submit to a set of conditions that get in my way? Answer: because, otherwise, I will be disbarred from the game.

But that only gives me a reason to go through the *motions* of submitting. The numerous doping scandals of the Olympic Games are strong evidence that, when the stakes are high, the rules can easily be regarded as expendable.

So, not only is competition an unwelcome imposition on capitalism from without, but the freeness and fairness of that competition is not part of it. Again, it is imposed from outside in the form of an alien power.

In short, freedom and fairness are not produced *from within* capitalism in an unproblematic extrapolation of consumer choice into the political arena. Again, the term 'free market' plays a part in concealing that. Leaving aside the problem of its analytic/synthetic credentials, discussed above, the term 'free' is morally ambiguous, as that word always is. It could mean 'unrestrained', in which case it implies the proverbial 'war of all against all', where guns and bombs are as legitimate as any other tools of contest. Alternatively, it could incorporate Isaiah Berlin's well-known distinction between 'freedom for' and 'freedom from'. But even that might not get us anywhere: 'freedom for' – understood, in Berlin's thinking, as self-mastery – becomes, in the term 'free market' (ie, as applied solely to the

---

[178] In Chapter 9 of If *This is a Man*, Primo Levi says that under conditions of virtually total scarcity, humanity separates into two groups. 'The Saved' are those who can lie, steal, plot and generally put themselves first.

market as opposed to society as a whole), incoherent. The participants in the free market all want to attain a monopoly. As a matter of logic alone, they cannot all succeed. To the extent that the market is 'free' in any moral sense – ie, placing ethical limits on what capitalists can do to each other in their quest for monopoly, thus providing all the players with the possibility of 'freedom for' – the conditions for that freedom must be imposed from outside.

In conclusion, it looks as if freedom and fairness precede capitalism, and it seems likely that they, not capitalism, are the underlying pillars of democracy. They are undoubtedly the achievements of working-class organisations and associations, discussed in the first part of this book.

The second bonus supposedly supplied by capitalism is science. To some extent, the idea that it is science-friendly is partly premised on the fallacy we have just exposed, that it is intrinsically competitive, thus delivering choice, thus delivering freedom, which more or less simultaneously gives us the 'open society' of civil liberties and the rule of law. But it is also based on the idea that capitalists must experiment to find out which goods appeal to potential customers, and they must be open-minded enough to alter direction whenever consumer preferences change.

The problem is that consumer preferences can be manipulated. To repeat: capitalism is a system in which an individual tries to make a profit from the sale of commodities. Science may help her – eg, by devising psychological stratagems, it may give her a means of consumer manipulation - but it may also get in the way, as, for example, when it reveals costs to stakeholders that reduce shareholder dividends, or when it invents new bombs to drop on factories during wars. The ideal customer is always an addict, so, as far as possible, capitalism will always try to produce addictive commodities. The pharmaceutical industry and the ultra-processed foods industry are legal exemplars of that, but, strategically, and as a form of capitalism, the illegal narcotics industry is entirely continuous with both.

Forced to serve a system comprised of actors whose sole purpose is to make a profit, science will produce good outcomes only to the extent that the good can be made to conform to the system's purpose. To the extent that the bad can be made to pay, it will work to produce that. So, under capitalism, science has given us MRI machines, MP3 players and a cure for smallpox, but it has also given us cigarette factories, Zyklon B and nuclear weapons.

Obviously, science and capitalism are different things; no degree of superficial resemblance can change that, but the confusion runs deep. We are often told that capitalism is making the world a better place. To give an example from Ingrid Robeyns:

> "In 2016, the economists Christopher Lakner and Branko Milanovic published a paper in the *World Bank Economic Review* which contained [a] graph that sparked a lot of interest. Nicknamed, 'the elephant graph' for its shape, this 'growth incidence curve' shows the percentage by which incomes increased in different groups of the world population between 1988 and 2008. It reveals that, overall, the poorest 70 per cent saw the greatest increases in income (with the exception of the poorest 5 per cent of the world's population, who saw an increase that was smaller than the global average. People on a median income experienced the greatest increases of all, about 75 per cent of the average… The optimists have used this

graph to support their claim that everyone wins under capitalism, especially the middle classes."[179]

On any reading of this evidence, the 'optimists' are wrong. To the extent that living standards have improved – not just recently, but for over a hundred and fifty years – we have science to thank, not capitalism. Science is not intrinsically dependent on capitalism, nor was it ever. A list of the biggest capitalist companies of the last century will not allow anyone to deduce a list of the greatest medical and agricultural advances during the same period. Capitalism deploys science for beneficial purposes only when it suits it.

Even so, things have improved. One wonders how much greater the improvement would have been had we spent the last century and a half living under a system that actually prioritised the use of science for human flourishing.

So, to get back to original question, can we imagine the end of capitalism? Well, yes: if we can imagine a free and fair, willingly competitive economic system, then yes: we can. Capitalism masquerades as such a system. On the other hand, science really *is* such a system.[180] Imagine a world in which whenever the need for something arises, different teams of scientists are asked to produce it. The winning team receives a significant one-off reward and the prestige. That was roughly how the marine chronometer came to be, in 1761; it is the principle behind the Orteig Prize, the X Prize Foundation and challengeworks.org.

And it is probably not too far away from what happens in the research and development departments of many capitalist

---

[179] Robeyns, Ingrid (2024), p21-22.
[180] Those convinced by Thomas Kuhn's 1962, *The Structure of Scientific Revolutions*, or Paul Feyerabend's 1975, *Against Method*, will naturally challenge this. In the first appendix to this book, I examine the ways in which science has been compromised under capitalism, which may go some way towards allaying such concerns.

enterprises already. The point is not whether it is workable (it is), but that we have just imagined a world without capitalism.

Capitalism's purpose is to make a profit, and since free and fair competition presents it with an extrinsic obstacle, it will take every opportunity to circumvent it. It will engage in industrial espionage, mislead or lie to consumers, lobby and bribe politicians, conspire with its putative competitors to operate a cartel, launder money, evade taxes, underpay its workers, and so on. Its artificial obligation to function within preconceived boundaries very much against its liking means that it will always behave in such a way as to corrupt the society it inhabits. The more powerful companies are of course the bigger corrupters, because they have more to gain, and they stand a better chance of getting away with it.

So why does society put up with it? Because (a) most people are doing moderately well, and it is always easier to stick with something than to make an effort to change it, and (b) everyone with any real power makes a huge amount of money. Ideology does much of the work in keeping the relatively powerless compliant, but the impression must be perpetually maintained that the present economic system is a free and fair competitive one from which democratic freedoms and scientific inquiry have emerged as natural extrusions. (In other words: there is no alternative, better world.) Along the way, we are transformed into varieties of *homo consumens*, shopping creatures self-governed by suspicion, pathological acquisitiveness, intransigence, short-termism and egoism. We become enemies of each other, and friends of commodities. And we do not notice that we are not living in a democracy.

Transcending *homo consumens* will take time. Any rational government would take steps to end capitalism's character as a never-ending game, ie, introducing Limitarianism. Ingrid Robeyns's thinking complements Wilkinson and Pickett's 2009, *The Spirit Level: Why More Equal Societies Almost Always Do Better*, and Oliver James's 2007, *Affluenza*.[181] But here we run into a brick wall. The last two paragraphs make sense on the assumption we have the power to implement changes. But can any of us really imagine any political party with a Limitarian agenda getting elected today?

Conventional Politics and Communist Command Economies

The answer, surprisingly, may be yes. We have seen that what might be called civil society – civil liberties, the rule of law, universal suffrage - is partly a container for capitalism, and, while it is frequently suborned, it is neither a product of capitalism, nor intrinsically compatible with it. If that were not so, there would be no need for capitalists to undermine it (by, eg, lobbying political parties, hiding dubious practices from journalists and inspectors, hiring lawyers to find legal loopholes, avoiding taxes, discouraging unionisation).

Today's democracies are the same: the two, four or five contending political parties (it is rarely more than five) in any country may sometimes be in the pockets of particular capitalists and, equally often, of capitalism in general, but that does not mean they are intrinsically the products of capitalism, or that they cannot be made to serve a higher end.

Britain and the USA are effectively two-party states. In Britain, the Labour Party and the Conservative Party have alternated for over a century now; in the USA, the Democrats and the Republicans have swapped places since 1852. In Britain,

---

[181] *Affluenza* is a much better book than is commonly admitted. Caricatured by its critics as mere 'pop psychology' dealing with an invented condition exclusively affecting middle-class cry babies, in fact Parts One and Three are a trenchant critique of capitalism's consequences for mental health. Two things let it down: its jokey title, which suggests a pseudo-illness, and which plays into the hands of its critics, and secondly, its refusal to grasp the nettle: it locates the source of the problem in 'selfish capitalism', as if 'selfish capitalism' is an aberrant subset of the category as a whole.

at least, voters tend to place a high value on politicians' personalities, particularly those of potential leaders; they tend to vote against, rather than for, a political party (Conservatives, not because they like the Conservatives, but because they dislike Labour, and vice-versa);[182] they are significantly swayed by what Adam Curtis calls 'the power of nightmares'; and for all the above reasons, they do not like to think deeply about politics until just before a general election. Even then, they often engage reluctantly.

In such an environment, any attempt to establish a new progressive political party is almost certainly doomed to fail (reactionary parties are a different matter, since capitalists may well provide significant political funding, as Elon Musk allegedly wants to do with Reform).

The alternating-two-parties narrative, however, may conceal a wealth of genuine variety. Margaret Thatcher's Conservative Party was significantly different to Ted Heath's, and in 2007, Gordon Brown (Labour) compared himself to Mrs Thatcher. Jeremy Corbyn's Labour manifesto was nothing like Tony Blair's, just as Neil Kinnock's vision for Labour bore little resemblance to Michael Foot's. Partly because the world itself changes, there are serious internal disagreements across time; there are radicals and traditionalists; there are visionaries and jobsworths.

The same holds true within the parties themselves. Theresa May and Liz Truss are ideologically antagonistic Conservatives, while John McDonnell and Liz Kendall occupy similarly distant points on the Labour spectrum.[183] And each party also contains 'fringe' groups, which may not be as marginal as that word makes them sound. In the case of Labour: CDS, Momentum,

---

[182] Cf. eg, https://electoral-reform.org.uk/latest-news-and-research/publications/a-system-out-of-step-the-2024-general-election/
[183] https://labourlist.org/2025/01/labour-mps-left-wing-right-wing-survation/ gives more details.

178

CLGA, Compass, Blue Labour, Open Labour, Red Wall Caucus, and so on. In the case of the US Democrats; the Democratic Socialists of America, EMILY's List, MoveOn, America Votes, Blue Dog Coalition, Indivisible, ActBlue – again, to name just a few. There is nothing 'entryist' about any of them: they are an essential part of the internal dialogue without which a modern political party cannot function (consisting, as they nearly all do, of free-thinking, intellectually evolving citizens).

Other political parties in other democratic countries are constituted in roughly the same way. The discussions are usually out of sight of the ordinary voter, but that does not mean they do not happen: it is one of the reasons why interesting-looking individuals can sometimes make a comfortable home in what appears to most people to be a 'boring' profession.

Arguably, under a two-party system, anyone hoping to implement something like the ten measures we listed above could do worse than join her own country's dominant left-leaning political party, be it the British Labour Party, the US Democrats, the Australian ALP, or the Brazilian MDB.[184] As regards the first, it is theoretically possible to become a member without assenting to any of the proposals in its manifesto, and since it is widely supported, constituted on democratic grounds, and has a membership of just over 300,000 people, all to a greater or lesser degree socialist, one has a better chance of reforming it, and thus (indirectly) the country, than one has of directly changing the country – with its sixty-eight million people of all political persuasions – via an outlier like the Communist Party of Britain, the Alliance for Workers' Liberty, the Anarchist Federation, or by creating one's own political party. On the other hand, outliers are important: some individuals, for reasons of conscience or temperament, will always feel that 'mainstream-ism' involves too many

[184] In countries with more multi-party systems, things would naturally be different. The key consideration is how realistic the chances are of achieving power.

179

compromises, and carries too many risks of corruption. They may be right.

To return to the question with which we ended the last section: can any of us really imagine any political party with a Limitarian agenda getting elected today? Well, yes, we can, assuming we can imagine (a) one of the established left-leaning political parties approving a candidate with a radical agenda, and (b) such a candidate gaining a victory at the polls. Such things have happened. They continue to happen, and they are not even particularly rare.

Much of the above, however, may be too optimistic for some readers. In *The Future of Anarchism*, Hugh Small discusses the way party politics has become self-serving, in ways that were first identified by Gaetano Mosca in 1896 and Robert Michels in 1911.[185] In both the USA and Britain, democracy was originally meant to be 'representative', ie:

"A faithful sample representing the composition of the whole electorate and all its various special interests. In today's politics, 'representative' has come to mean something very different. A modern 'representative of the people' is an individual specially qualified in electioneering and explaining the party manifesto to voters. The selection of representatives does not nowadays replicate the composition of the population ... Party theoreticians study long into the night to identify 'wedge' issues, however trivial or irrelevant to people's welfare, that will divide the nation and demonstrate that the party system is 'necessary'. Our political parties are playing into the hands of the world's worst dictators who are gleefully mocking the social disharmony produced by these political parties in search of power."[186]

---

[185] Cf. also Oborne, Peter (2007).
[186] Small, Hugh (2019), p105, 119.

As a way to restore true representation, Small proposes 'electoral anarchism: the anti-party vote', which he outlines specifically in terms of UK elections (although it is transferable elsewhere). The aim would be to create "100 independent MP's free of any party discipline."[187] The means would be tactical voting, carried out by two electoral groups: those who usually decline to vote at all, and those accustomed to vote for 'no hope' parties. Since each group amounts to around 20% of the electorate, their combined involvement could be decisive. Small's proposal is that they be encouraged to vote for "whichever candidate in last in the alphabetic order on the list."[188]

"One hundred independent MP's free of any party discipline will resist any attempt by the two major parties to sideline them and dominate the chamber. The smaller parties (in this 'thought experiment' retaining about 50 of 650 seats) would combine with the 'independents' in this resistance. Cabinet ministers would have to be appointed by free parliamentary vote, not chosen by a party. The biggest party's ability to spend taxpayers' funds on grandiose projects with uncertain payback would be curtailed. These changes will erode the centralised power of the state and create the 'representative government' envisaged by democracy's American and British founders."[189]

I will leave the reader to consider the feasibility of this – although there is nothing incredible about it in principle.

However, partly out of despair at the perceived unlikelihood of change by conventional means, partly because of a cynicism

---

[187] Ibid. p124.
[188] Ibid. p121.
[189] Ibid. p124.

about politics generally, and partly as a result of the self-aggrandisement of China (with its high growth and burgeoning infrastructure), many young people have been seduced by the supposed virtues of central state capitalism. Arguments against the free market are then taken to be arguments for command economies.

But in fact, although China is skilled at trumpeting its own virtues - a mission in which it is helped by its highly vocal middle class - it is a police state. It crushed democracy in Hong Kong, it has committed crimes against humanity in Tibet and Xinjiang, and it hopes to invade Taiwan someday soon. We do not know how successful it really is: for example, how effectively it has managed homelessness, or mental illness. Only the CCP knows that, and we can have no confidence that it tells the truth on any particular occasion. At the time of writing this paragraph, a 19-year-old Chinese choirgirl-turned-democracy-activist, living in Britain, has been declared an enemy of the Chinese state, and a $100,000 reward offered for her capture abroad, simply because of a blog post in which she described Hong Kong police brutality in 2020.[190]

China regularly pursues overseas dissidents. It is not the friend of any version of progressivism, nor was the USSR, for all its occasional growth successes.[191] Western capitalism has fared better in terms of upholding human rights – and probably better than most other countries in the world - but, as we have said, that is the result of a containment structure which pre-dates it, and which continues to hold it unsteadily in check. As the

---

[190] https://www.bbc.com/news/articles/c93lp2wd0qzo

[191] See eg, Spufford, Francis (2011), Dean, Jodi (2011). We might add Lea Ypi's 2021 memoir, *Free* to the list of books that could be read as (guarded) praise for command economies. In the latter case, it is Albania. Such economies undoubtedly do work for some citizens, especially conservatives and conformists. Minorities, nonconformists and those who simply think things can be changed for the better tend to fare considerably less well.

Conservative thinker, Edmund Burke, warned us long ago, we methodically dismantle that structure at our peril.

The 'Subject' of 'the Revolution'

Razmig Keuchyan's comprehensive 2014 *The Left Hemisphere*, begins with two claims: firstly, that any attempt to understand contemporary critical theory must recognise that it begins with the experience of the defeat of the left.[192] Secondly, that all the powerful working-class organisations of the first half of the twentieth century, which were often led by Marxists, have now gone. "Nothing similar exists at present or, probably, for the immediate future."[193]

The search is therefore on for a new 'subject' of emancipation, a social class that can combine the role of 'oppressee' with the potential to carry through a revolution on behalf of oppressees everywhere. As McKenzie Wark puts it, "What such theories have in common is the fixed idea that capitalism only comes to an end when it is negated by the force of an agency coming from below."[194] Candidates have included 'the multitude', the cognitariat, the lumpenproletariat, a coalition of marginalised groups, the 'subaltern' classes, the *sans-papiers*, and so on. The second half of Keuchyan's text – entitled 'Subjects' – is wholly devoted to this vexed question. The increasingly conventional move to define the lumpenproletariat in terms of the unemployed, etc. is recognisably part of this same quest. In chapter 4 of the present book, we spent a long time examining the revolutionary potential of a probably-impossible-to-pin-down section of the middle classes.

---

[192] Keucheyan, Razmig (2014), p7. According to the author, the seminal failure was the attempted German revolution of 1919.
[193] Ibid, p4.
[194] Wark, McKenzie (2015).

A replacement for the proletariat, at least as Marx and Engels conceived it, is a very tall order. The proletariat was supposed to be the class that was not a class, and, precisely because it came from nothing, it was supposed to be capable of effecting a universal liberation. In the words of *The German Ideology:*

> "The communist revolution ... does away with labour, and abolishes the rule of all classes with the classes themselves, because it is carried through by the class which no longer counts as a class in society, is not recognised as a class, and is in itself the expression of the dissolution of all classes, nationalities, etc. within present society."

The modern reader might detect a heavy dose of Judaeo-Christian mysticism here, mixed with a Hegelian fondness for opposites crashing into each other to produce a 'negation' – in this case, a once-and-for-all negation of injustice. It strongly resembles Biblical claims that God had to make Himself nothing in Jesus Christ, since only that 'self-emptying' could open the door to universal salvation[195]. But there is not the slightest evidence that the proletariat was ever capable of fulfilling such a role, nor that any contemporary class can be expected to rise to the (impossible) challenge.

The disinterested reader might be tempted to ask why a 'subject' is needed for a present-day revolution at all, and, indeed, whether the search for one conceals a fundamental pusillanimity. The searcher seems to require a social class to carry out a revolution *for him*, and yet *for its own* benefit, a process in which he hopes to play a part, either as a 'fellow-traveller', or in some sort of 'vanguard', all the time preferring not to be identified the primary mover. Surely, our disinterested

---

[195] Eg, The Letter to the Philippians, Chapter 2 verse 7. Such passages probably have their ultimate source in the 'Suffering Servant', in Isaiah chapter 53.

reader might go on, the important thing is that the revolutionary programme should be morally and intellectually coherent, and that it should be implemented effectively; by 'who' is a comparative – if not a complete - irrelevance. The real question of *who* the revolutionary 'subject' is should really have but one answer: anyone who wants to be.

So far, we have been arguing from facts towards a thesis claimed as factual. The proposal has been that we have existed since the beginning of history within a human-constructed world defined primarily by whatever means of securitisation prevails at the time (although the inside/outside, have/have not distinction has retained a roughly uniform character throughout); that so living has made us suspicious of, fearful of, and hostile towards one another; that the present social system is generally one in which lumpenproletarian capitalism (which, in principle, includes all capitalism) pulls in one direction, while the middle classes pull in another; that both pullings are malign; that, while these two groups (only one of which qualifies as a 'class' in the sociological sense[196]) are technically at odds with each other (because they have long-term conflicting purposes), yet they live side-by-side in a reluctant collaboration, which is also, partly, a standoff.

The purpose of this book has been (1) to show how the means of securitisation has always been central to the organisation of any society and (2) to more accurately delineate the nature of capitalism. Some readers may have concluded that the ultimate purpose of (1) was to advocate for the 'overthrow' of the means of securitisation, but a moment's thought shows the impossibility of such a thing. Biology itself is a network of securitisation mechanisms, and our physical bodies are entirely continuous with that. Humans are part of nature; we cannot

---

[196] Although even that is debatable. We noted Erik Olin Wright's reservations about the coherence of the middle-class, above.

exist except within a network of securitisation devices such as shelter, community and medicine.

Nevertheless, we cannot ignore the question of whether we have been *over*securitised, and whether, on the whole, we have been *securitised against*. This book contends that, on both counts, we have. We need to construct a society which serves all our interests, which itself is securitised *for,* and within which we ourselves are securitised for.

The Securitisation of the Imagination

As Nick Hayes puts it in his 2020, *Book of Trespass:*

> "Many of our liberties, and the restrictions placed on them, are expressed in terms of land, parameters and property, so much so that it is hard to tell which is a metaphor for the other. If someone has *crossed the line*, they have strayed over the limits of acceptable action and their words or deeds are deemed to be *beyond the pale* (the old Saxon word for fence). We talk of *access* equally in terms of the physical, with disability rights and the right to roam, and in the abstract realm, in terms of education, health and opportunity. Segregation, which directs the mindset of race and gender, is a word whose Latin root means to be cast out of a flock, and which reinforces the prejudice that racial groups can be distinguished by a line alone … To *wander* and to *roam* are implicitly connected with moral failings and the word 'vagrancy' has as much sense in morality as it does in legal cases concerning homeless people. A *deviant* is someone who has turned off the right way. To *stray from the path* suggests a clearly marked line of righteousness, signposted by societal or religious doctrines. And the most fundamental link

between the physical world of trespassing and its moral parallel, is the origin of the word itself. *Trespasser* is the French verb meaning to cross over, which came from the Latin word *transgredior*, from whose past participle we get the English word: transgression."[197]

But the securitisation of the imagination goes even deeper. The attempted destruction of human rights movements and individuals by despotic regimes globally is well documented, but the persecution of alternative worldviews is probably just as prominent. According to a 2021 report by The Pew Research Centre, forty-one countries ban religion-related groups, with Jehovah's Witnesses, Baha'is and Ahmadis being the biggest targets.

There is some method in this apparent madness. The banned group often represents an active vision of an alternative society, what might be called a 'countersociety'. Obviously, the ultimate ideals of all religions are sharply opposed to the status quo – even when the religion in question is the official state one - but in most cases, these religions exist in a state of practical accord with the powers that be. Adherents may *formally* assent to such injunctions as 'forgive your enemies' and 'love your neighbour', but *in practice* they tend to live by more 'realistic' rules.

Where that does not happen – and new converts often represent a problem, since they are more likely to take the religion's injunctions more seriously - and under a government whose prime goal is to hold on to power indefinitely, the groups in question are routinely perceived as a threat to the established order, even in virtue of their continued existence (because that existence implicitly entails that state's tolerance of divergent views and of, at the very least, tacit criticism). In general, swift measures must be taken to liquidate them.

---

[197] Hayes, Nick (2020), p18.

Under Western capitalism, the situation is different. By and large, all such groups are tolerated under the proviso that they do not engage in, or preach, violence. But they are also kept in check by what we have called the securitisation of the imagination.

'Countersociety' is a neologism, but in the late 1960s, so was its ancestor, 'counterculture'. The latter term first appeared in print in 1969 - in Theodore Roszak's *The Making of a Counter Culture* - since when it has become firmly established in everyday discourse.

And yet, the movement Roszak was describing was obviously as much of a counter*society* as a counter*culture*. What happened in Haight-Ashbury in 1967 was never intended to stay in Haight-Ashbury. Why, one might ask, in all the years since Roszak's book was published, has no one thought to coin the term 'countersociety'? Radical alternative societies are variously labelled 'protest groups', 'intentional communities', 'collectives', 'social experiments', 'communes', 'prefigurative political movements', 'cooperatives', 'neighbourhood associations' – but never countersocieties. And yet, that is clearly what, in most circumstances, they are.

We will return to the question of *real* countersocieties later when we consider prefigurative politics, but for the rest of this section, I would like to consider the *concept*, since I think it sheds light on a number of philosophical problems.

Every negative has a positive: an anti-capitalist may not necessarily be a pro-communist, but he or she must be committed to a *world* in which capitalism is tightly constrained if not wholly absent. A protestor must be protesting against something, and must be at least implicitly committed to a world without that thing, even allowing for the fact that they may only object to it in certain walks of life (in which case they are committed to a world without it in the relevant walks of life).

Talk of 'possible worlds' is a staple of philosophical metaphysics, but not, currently, of ethics. However, if I am against, say, octopus farming, I must be committed to the realisation of a fairly specific possible world, ie, one in which no one farms octopuses. If, in addition, I am also against sexism and tax avoidance, then the possible world to which I am committed contains at least two more significant features distinguishing it from the one I actually inhabit. Kantian moral absolutists might claim that, because moral rules must be consistent with one another they all point to the same possible world, namely, the one Kant himself called 'The Kingdom of Ends', where everyone treats others as an end, never as a means.

In his *Critique of Practical Reason*, Kant himself proposed three 'postulates of the moral life' – unprovable premises without which the moral life does not make rational sense.

> "These postulates are those of *immortality*, of *freedom* considered positively (as the causality of a being insofar as it belongs to the intelligible world), and of *the existence of God*. The first flows from the practically necessary condition of a duration befitting the complete fulfilment of the moral law; the second from the necessary presupposition of independence from the sensible world and of the capacity to determine one's will by the law of an intelligible world, that is, the law of freedom; the third from the necessity of the condition for such an intelligible world to be the highest good, through the presupposition of the highest independent good, that is, of the existence of God."[198]

Freedom is, of course, necessary for the notion of moral choice, but, arguably, immortality and God are not. The

---

[198] Kant, Immanuel (2015), p106-07. Italics mine.

'complete fulfilment of the moral law' on which Kant grounds his immortality requirement could be satisfied by historical progress that terminates in the societal realisation of the Kingdom of Ends, and the latter could just be defined as the highest good *in itself*. If we require God to make it the highest good, we enter a kind of Euthyphro dilemma to the effect of 'What makes God good?' No, there are only two postulates of the moral life as that life is conceived in Kant: freedom and the Kingdom of Ends. The latter would be conceived historically, as a society devoid of injustice insofar as everyone treats everyone else as an end. It is not necessary for me, personally, to inhabit that world, only for me to be (implicitly) committed to the possibility of its realisation.

Talk of 'possible worlds' in ethics would really be talk of 'possible countersocieties', since the ethical features of any world whatsoever are necessarily social features. 'A world without lies', 'a world in which there is no murder', and even 'a world in which no one harms animals' could all be *this world* as regards its non-moral features, but they could not be *this society*. By contrast, the 'possible worlds' of Leibnizian modal logic do concern non-moral features, and thus refer to states of affairs external to *any* society: monkeys using typewriters for eternity, Achilles agreeing with a tortoise to enter a race, or a demon who knows the position and momentum of every particle in the universe.

The notion of possible countersocieties has several advantages over the individuating tools of traditional moral discourse. (1) It can be used to test the coherence of an individual's moral stance: is the possible world rendered by his or her moral beliefs internally consistent? (2) It also requires a holistic understanding of moral values, an understanding that moral values do not exist in isolation, rather they are component elements of a different world-constitution. And (3) it effaces the artificial distinction between morality and politics, which is another way in which language has been securitised: the restriction of moral discourse to private affairs. The notion of possible countersocieties is not so different from the age-old notion of Utopias, and, notwithstanding Marx's distaste for 'Utopian Socialism', some modern thinkers have underlined the value of Utopian thinking for bringing about positive change.[199] Finally, (4) it may make some contribution to a closure of Hume's is/ought gap: my moral values have a grounding in some (counter-) factual state of affairs.

Admittedly, it also makes morality more complex. One hundred members of Amnesty International may represent one hundred different countersocieties whose only intersection is at the point where universal human rights are realised.

But obviously (and leaving Kant to one side for a moment), it would be strange if the many countersocieties projected by different people all entailed *the* same possible world (and of course, there are plenty of fascist countersocieties). If the contradictions can be overcome, it will be by seeing the problem as one for the long-term, and perhaps – this is a speculation which there isn't space to develop here - by bringing Jürgen Habermas's Discourse Principle and Moral Principle to bear. The Discourse Principle tells us when the application of a moral principle is valid; the Moral Principle tells us when it can be accepted.

In any case, the notion of moral behaviour as an implied countersociety arguably encourages discussion of a better future and how to get there. But more than that, once we push past the current securitisation of language to consider the various movements which have defined themselves *vis-à-vis* the current system as anti- or 'protest', we can see them in their hitherto hidden aspects, as they really are. They look like dark stones whose undersides glow. On turning them over, it transpires that

---

[199] Cf. eg, Marcuse, Herbert (1969), Coverley, Merlin (2012), Claeys, Gregory (2024), Segal, Lynne (2017).

the prevailing system is not as dead as one supposed: it is full of little light sources whose net effect is to illuminate a state of affairs beyond it.

The Altersociety

Every economic system generates social norms whose function is to make it easier for individuals or communities to benefit to a greater or lesser extent from the means of production. But in each age, it also generates individuals and communities who deliberately deviate from, or subvert, those norms. Capitalism is no different. In creating a very specific form of society, it also fashioned its own 'altersociety', its own underbelly of communities loosely united by a conscious rejection of its principal norms - including, in this case, its socially-backed aspiration to accumulate money – and an equally fervent adoption of *values-in-themselves* in the form of painting, poetry, music, dress, dance – the whole spectrum of 'art for art's sake.'[200] In his 1907, *Bohemia in London*, Arthur Ransome summed the phenomenon up:

> "The men who really care for their art, who wish above all things to do the best that is in them, do not take the way of the world and the regular salaries of the newspaper offices. They stay outside, reading, writing, painting for themselves, and snatching such golden crumbs as fall from the tables of publishers, editors and picture buyers. They make a living as if by accident."[201]

---

[200] Medieval society also had an altersociety, of course. Its rejection of wealth was the same; however, its adoption of values-in-themselves was much more likely to be religious in character. However, it also contained the wandering minstrels whose artistic endeavours gave rise to the notion of courtly love. In general, it is the positive choices of the altersociety that gives it its distinctiveness in any given economic era.

[201] Ransome, Arthur (1984), p195.

At the end of the nineteenth century and the beginning of the twentieth, it was not unheard of for such men and women to starve to death. By doing so, most of them cemented their invisibility to posterity. Somerset Maugham's 1915 semi-autobiographical *Of Human Bondage* contains an account of just one such demise.

Any altersociety is necessarily impossible to delineate most of the time: it subsists as a perpetually morphing shadow of the society whose members populate and sustain the dominant economic system, what we might call 'the master society'. We can discern its occasional irruptions into conventional social interaction with hindsight, but it is always more difficult to detect in the present. Its history can seem to be the history of its middle-class, wealthy actors[202] – especially under capitalism, where the rejection of money only means anything, it might be held, to the extent that the opposite is a realistic possibility; for those immured in poverty by, eg, discrimination, disability or political misfortune, it is, at best, an empty gesture. We will return to this later.

In any case, as we mentioned above, the capitalist altersociety is distinguished by a twofold gesture: the rejection of money is merely a felt precondition of the pursuit of transcendence, usually in the form of one or another kind of artistic achievement, but also, sometimes, also more directly, in the form of magic, the occult, orthodox religious mysticism, esoterism. Its poorer members – who are always numerous – nearly all live and die in obscurity, as the poor usually do.

---

[202] Jerrold Siegel accurately captures the relation of bohemianism, here, to the master society: "From the start, Bohemianism took shape by contrast with the image with which it was commonly paired: bourgeois life… But the quality revealed by the scraping away of that false opposition is seldom hypocrisy. Like positive and negative poles, Bohemian and bourgeois were – and are – parts of a single field: they imply, require, and attract each other." (Siegel, Jerrold (1986) p5).

The capitalist altersociety is intrinsically linked to the notion of the psychogeographical city-walker – a figure Merlin Coverley has shown to be far older and more complex than the Baudelairean *flâneur* – for whom the city is "a dreamscape in which nothing is as it seems and which can only be navigated by those with secret knowledge."[203]

In its capitalist instantiation, we may assert, very roughly, that the altersociety began with Rousseau in the eighteenth century[204], then reappeared in British Romanticism, as exemplified initially by Thomas Chatterton, then by Byron, Keats, Shelley and the early Wordsworth. In the 1830s, we find it in back in France under the name 'Bohemianism' and associated with Théophile Gautier, Alexandre Privat d'Angelmont, George Sand, Gérard de Nerval, Philoxène Boyer and Henri Murger, among many others (summing up whose general approach to life Augustin Challamel wrote in 1885: "They elevated poverty into a system. They were riddled with debts, and they laughed at their deliberate insolvency.") French Bohemianism eventually morphed into Symbolism[205] and the Decadent movement (in both of which, altersociety ideals achieved a particularly developed form), then Surrealism, Dada-ism, Letterism and Situationism, before breaking onto the capital's streets in May 1968, after which it appeared to go underground. In Britain, it declined after the Romantics, though George Borrow, Aubrey Beardsley and Oscar Wilde kept it alive in different ways, but it reappeared in force at the end of the

---

[203] Coverley, Merlin (2006), p17.

[204] Although Ransome (1984, p8) traces it as far back as the medieval poet, François Villon (1431-1463).

[205] Robert Goldwater asserts that "Certain of the Symbolists had a desire to bring art to the people. They were a decided 'gang', and their ideas were unwelcome to the purists… As Fénéon wrote in *Le Symboliste* (1886): 'A day will come when art will be part of the life of ordinary men. When it does, the artists won't look down on the worker from his celluloid collar: the two of them will be a single one. But to achieve this, the Revolution must get up steam and we must build a completely anarchist civilisation.'" (1979), p71.

nineteenth century as an import from Paris. Augustus John, Roy Campbell, Dora Carrington, Isadora Duncan and the Bloomsbury Circle all undertook audacious 'experiments in living' diametrically opposed to the prevailing expectations of capitalism. As Virginia Nicholson tells us:

> "[They] felt that they were inheritors of a kingdom where the rich man cannot penetrate. Being penniless qualified one for a higher form of life than that offered by Victorian society… If poverty is an imperative for the artist – as many believed it to be – then wealth was to be derided, regarded as sordid and corrupting to the integrity of the artist. Bohemia on the whole felt a psychic distaste for Mammon."[206]

A related movement had appeared in Germany in the late eighteenth century as *Sturm und Drang*. By the early nineteenth century, it had become a form of Romanticism, appearing significantly first in Jena, then in Berlin. In *The Roots of Romanticism*, Isaiah Berlin defined it mainly in terms of a felt cultural inferiority to Britain and France; nevertheless, it had a formative influence on Karl Marx, who, prior to his conversion to Hegelianism in 1841, had been a prolific poet, a "follower of Kant and Fichte, [a] romantic subjectivist who considered the highest being to be separate from earthly reality."[207] David McLellan tells us:

> "[Marx's] process of giving up his romantic idealism and delivering himself over to 'the enemy' was an extremely radical and painful one. He described the immediate results: 'My vexation prevented me from thinking at all for several days and I ran like a madman

[206] Nicholson, Virginia (2002), p7.
[207] McLellan, David (1973), p28.

around the garden beside the dirty waters of the Spree
"which washes souls and makes weak tea". I even went
on a hunting party with my landlord and rushed off to
Berlin and wanted to embrace every street-loafer I
saw… My fruitless and failed intellectual endeavours
and my consuming anger at having to make an idol of
a view that I hated made me ill.'"[208]

Probably not enough scholarly attention has been paid to
this period in Marx's life, and the question of how far it
conditioned his future thinking. His rupture with Romantic
ideals was obviously traumatic, and must have influenced his
subsequent thought; intellectual breaks are rarely that clean.
How far, here, was 'the child the father of the man'?

In any case, the Germanophone world perhaps discerned the
vague outlines of the capitalist altersociety before anyone else:
that society appears as the negation of the present system in
Hegel, as Dionysius to conventionality's Apollo in Nietzsche,
and as the disturbing, subversive Unconscious in Freud.

In the USA, Bohemianism, until the early twentieth century,
was chiefly a foreign import, and sometimes even an affectation
amongst middle-class intellectuals;[209] the reason perhaps being
that, for most of the preceding period, land was plentiful
enough for *real* experiments in living: Fourierists and Owenites
tested their ideas there in a way they could not have done at
home, while Ralph Waldo Emerson, Henry David Thoreau and
Joaquin Miller, have none of the hallmarks of self-conscious
extroversion usually associated with Bohemianism. In general,
Bohemians are an urban phenomenon. They do not necessarily
originate in cities, nor are they necessarily produced by them,

---

[208] Ibid. p29-30.
[209] Emily Hahn writes: "From the 1850s until the early 1890s, American Bohemia
had to feel its way with caution. At first, it derived wholly from Europe, but
American artists and writers soon found their own paths." (1967), p292.

but cities offer 'altercitizens' the tempting prospect of becoming a 'man of the crowd'[210] and of finding a community of like minds.[211] Nevertheless, Adah Isaacs Menken and Edgar Allan Poe demonstrate that genuinely home-grown Bohemianism was far from non-existent during this period.

Bohemia only properly emerged in the USA at the end of the 19th century. It first appeared in Greenwich Village, and more or less simultaneously in the Deep South (and Chicago) with the advent of black musicians like Robert Johnson, Big Joe Williams, Ike Zimmerman and Son House, travelling between 'juke joints', playing 'the devil's music', plus artists like Moms Mabley, Ethel Waters and Gladys Bentley performing on the so-called Chitlin' Circuit.[212]

The frequent impossibility of the renunciation of money under Jim Crow conditions is not insignificant (Bessie Smith was probably far from alone in beginning her career as a busker on street corners): necessity frequently made the pursuit of art a matter of Hobson's choice.

It is clear that here we have a bohemianism that reverses the French version by compulsion of circumstance: it begins from nothing, and tries to extract money from capitalism through its artistic accomplishments. Bohemianism it nearly always is, however: one need only look at Charley Patton, a 'hard-drinking' cocaine taker, or Little Walter, who died from a combination of alcoholism and injuries sustained in fighting, or Moms Mabley, a comedian who came out as a lesbian in 1921 (and who, like George Sand in Paris, dressed in men's clothing). The extroversion, the rejection of the status quo, the dogged pursuit of artistic excellence – all are present.

---

[210] After Poe's short story of the same name, which heavily influenced Baudelaire.
[211] "There are no bohemians in the desert." Ransome, Arthur (1984) p278.
[212] For an excellent summary of this version of Bohemianism see http://www.queerculturalcenter.org/Pages/Bentley/QueersinJazz.html

On the other hand, artistic excellence is always a matter of doing much more than capitalism strictly requires, and it may rebound on the artist, and become a kind of self-hindrance, depending, among other things, on how far the artist is 'ahead of his time.' Mance Lipscomb did not even release an album until he was in his late sixties; Mamie Smith and Lead Belly both died penniless. Because the early blues originated with a class of relative 'invisibles' (to draw on Ralph Ellison's phrase), the casualty list is probably much higher than any list of recoverable names might suggest.

Not insignificant here is the well-known story of Robert Johnson's midnight meeting with the devil, at a crossroads somewhere in the Mississippi Delta, in which he is supposed to have sold his soul in exchange for guitar mastery. The same story is also connected, at an earlier date, to the bluesman Tommy Johnson (no relation), and NN Puckett's 1926 *Folk Beliefs of the Southern Negro*[213] cites the central framework as an established superstition. The point is partly that it came to be seen as emblematic of a contextually specific relation of one kind of artist to his craft, to the point where Robert Johnson is nowadays the only blues player whose name many people know, and usually in connection with that story.

In Europe, of course, stories of 'deals with the Devil' go back at least to medieval times, and achieve their best cultural expression in the plays of Marlowe and Goethe. Since, for individuals in absolute poverty, the double gesture of European Bohemianism – the rejection of money and the concurrent embrace of art as a value-in-itself – cannot necessarily be replicated, for lack of the former, it is re-expressed in a myth in which, the soul (ie, the only remaining possession of the actor) is renounced *in place of* mammon. The double gesture is thus preserved.

---

[213] I am indebted to Benjamin Allmon for this: https://opossumlit.com/devil-in-the-detail-a-history-of-musicians-and-the-crossroads/

In mid-twentieth century British-American society, the juke joints and the Chitlin' Circuit produced jazz music, Isadora Duncan, the Harlem Renaissance, the culture of *The Lonely Londoners*, the Beats, the 'hippies', the punk rock movement, early rap and hip-hop, the Craftivist movement, and in the UK the 'New Age Travellers'. In the 21st century, Barbara Ehrenreich recognised its ever-presence in *Dancing in the Streets*. As Huston, Wadley and Fitzpatrick pointed out, Bohemia was, and is, a global phenomenon:

> "Though potentially elusive and surrounded by mythical domains such as Vagabondia, Licentia, Philistia, and Saevitia (Nathe, 1978), [it] has been noted in various cities around the world. Among them are Montmartre and Montparnasse in Paris; Chelsea, Fitzrovia, and Soho in London; Mitte in Berlin; Schwabing in Munich; Skadarlija in Belgrade; Tabán in Budapest; Cais do Sodré, Mouraria, and Alfama in Lisbon; Greenwich Village in New York; North Beach in San Francisco; Venice and surrounds in Los Angeles (Deener, 2012); Topanga and Tiburon elsewhere in California; Fremantle in Perth; Newtown in Sydney; and Fitzroy in Melbourne, a city which, from 1939 to 1967, produced a journal called *Bohemia* under the auspices of the all-male, art and literary 'Bread and Cheese Club.'"[214]

Throughout all this, the altersociety emitted a constant background 'noise' to the effect that subjectivity could not be quantified and was not to be extinguished: Stirner, Kierkegaard, Nietzsche, Dostoevsky, Kafka and Camus all belong to this *chorós*.

---

[214] Huston, S, Wadley, D and Fitzpatrick, R (2015), p314.

We may make several observations concerning the altersociety. Firstly, it keeps bursting into the conventional one in different guises, all with a similar ethos: a marked anti-commercialism and anti-conventionalism, an urge to get outdoors, to travel, a longing for transcendence (which it tries to satisfy with an eclectic mix of religious or esoteric devices, and/ or by a commitment to one or another form of art: poetry, prose, painting, music, dance). The master society's attitude to it is highly equivocal: capitalism perpetually and systematically plunders it, mainly for commercial gain, but also in the hope of acquiring a semblance of transcendental authenticity.[215] Some – occasionally, most - of its members will 'sell out', and mostly, in so doing, will wither on the vine. Meanwhile, the question of whether or not the individual bohemian has 'artistic talent' is of interest to capitalism, but of no interest to bohemia itself, where the pursuit of art is more in the nature of a spiritual quest than a financial gamble. Of all the art forms, capitalism finds poetry the most difficult to co-opt. It may be un-co-optable. Capitalism always prefers dead artists to living, since death removes the possibility of unpredictability, and of biting the hand that feeds them.

The altersociety has little self-awareness. Its default attitude to politics is probably indifference[216] – politics is a concern the mainstream culture, and is an intrinsically sordid business – but, although it is logically linked to anti-capitalism, it will

---

[215] In the context of the first decades of the 20th century, Virginia Nicholson comments: "The existence of a rich Bohemia presented artists with a different problem. The invasion of their inviolate territory by the moneyed world was in some respects welcome, providing as it did, a market for creativity, and yet it was also deeply distasteful… The artist's challenge to society was devalued by its reduction to the status of a commodity; this was, and still is, a bitter pill to swallow." (Nicholson, Virginia (2002) p29).

[216] Henri Murger's father – a proud veteran of the Napoleonic campaigns - hated his son for his indifference to the political issues of the day. Murger – or perhaps his work - has an enduring claim to be the quintessential 'bohemian'. Easton (1964) also remarks on the indifference of most of the early French bohemians to politics, eg, p59f. Jules Vallès (1832–1885) was a notable exception.

sometimes express itself in the apparel of the political right, even the extreme right: so, Ezra Pound supported Mussolini; the Italian Futurists glorified "militarism, patriotism... and scorn for woman"[217], and Hitler began his career as a penniless painter on the streets of Vienna. Yet the logic of the altersociety cannot be reduced to the individual reasoning of some of its members or factions: in its essence, it is the negation of capitalism and the embracing of some concrete creative pursuit largely or wholly for its own sake.

Its ambiguity of political allegiance may be attributed to the fact that it is necessarily a double phenomenon: simultaneously moral and aesthetic. To the extent that the latter dominates, it has the potential to turn fascist. Sometimes, when that happens, it is the outpouring of a purist fantasy, a childish rebellion against the 'untidiness' of the world; sometimes it is because, as Barbara Ehrenreich says, fascism is fond of creating aesthetically appealing, tightly choreographed 'spectacles'[218]; but sometimes it is the result of a Nietzschean despair of the 'herd' and the seeming ubiquity of market values. Right-wing leaders and their cultural enforcers do not usually assume power until later, and by that time, one's mistake may have become obvious (unless one ends up in government). To the extent that the genuine altersociety persists in such circumstances, it is always condemned as 'decadent', and sometimes even 'debauched' and 'depraved'.

But there *will* always be right-wing denizens of the altersociety, partly because it confers no automatic induction to intellectual prescience. As Joanna Richardson remarks, in the context of the nineteenth century:

---

[217] *The Futurist Manifesto* (1909), online at:
https://monoskop.org/images/7/73/Futurist_Aristocracy_1_1923.pdf
[218] Ehrenreich, Barbara (2008), chapter 9 'Fascist Spectacles', p181-206. A similar interpretation of fascism as a significantly aesthetic phenomenon can be found in Walter Benjamin, Ernst Bloch and Siegfried Kracauer.

"The Bohemian movement had been born of political disappointments and Romantic ideals. It had owed much to the *mal de siècle*, and much to the aspirations of the young. Bohemia had always offered an escape for the parasite and the social misfit, for the unscrupulous and the unstable. It had sheltered those who had lived in fear of reality; it had given an ideal opportunity to adults who could not accept the challenge of reality."[219]

Finally, there is no rigid border between a society and its attendant altersociety – the two are always in intimate communication – so there is also a wide latitude for fraudulence, inauthenticity and cultural embezzlement. Richardson believed that the Parisian Bohemians of the 1830s possessed a genuineness their successors found increasingly difficult to sustain. "In the Romantic age," she wrote, "Bohemia had its brilliant inhabitants. They had a colour and panache, a gaiety and often a distinction which no later Bohemians recaptured."[220] And Nicholson writes of the British version: "By the late 1930s the problem for Bohemia was already prefiguring our own tourist explosion. It was now beginning to seem impossible to escape from dilettante Bohemia-watchers."[221]

The use of 'bohemian' to describe a member of the altersociety nowadays is arguably anachronistic. How far the bohemians partly evolved to become 'Bobos', a term coined by David Brooks in 2000 (a combination of 'bourgeois' and 'bohème'), is an open question. There is a strong conceptual overlap between 'bobos' and the 'cognitariat' (see above), with the difference that the former are left-leaning progressives and usually to be found in the creative industries. According to Gilles Saint-Paul, they tend to support greater investment in

---

[219] Richardson, Joanna (1969), p168.
[220] Richardson, Joanna (1969), p26.
[221] Nicholson, Virginia (2002), p235.

collective urban amenities and socialised recreational events, reduced urban space for the automobile, more investment in public transportation, and a promotion of 'social mixity' and 'diversity'.[222] Assuming they exist as an identifiable social group, they are one way in which the altersociety can ameliorate the conventional one.

In any case, the altersociety will keep throwing up radical movements of one form or another. As long as the master society exists, so will it exist, and it cannot do otherwise. And because it is essentially the rebuttal of capitalism, it is to be expected that it will throw out more left-leaning than right-leaning ones. Meanwhile, the end of history will occur not as a complete obliteration of capitalism, but as a synthesis in which master society and altersociety are united and simultaneously overcome. The Kingdom of Ends will not simply be the realisation of moral values, but also of all aesthetic values. It will be the kind of place Nietzsche himself could have felt at home.

Countersocieties Past and Present

Because the means of securitisation has had a relatively uniform effect throughout history – dividing societies into haves and have-nots, rulers and ruled, insiders and outsiders – it has always had the side-effect of generating countersocieties where outsiders become insiders. The Pythagoreans, the Essenes, the Epicureans, the earliest Christians, the Buddhist Sangha, the Hindu Ashram, the Bacchae, the Cathars, the Anabaptists, the Diggers, the Sandemanians the Owenists, the Amish, the Bruderhof, the Hippies, the New Age Travellers, New Monasticism, Diggers & Dreamers – understood together, constitute a critical commentary on history as it is ordinarily conceived.

---

[222] Saint-Paul, Gilles (2015), p1-2.

Of course, not all of these groups have been healthy or good. Countersocieties often have a way of becoming worse than the communities that engender them, and, historically, most of them had no sense of having made a political gesture: they were escapist.

The Catch-22 is that it would take communist persons to bring about a communist revolution; but we cannot have communist persons until there has been a successful communist revolution. Mere doctrinal purity is not enough.

To put it another way, the problem outlined by Plato two and a half millennia ago has never gone away, and has never been solved, viz. the people most suited to rule will recognise the responsibilities of the office before the rights, and they will shy away; those least suited will recognise the rights first, and will thrust themselves forward. The upshot is that political parties – coalitions of future-oriented ideologues - will often replicate, in miniature, the failings of the societies they allegedly want to reform.

One way of solving this problem has been through the idea of 'prefigurative politics'. First introduced by Carl Boggs in 1977[223], it has gained increasing traction in recent years. According to Paul Raekstad and Sofa Saio Gradin's 2020 book on the subject:

> "A successful revolutionary movement needs to be able to survive and struggle effectively in the present and make itself capable of changing society in the ways it wants. For advocates of prefigurative politics, this requires forms of organising that develop people's powers, drives and consciousness in the right ways … The organisational means employed in the present must prefigure the kinds of social organisations aimed

---

[223] Boggs, C, (1977).

for in a future society... A successful socialist revolution requires a prior process of evolution, planting and nurturing the seeds of the future society within the soil of the old."[224]

Raekstad and Gradin's discussion ("the first dedicated book on prefigurative politics as a concept and idea"[225]) – which contains a good discussion of the First International and early modern socialism - was recently joined by an anthology, edited by Lara Monticelli, and published by Bristol University: *The Future is Now*. Both books contain promising lines of thought, but look a little too deferential to neo-Maoism. Raekstad and Gradin begin with the semi-apologetically announcement that they are "two white people with PhDs who work in Western European universities", while Monticelli worries that, "research on prefigurative politics hasn't paid enough attention to the way intersectionality between class, gender, race and ethnicity affects individual access to, and participation in, prefigurative initiatives and movements. In fact, some critics have pointed out that prefigurative politics is inherently exclusionary, attracting mostly Western, white, middle-class individuals."[226]

Both books have arguably been rendered comparatively irrelevant by Vincent Bevins's 2023 *If We Burn*, a rigorous denunciation of many aspects of anarchist prefigurative politics. Drawing on Jo Freeman's 1972 essay, 'The Tyranny of Structurelessness'[227], Bevins examines seven different popular uprisings between 2010 and 2020, at some of which he was present. The book's subtitle, 'The Mass Protest Decade and the Missing Revolution' provides a spoiler: here were seven

[224] Raekstad, Paul and Gradin, Sofa Saio (2020), p69-70.
[225] Ibid, p11. One has to exclude Marina Sitris's 2006 *Horizontality* (discussed later) to support this conclusion. The Sitris text is included in the bibliography of Raekstad and Gradin's book, but it is nowhere discussed.
[226] Monticelli, Lara (Ed.) (2024), p6.
[227] Available online at https://www.jofreeman.com/joreen/tyranny.htm.

significant opportunities for real change, all of which ended not only in failure, but in a significant worsening of the initial conditions.

The idea behind prefigurative politics is that the organisation concerned must be egalitarian, on the grounds that the society it aims to bring into being will be egalitarian. Bevins convincingly shows that this creates a number of problems: to begin with, it makes decision-making an unreasonably long process since, in practice, it is too often taken to require unanimity. The 2005 Brazilian *Movimento Passe Livre* was founded on such lines:

> "In its founding 'charter of principles', the MPL declared that it would be a fully independent, 'autonomous,' and 'horizontal' organisation. There would be no leaders or specialised role, and decisions would be made by consensus. Every single member should agree on any course of action… In this model, the majority should not be able to force any individual to do something they didn't agree with. This approach was partially inspired by some of their neighbours in South America."[228]

By 'neighbours' Bevins probably is probably referring above all (though not exclusively) to Argentina. The MPL's guiding principles here are recognisably (a point Bevins himself makes) those outlined in Marina Sitrin's 2006, *Horizonalism*, a compilation of interviews with Argentinian activists belonging to different direct democracy initiatives during the years following the anti-IMF protests in 2001. Sitrin is American; she travelled to Argentina because she heard about the new movements, and felt that, in sharing whatever discoveries she

---

[228] Bevins, Vincent (2023), p67-68.

made about them, she "could be useful to people who are committed to social change."[229] The central terms in her presentation include *horizontalidad* ("democratic communication on a level plane ... and anti-authoritarian creation rather than reaction"), *autogestión* ("a word that has no exact English translation ... implying directly democratic decision-making processes and the creation of new subjectivities along the way"), and *política afectiva* ("a base that is loving and supportive, the only base from which one can create politics"). She writes:

> "Over the last ten years, the world has been witnessing an upsurge in prefigurative revolutionary movements; movements that create the future in the present. These new movements are not creating party platforms or programmes. They do not look to one leader, but make space for all to be leaders. They place more importance on asking the right questions than on providing the correct answers. They do not adhere to dogma and hierarchy, instead they build direct democracy and consensus. They are movements based in trust and love."[230]

And yet, for all her enthusiasm, she is not blind to what Bevins would later identify as horizontality's major weaknesses:

> "The years after the [2001] rebellion have witnessed a significant decrease in the organisation of, and participation in, neighbourhood assemblies. Many dozens are still active, but this is much less than the hundreds that instantly emerged. While we will explore the reasons in the interviews ahead, some

---

[229] Sitrin, Marina (2006), p12.
[230] Ibid, p2.

recurring themes are: the intrusion of left political parties, a lack of concreteness in activity, and interference from the state."[231]

Bevins does not examine the Argentinian phenomenon in much depth – it falls outside his chronological remit - but the movements he examines all share, to a greater or lesser extent, its principles. They are all inspired by the American 'New Left', the 'Old Left' having been "smashed by McCarthyism" by the end of the 1950s.

> "Perhaps the thing that was truly 'new' about the New Left dictated that they should adopt organisational forms now that they would like to see in the world they wanted to create. The name given to this was 'prefigurative politics' – what you are doing will prefigure, or show a glimpse of, the world you would want to live in tomorrow."[232]

The weaknesses of an organisation based in *horizontalidad*, *autogestión* and *política afectiva* become particularly glaring, Bevins thinks, in the context of a major social upheaval, such as happened in Tahrir Square in 2011 and in Brazil in 2013. He argues that movements thus organised have difficulty (a) adapting to rapidly changing circumstances (since their decision-making processes are cumbersome), (b) deciding what to do about enthusiastic new members who simply 'turn up' (ie, working out how to gauge the sincerity of their commitment, and integrate them into an organisation "based on the ties of close personal friendship"[233]), (c) providing official representatives to put their demands to the authorities (since

---

[231] Ibid, p10.
[232] Bevins, Vincent (2023), p37.
[233] Ibid, p265.

they cherish their own leaderlessness), (d) preventing the 'message' of the protest (whatever it eventually is – if anything) from being rewritten by a hostile media, or by intruders from rival organisations, some of whom may be reactionary. The nationwide protests unleashed in Brazil by the MPL's campaign for a reduction in public transport fares were eventually hijacked by the right, and ended, shockingly, with the impeachment of one of the country's most progressive presidents by a virtual kangaroo court of reactionaries, an outcome none of the protest's original movers had wanted. By the end of the process, the MPL was entirely sidelined.

> "Since 2010, a pattern had emerged in the evolution of mass street protests. They start over something very specific; then they explode to include all kinds of people, accommodating numerous competing or even contradictory visions; finally, a resolution imposes very specific meaning once more. In the middle, infinite possibilities present themselves. At the end, any concrete outcome of the days of quick-thinking and unpredictable actions and reactions will disappoint some people."[234]

The biggest problem for a horizontalist movement is addressing the question, 'What comes afterwards?' Once your demands have been met, what do you do? In the case, of the MPL, "People would ask what they were doing next. But making such a decision would have required every single member to agree."[235]

> "To understand what might happen after any given protest explosion, you must not only pay attention to

---

[234] Ibid, p221.
[235] Ibid, p195.

who is waiting in the wings to fill a power vacuum. You have to pay attention to who has the power to define the uprising itself… Movements that cannot speak for themselves will be spoken for."[236]

Bevins thinks that horizontalist movements are subtly grounded in a version of liberal optimism that was inspired by the fall of the Berlin Wall in 1989, and which achieved its best expression in Francis Fukuyama's 1992, *The End of History and the Last Man*. The central pillar of that optimism is that full political freedom is, in the long run, everywhere historically inevitable; there might well be setbacks along the way, but ultimately one only has to keep clearing the obstacles.

For Bevins, horizontalism implicitly accepts this reading of history. However,

> "History does not possess a supernatural, metaphysical quality that pushes it forward relentlessly. Many people in my generation (and I think I, too, was guilty of this teleological mode of thought at the beginning of the decade) thought that if you simply gave the thing a kick, it would come unstick. Paradoxically, liberals, socialists, conservatives, and anarchists alike have all thought that way, even as they define 'the right direction' rather differently."[237]

But he also agrees with the Italian sociologist, Paolo Gerbaudo, that horizontality is grounded in individualism. "This might, indeed, make sense for a movement that had so much overlap with a musical subculture born out of generational warfare and absolute rebellion."[238]

---

[236] Ibid, p361-62.
[237] Ibid, p337-38.
[238] Ibid, p355.

Ultimately, *If We Burn* is an argument for a 'vanguardism' of the type the 'Old Left' favoured.

> "If you believe that you can forge a better society, if you are willing to run the risk of trying, then you should enter the vacuum yourself. But a diffuse group of individuals who come out on the streets for very different reasons cannot simply take power themselves, at least not as an entire diffuse group of individuals. Once someone goes in there and takes power in the name of the masses, you are talking about a kind of vanguard – a minority of people who dare to try to represent the rest of the population. In some of the more utopian strains of anti-authoritarian thought, the riot is supposed to become the new society, but this has not worked out so far. If some new group boldly steps into the vacuum, manages to stay there, and transforms a society, then that's a revolution. But if you find your political system broadly acceptable, or you don't think you can replace it with something better, then the thing to do is negotiate. That is called reform. You can use your power on the streets to extract concessions, if you play it right. But once more, this necessarily entails representation."[239]

Does this mean that the kind of horizontalism described by Sitrin is a dead-end? Such a conclusion would be a serious misreading of *If We Burn*. Sitrin is describing what I have described as 'countersocieties', groups of individuals creating self-contained 'utopian' collectives in the here-and-now. "Some participants say that they are not political, or that they are anti-political," she writes.[240] By contrast, Bevins is concerned with

---

[239] Ibid, p345-46.
[240] Sitrin, Marina (2006), p4.

street protest movements whose goals are relatively specific. He cites Rodrigo Nunes's 2021, *Neither Vertical Nor Horizontal* with approval: "He [ie, Nunes] writes about an 'ecology' of organisations and affirms that different types of organisational schema can, and should, interact with one another."[241]

But Nunes's idea that "Leninists, anarchists, autonomists, populists, verticalists and horizontalists" should organise in a way that "ceases to be an arena for the endless reiteration of fixed positions and becomes instead a shared worksite in which everyone has to deal with the same set of problems, even if coming at them from different angles" seems to be vulnerable to the objection already raised by Bevins: given the disjunction between the different perspectives, what is to stop any solution to the 'set of problems' being hijacked by one group within the coalition for its own ends? In any case, are these groups not talking to each other already?

Bevins adds that, in any case,

> "In a political movement, the 'leaders', the people who make strategic decisions or stand in front of cameras should not be seen as superior to the people delivering food, or risking their lives in battle, or caring for the sick and wounded."[242]

One can take this need for a vanguard too far. In his 2004 *Revolution at the Gates*, Slavoj Žižek argues that the left, as it stands, is too squeamish to rehabilitate Lenin. Turning ideals into a concrete social order is bound to involve cruelty at some stage, and one needs the courage to grasp the nettle. Lenin, Žižek thinks, is due a reinstatement.

However, given that some sources estimate the number of people executed during the Russian 'Red Terror' of 1918-1922 at

---

[241] Bevins, Vincent (2023), p363.
[242] Ibid, p355.

roughly one and a three-quarter million, and that even conservative estimates put it at around fifty thousand, maybe a degree of reluctance is justifiable. Leninism is a party philosophy based in violence; in 1917, violence was probably unavoidable, the die having been cast in 1905, when the Tsar's soldiers opened fire on a peaceful march in Saint Petersburg. After World War 2, the authorities in the West became less likely to deploy such indiscriminate means of quashing protests, however, the idea of revolutionary violence was kept alive by Jean-Paul Sartre and his disciples, Frantz Fanon and Ali Shariati Mazinani. As Adam Curtis pointed out, that philosophy found its logical conclusion in Pol Pot's Khmer Rouge. Today, no one can argue that murder is a justifiable tool in the anti-capitalist toolkit.

And, of course, it is not clear that political parties – 'vanguardist' institutions – are any more capable of answering Bevins's question, 'What next?' than are horizontalist movements. How often do such parties jettison their manifesto pledges on gaining power? In practice, their focus tends to shift to consolidation of their own position. And while anarcho-syndicalism claims to find an answer in a coalition of workers' unions, corrupt union bosses may be more common than the law has been able to reveal (especially, if, as a sceptic might say, police investigators are inclined to be sympathetic to capitalism).

Bhaskar Sunkara insists: "A loose network of leftists and rank-and-file workers isn't enough. We need a political party."[243] Alongside the potentialities of conventional politics, the solution may lie in the creation of an informal family of separate movements, all sharing a similar philosophy (so nowhere near as diverse as Nunes's list, above), whose constitutions allow for a top-down leadership (of the

---

[243] Sankara, Bhaskar (2019), p229

representative, democratic kind) during emergencies; which are horizontal where horizontalism fits the situation, but appropriately vertical and vanguardist during significant social upheavals and crises. Such movements would be capable of a real internal dialogue, but would not necessarily be hamstrung by a felt need for unanimity. They would have to be flexible. On the whole, they would not be political parties in anything like the modern sense. They would not necessarily be paralysed by Bevins's question, 'What next?'

Love/Care

No society can do without a means of securitisation, but what people want is choice. The prisoner in a cell is securitised. To what extent are we all today, in that position? We do not know, because we have grown into the world we inhabit, so we take it for granted. But we spend most of our lives on repeat: home, to car, to work, to computer, to car, to home, to TV. In the intervening periods, we are often on our phones – arguably, because we are addicted to them. We are securitised at every point. For whose benefit?

Walk out of your front door. Go deep into the countryside. Lie down where no one can see you. Look at the sky. You are now, at least temporarily, outside the means of securitisation.

Or: meet up with someone you truly love, and do something you both enjoy. Again, you are now, at least temporarily, outside the means of securitisation.

Thirdly: imagine your elderly father can no longer supply many of his own needs. You call him every night, shop for him twice a week, and visit him at weekends.

In the first of these three cases, you are outside the means of securitisation... but not yet in a countersociety. In cases two and three, you are both.

As Marina Sitrin suggested in *Horizontality*, love and care always put you in a countersociety, however small, because they form the premise of that society, and negate the pursuit of unlimited wealth. Cases two and three are the smallest possible – just a couple of people.[244] But small or large, all countersocieties have radical potential; they can all shake the world to its foundations.

It will quickly be objected that both *pairs* of persons just mentioned (in cases 2 and 3) are not *at all* outside the means of securitisation. As regards the first: they will be named individuals, probably tracked by CCTV, and if whatever they enjoy doing together costs money, then they will pay for it either with a credit card, which is a securitisation device, or with cash, which will need to be kept in a pocket, a bag, a purse or a wallet, all of which are securitisation devices. They will walk into or between buildings, which are securitisation devices ... and so on.

The answer consists in examining the priorities of the individuals themselves. Nothing in any of the securitisation devices we have just mentioned entails that *the individuals themselves* have been securitised – ie, that their behaviour has been rendered entirely 'safe' (from the point of view of the things that are being securitised) and predictable. They could spontaneously decide to drop everything and run away together, in which case all the securitisation devices in the world did not prevail against them.

Love is adventurous. It is open-ended. It takes risks. It is always *potentially* a dropout. If the love of the two people in our little thought experiment is powerful enough, it may trump the means of securitisation.

Care too. War may come; we may lose everything and be forced to flee the country. If I truly care for my father, I will not

[244] As Alain Badiou puts it, in *In Praise of Love* (Serpent's Tail, 2012), "Yet another possible definition of love: minimal communism!" (p90).

leave him behind, even though taking him with me – on my back, if need be - jeopardises my own safety.

Obviously, the words 'love' and 'care' strongly overlap. But what specifically do they signify?

Love first. Over the last century, philosophers, sociologists and psychologists have had a hard time overcoming their reluctance to say much about it. To the extent that they have succeeded, they have focused on romantic love. Which is certainly powerful enough to break securitisation's chains, but unreliable: its intensity usually dwindles over time. In many respects, maybe, it is a fabricated emotion: invented by bards, minstrels and aristocrats for literary purposes during the medieval chivalric period.[245]

However, second-wave feminists pioneered a more positive evaluation of love grounded in its expression not as a romantic passion, but in family and community connections: love as care. Care for children, neighbours, siblings, parents and relatives, and other members of society. Care was first brought into ethics as a significant factor in its own right by Carol Gilligan in her 1982, *In a Different Voice*. Gilligan claimed that by and large, men and women tend to view morality in different ways (although ultimately, the difference transcends gender): men focus on utilitarian calculations and/ or rights, women on longer-term care and/or responsibilities. Nel Noddings developed Gilligan's insights in 1984. Subsequent feminists have built on their insights, often by talking about love and care interchangeably. Virginia Held, Annette Baier, Joan Tronto and Eva Kittay are some of the thinkers who made huge strides in this regard.

But love has an abstract dimension that proceeds beyond the concrete day-to-day concerns of care for individuals. In her long

---

[245] Although, at that point, it may have had a religious aspect which it has now lost: see, eg, CS Lewis, *The Allegory of Love: A Study in Medieval Tradition* (Oxford 1936).

discussion of the value of love in her 2017 *Radical Happiness*, Lynne Segal writes:

> "Knowing also that we can, in different ways, fall in love with ideas, ideals, places, sounds, anything that inspires and uplifts us, I cannot possibly do justice to all that we might call 'love', if I am ever to conclude my thoughts on the subject. It is often because people we have loved have introduced us to other aspects of life that those particular objects or experiences retain their power over us. Love is obviously not one thing, but a set of emotions that takes many forms depending on its object; indeed, it may be easy, some have suggested, even easier, to keep loving the dead and feel them still beside us, years after they have departed."[246]

However (and obviously), if we intend to rely on 'love' as the ground for anything as significant as a (counter) society, we need to reckon with the so-called Dunbar number.

In the 1990s, the British anthropologist, Robin Dunbar, claimed to have discovered an upper limit on the quantity of meaningful relationships an individual person could sustain[247]. Based on his investigations into primate brains, the number he suggested was 150. Others have since attempted to revise it up or down, but the important point, from our point of view, is that there may well be a maximum.

This affects the problems philosophers have when assessing love/care as a basis for ethics. To what extent is love an emotion, and assuming that emotional attachment can only extend to so many people, how can it work for more abstract states of affairs, as for example, when I must decide whether to contribute to a charity whose beneficiaries all live thousands of miles away?

---

[246] Segal, Lynne (2017), p154.
[247] Dunbar, RIM (1992).

These are people I have never met and likely never will. What sense does it make for me to seek a resolution of my dilemma in love/care?

The answer may lie in seeing the 'love' in this case as an *extrapolation* of the emotion I feel for the one hundred and fifty: ie, I imagine those distant people as being equivalent to them, and recognise the emotion they inspire as being the same, but considerably less intense. Since I can love my best friend more than I love my next-door neighbour and my mother more than either, it follows that I can recognise degrees of love. The love I feel for people thousands of miles away may be very weak, but I still recognise it *as* love, and as such, it has the same categorical power.

Under capitalism, the Dunbar number holds fairly universally: most people feel affection for a limited number of family members, friends, and acquaintances. Outside the Dunbar number, however, love all too often evaporates, even in the diluted sense in which we have just discussed it. It turns instead, into its opposite: an unnameable mixture of suspicion, hostility, and rejection. As we have already suggested, the mystery may be that love exists in such a system at all. Such persistence may be taken as evidence that human nature is essentially good, but, as Rousseau thought (in *Emile*, for example), corrupted by society.

The best attempt to create an ethics based on love draws on the New Testament (and before) notion of *agape,* and is to be found in the works of Christian Situation Ethicists such as Paul Tillich, Gabriel Marcel, Rudolf Bultmann and Reinhold Niebuhr. In the English-speaking world, its most popular expression is found in the works of John AT Robinson and Joseph Fletcher, and its most prominent contemporary champion may be the American thinker, Thomas Jay Oord. Fletcher himself insisted that there is nothing necessarily Christian about it, albeit Christians have been at the forefront of developing it, and Humanists also recognisably subscribe to the same ideal. "The problem solver will see," Fletcher wrote, "that Situation Ethics is not particularly Catholic or Protestant or Orthodox or humanist ... Properly used [it] is applicable to any situation-sensitive decision-making, whether its ideology is theological or non-theological – eg, either Christian or Marxist."[248]

For Fletcher love is basic: it cannot be defined or described, and it is arguably not even an emotion anymore. The reason for this is that it must proceed beyond the Dunbar number, but as we have just shown, that is not a conclusive objection. At worst, it simply places the theory within the (much more academically respectable) parameters of Intuitionism, which also appeals to an undefinable subjective ethical source. Fletcher appeals frequently to GE Moore, whose 1903 *Principia Ethica* remains one of the foundational texts of Intuitionism.

As expected, care ethics and situation ethics exhibit a strong overlap. Just as Fletcher endorses a relativism in which there can be no universally applicable rules, so Noddings insists that care must always be contextual: again, there can be no one-size-fits-all solutions. There are, of course, other strong resemblances. Nevertheless, love itself is always central, which strongly undermines its putative relativism.

Another attempt to centralise love – again, abstractly defined – in public affairs, is arguably to be found in the work of Alain Badiou. As is well known, Badiou sees art, love, politics, and science as four independent 'truth procedures.' Love is a supplement to the isolated individual, one that provides support for a universalism emptied of object relations. For Badiou, it is not opposed to logic: yet from a series, it generates a number that is seemingly outside the series. "Love can only consist in failure ... on the fallacious assumption that it is a

---

[248] *Situation Ethics*, Fletcher J (SCM 1966), p13,14.

relationship. But it is not. It is a production of truth," as he puts it in *Conditions*.

If love/care constitutes the ground of a meaningful countersociety, the family represents its microscopic form. This will strike many readers as strange, since the left has traditionally regarded the family as an institutional shackle to be cast off.

A Communist Philosophy of the Family

In Part 2 of his 2011 BBC TV documentary series, *All Watched Over by Machines of Loving Grace*, Adam Curtis ends by passing judgement on the communes that emerged from the 1960s counterculture in the USA. "They all failed," he tells us.

> "Most lasted no more than three years, some for less than six months. And what tore them all apart was the very thing that was supposed to have been banished. Power. The commune members discovered that some people were more free than others. Strong personalities came to dominate the weaker members of the group, but the rules of the self-organising system refused to allow any organised opposition to this oppression."

One of his contributors says:

> "The original idea was very positive indeed. It was to create an egalitarian society in which everyone would both be free to be themselves and also be able to contribute to the group in a really positive way. But the very rules that kind of set up this egalitarian group resulted in the opposite of the dream. They resulted in creating a hierarchical structure in which some could be

dominant over others because everyone is not equally powerful in their voice against one other person."

Curtis ands by expressing a thoroughgoing pessimism about prefigurative politics.

> "The failure of the commune movement and the fate of the [2003 European and Asian] revolutions show the limitations of the self-organizing model. It cannot deal with the central dynamic forces of human society: politics and power... It is a very good way of organising things, even rebellions, but it offers no ideas about what comes next. And just like in the communes, it leaves us helpless in the face of those already in power in the world."

This was roughly Bevins's verdict too. William Golding's 1954 *Lord of the Flies* depicts a world similar to that of the communes in *All Watched Over*. It is a world without families, in which young people try to build a community in their capacity as atomised individuals of roughly the same age. It is arguably a disaster not because of the model, but partly because the participants are mutually-repelling products of the very system they are trying to escape. In addition, they are all at the same stage in the human-biological development process, and that relative sameness forces them to compete for the same social niche.

We might well wonder whether a community based in family units would do better. All the most enduring countersocieties – the Amish and the Bruderhof, for example – have been family-based - although both are also deeply grounded in conservative religious ideologies that most libertarians would reject.

But libertarians might reject such a possibility anyway. One of the reasons the right has so often been able to defeat the left in the popular imagination is that the latter has so often declared the family to be a reactionary institution. Rightly or wrongly, most people probably feel loyalty to their families, however much they may find them wanting in practice (as most families probably are). Marx was far from the earliest family-sceptical socialist when, in *The Communist Manifesto*, he dismissed 'the bourgeois family'.

Friedrich Engels's much later, *The Origin of the Family, Private Property and the State* claimed to be partially based on notes Marx made on the writings of the anthropologist, Lewis H Morgan. Hardly anyone accepts Morgan's views today: he thought that the family was originally matriarchal, but the introduction of private property had turned it into a patriarchy. A novel idea, but with virtually no empirical support.

Subsequent Marxist writings seemingly had little time for the family. In 1917, Alexandra Kollontai, the Russian 'People's Commissar for Welfare', denounced its 'old' incarnation, and the new Soviet Union adjudged its nuclear version pathological. Marxists ever since have tended to agree.

However, that was rarely a wholesale rejection of the family. It was nearly always and only a rejection of a certain model, one in which the father dominated, in which the mother had no choice but to stay at home, and in which both of them were institutionally co-opted to make their children conform. Other models of the family – some radically different to the 'old' one - have always been both possible and actual. There is nothing remotely absurd about the matriarchal family, the family in which the mother is in charge. Such families have existed throughout history, and have almost certainly become increasingly common in the 21st century.

In his 1994 paper, 'Marx, Engels, and the Abolition of the Family', Richard Weikart wrote:

"Despite their emphatic rejection of the family institution... [Marx and Engels's] rendition of the place of the family within the materialist conception of history left an ambiguous legacy that has plagued socialists and feminists down to the present. If the family is a mere epiphenomenon reflecting the economic structure of society, a thoroughgoing critique of the family is superfluous or, worse yet, a distraction from more crucial matters. If, however, the family is an independent factor interacting with the economic structure, then greater emphasis could be accorded to a critique of the family." (*History of European Ideas*, Vol. 18, No. 5, pp. 657-672, 1994)

Hegel's division of social reality into the family and civil society, which Marx seems to have accepted up to a point, would suggest that the family is an 'independent factor', as Weikart puts it; but so, too, would the fact that families have existed, in different forms, from time immemorial under myriad types of social system.

So what is 'The Communist Family'? This will seem either an odd, or a redundant, question, depending on one's point of view, and the level of one's familiarity with the writings of self-declared Communists.

The family is undeniably a plastic entity, capable of being moulded to suit the ideological purposes of the particular prevailing variant of civil society. Germaine Greer makes the same point in *The Female Eunuch* when she says, "The single marriage family, which is called by anthropologists and sociologists the nuclear family, is possibly the shortest-lived familial system ever developed."[249] Earlier, she remarks:

---

[249] Greer, Germaine (2012) p248.

"Modern Christianity developed its own paradigm of the nuclear family and considered it reflected in the natural law. The structure of the state, naively considered as no more than a collection of families, reflects the natural principle: the king/president is a benign father of a huge family. The Church also acknowledged one head, a *locum tenens* for God Himself. The man was the soul, and the woman the body: the man was the mind and the woman the heart; the man was the will and the woman the passions. Boys learnt their male role from father and girls their female role from mother. It seems clear, simple and immutable… The chain of command from the elders to the poorest vassals was complete."[250]

Engels was clearly making a similar point in *The Origin of the Family*. In a society where men dominate, the father will be the delegated representative of the established order within the comparatively closed micro-community of the family unit, and his relative privilege in civil society will lend him the power to fulfil that role. His unofficial job will be to act variously as a go-between, a guarantor of ideological continuity, and to some extent, a policeman.

Nevertheless, if he has any emotional investment in his family at all, it is likely that he can never be simply these things, and he can always potentially turn traitor. The nuclear family may be malleable, and it may be capable of being suborned, but, for good reasons, no family is ever beyond suspicion by the political establishment. True, nuclear families may often produce conformists, but they also produce radicals, dropouts, rebels, and violent revolutionaries – and sometimes

[250] Ibid p246-7.

intentionally. They are not 'designed' to do either thing: they are only ever drafted, and more or less effectively. Over the past seventy-five years in the West, the nuclear family has grown weaker and weaker. The same cannot be said of capitalism, and, even if it could, a social scientist would be hard-pressed to demonstrate the connection.

Besides which, we should not pretend that Marx and Engels were in any way experts on the family – Marx seems to have inherited his negative assessment of it from Robert Owen and Charles Fourier – or, indeed, that any real expertise even existed in their day. The fact that someone as wide of the mark as Lewis H Morgan could command widespread respect shows how uncharted the territory was. Marx's 'bourgeois family' was, in reality, probably very little different from rural peasant and working-class families: for reasons to do with Western Christian prohibitions on cousin marriage, and fully discussed by Joseph Henrich in his 2020, *The Weirdest People in the World*, they were all more or less nuclear, and had been since at least the medieval period. Moreover, if Henrich is right, the nuclear family gave us not only capitalism, but also civil liberties, including ultimately, rights for women.

Although communists have tended to denigrate the family, like all micro-communities it is probably neither good nor bad in itself, but only so in virtue of its specific members. The reality of domestic violence should not be overlooked: it is a truism that families can sometimes be prisons in which violence is the norm. However, they can equally well be places of safety and security. As Benedict Anderson puts it:

> "While it is true that in the past two decades, the idea of the family-as-articulated-power-structure has been much written about, such a conception is certainly foreign to the overwhelming bulk of mankind. Rather,

225

the family has traditionally been conceived as the domain of disinterested love and solidarity."[251]

In the third decade of the 21st century, in the West, the family exists in more varied forms that at probably any other time in history, and men are not necessarily the ones in charge.

The Marxist dilemma outlined by Weikart, above, in which the family is either an epiphenomenon or a biological limitation is arguably based on a false dichotomy. The reality is that, in itself, the family is a blank slate. It is neither wholesome nor unwholesome, neither a help to social progress nor a hindrance. In practice, it is usually conscripted by the ruling powers, and shaped to serve their purposes.[252] The communist mistake may have been to talk about it as if it has an essence, rather than as if it were like any other social phenomenon: always shaped by external forces

In what follows, I will discuss the 'ideal' family - not in the sense of the best possible, or even the non-problematic, but in the sense of what most people who think it is a good (or at least not a bad) institution consider to be a reasonable and healthy instantiation; a family whose members all relate to one another with normal levels of love/care. Some readers, of course, will claim that even that is pathological.

But perhaps that 'pathology' is precisely its strength. When we imagine being in a revolutionary movement, we imagine being alongside our friends, people who resemble us, like-minded people. But, as in *All Watched Over*, that may be a major reason why such movements fail. Society is made up of people who are not our friends; people we probably would not choose as such, with divergent minds of their own. A successful revolutionary movement, though it may begin with like-minded

---

[251] Anderson, Benedict (1991), p147.
[252] To borrow a distinction from Jürgen Habermas, it is a 'lifeworld' that has been colonised by 'the system'.

individuals, can never be a success until it includes people who differ significantly from each other.[253] The family trains us to build such a thing. Very little else does.

Human beings are best when they know their limitations. The way in which they develop within families requires mutual adjustment in a process that probably never ends: at some point, everyone has to know when and how to compromise. The individual person is never a finished article (although, if asked, most family members will probably claim that they are relatively complete in comparison to the others), but always a project, and the family presents continual reminders of one's own relative inadequacy. It militates against conceitedness. Mostly, one's fellow members will not be friendship-material: they will be in a different age-group, and/or their tastes, attitudes and beliefs will be dissimilar. Throughout our lives, it keeps us in touch with the very young and the very old, and most age-groups in between. It gives us the opportunity to learn from them, teach them, support them, share different experiences with them, care for them. In all these ways, the family involves us in a conflictual process of self-development in which we are perpetually buffeted by I-Thou contraries, and painfully confronted with our own imperfection. If we were to set up a schoolroom for good citizenship that began at birth and ended at death, something like the family is probably what we would devise. The fact that it fails so frequently is partly because it is almost always under external pressure to incorporate the values of the cultural and political establishment, but also

---

[253] The extent to which the Western countercultural revolution of the 1960s and the Chinese Cultural Revolution were actually manifestations of the same underlying phenomenon has yet to be fully investigated. Perhaps the chief difference was that one had the enmity of the establishment, the other its enthusiastic backing. Joan Didion's contemporaneous analysis in *Slouching Towards Bethlehem* (1968) documents some of the similarities, but Bob Dylan's *The Times They Are A-Changin'* (1964), often seen as a progressive soundtrack to US counterculturalism, could just as easily work as a foreshadowing of what happened in China.

because learning to be a good individual is hard, and some of us may find it too hard. The family is fragile. If all the members do not pull their weight, it can easily go off course, and sometimes it will crash. If, or when, I choose to leave, it need not be remotely my fault. Alternatively, I may try to control the variables.

All one requires from 'the communist family' is that it should incorporate the old, the middle-aged and the young (the greater the spectrum of ages the better), that its members should be united by lifelong ties much deeper than friendship (which need not be genetic ties), and that it should be capable of acting as a unit (which may not be internally unanimous) within a bigger collective. Families are the way right- and left-wing views, in society more widely, remain in dialogue. Without that, both young and old become prey to *idées fixes*, and divisions deepen. In any event, eventually, the young become the old, and the cycle carries on.

A meaningful countersociety, if it reaches any sort of size, must take its cue from the family. It cannot be anything like Adam Curtis examined. It must include a diverse spectrum of individuals – diverse in beliefs and values, not just ethnicity/skin-colour (which on its own, is a fairly banal form of diversity) – and it must be grounded in the sort of care/love that inspires a permanent dialogue.

Such a thing may become more possible as technology develops. In their 2023 book, *The Coming Wave*, Mustafa Suleyman and Michael Bhaskar discuss the way in which the Iran-backed terrorist group, Hezbollah, operated as a 'state within a state' within Lebanon, prior to Israel's 2024 invasion of that country. They think such setups could become more common.

> "The coming wave could make a range of small, state-like entities a lot more plausible. Contrary to

centralization, it might actually spur a kind of 'Hezbollahization', a splintered, tribalized world where everyone has access to the latest technologies, where everyone can support themselves on their own terms, where it is far more possible for anyone to maintain living standards without the great superstructures of nation-state organization. Consider that a combination of AI, cheap robotics, and advanced biotech coupled with clean energy sources might, for the first time in modernity, make living 'off-grid' nearly equivalent to being plugged-in. Recall that over just the last decade the cost of solar photovoltaics has fallen by more than eighty-two percent and will plunge further, putting energy self-sufficiency for smaller communes within reach. As electrification of infrastructure and alternatives to fossil fuels percolate, more of the world could become self-sufficient - but now equipped with an infrastructure of AI, bio, robotics, and so on, capable of generating information and manufacturing locally."[254]

The greatest countersociety movement of the nineteenth century was undoubtedly Owenism. For Karl Polanyi, it was that movement's founder, Robert Owen, and not Karl Marx, who best understood the complex dynamics of the age. "Owen alone," he tells us, "discerned behind the market economy the emergent reality: society. However, his vision was lost again for a century."[255] And again: "No thinker ever advanced farther into the realm of industrial society than did Robert Owen."[256] Marx – or at least, his followers - shared the error of the free-marketeers that the economy was overridingly determinative.

[254] Suleyman, Mustafa and Bhaskar, Michael (2023), p197.
[255] Polanyi (2024), p98.
[256] Ibid. p148.

"Upholding the viewpoint of opposing classes, liberals and Marxists stood for identical propositions."[257] Owen's countersocieties all collapsed, but, if Suleyman and Bhaskar are right, any twenty-first-century equivalents would not be bound to repeat that failure (nor the failure of the USA's 20th century countercultural communes).

For the neoconservative philosopher, Joshua Muravchik, Owen - and other practical utopians like Charles Fourier - had strengths that Marx relinquished.

> "Karl Marx disdained the utopians as so many 'organizers of charity, members of societies for the prevention of cruelty to animals, temperance fanatics, hole-and-corner reformers of every imaginable kind.' In contrast, he offered 'scientific socialism.' This was a spectacular inversion. What is science but the practice of experimentation, of hypothesis and test? Owen and Fourier and their followers were the real 'scientific socialists.' They hit upon the idea of socialism, and they tested it by attempting to form socialist communities… Then along comes Marx and says, never mind with these experiments at bringing about socialism by human devices, it will be brought about by the impersonal force of history. In other words, under the banner of 'science,' Marx shifted the basis for socialism from human ingenuity to sheer prophecy."[258]

In her 1982 *Eve and the New Jerusalem,* Barbara Taylor points out that, in any case, virtually everything in 'Marxism' was

---

[257] Ibid, p176.
[258] Muravchik, Joshua, https://www.aei.org/research-products/speech/the-rise-and-fall-of-socialism/ Muravchik claims that all of Owen and Fourier's experiments failed 'utterly and disastrously', which makes it sound as if everyone concerned was killed. If the failure of experiments was a good reason to stop experimenting, we would still be living in caves.

present in Owenism at least a decade before Marx put pen to paper.

> "In 1833, [Owen] unfolded his plan for the complete takeover of the British industrial system by combinations of workers and sympathetic employers, who would then delegate representatives to a House of Trades which would eventually supersede the capitalist state ... 'The Trades Unions will not only strike for less work and more wages,' one activist in the Operative Builders Union, a strongly Owenite-influenced body, explained, 'but they will ultimately ABOLISH WAGES, become their own masters and work for each other.'"[259]

But of course, Owen was only one part of a much bigger movement whose most significant membership would extend as least as far back as Gerrard Winstanley, and would include Étienne Cabet, Charles Fourier, Bernhard Müller, George Rapp, Philippe Buonarroti, Henri de Saint-Simon, Frances Wright and Josiah Warren. Like Owenism, many of the connected movements founded experimental communities in the United States. There were Fourierist communities in Ohio, New York State, Massachusetts, Texas and Kansas. Cabet founded communities in Illinois and Texas, Müller and Rapp in Pennsylvania, Wright in Tennessee, Warren in Ohio.

The year 1848 can be seen, in retrospect, as the end of a certain highly energetic, disparate, universal, practical and creative socialism in favour of a much more uniform, technocratic, fundamentalist and aggressive one. This is, of course, the year in which *The Communist Manifesto* appears. Hegel's words in the Preface to the *Philosophy of Right* seem apt

---

[259] Taylor, Barbara (2016), p86.

in this context: "When philosophy paints its grey in grey, one form of life has become old, and by means of grey it cannot be rejuvenated, but only known. The owl of Minerva takes its flight only when the shades of night are gathering."[260] What he means, of course, is that serious and sustained reflection often begins only when a movement has expended its original energy and begun to decline.

Concerning what was lost, Barbara Taylor says:

> "As the utopian imagination faded, so did the commitment to a new sexual order. As the older schemes for emancipating 'all humanity at once' were displaced by the economic struggles of a single class, so issues central to that earlier dream – marriage, reproduction, family life – were transformed from political issues into 'merely private ones', while women who persisted in pressing such issues were frequently condemned as bourgeois 'women's rightsers.' Organised feminism was increasingly viewed not as an essential component of the socialist struggle, but as a disunifying diversionary force, with no inherent connection to the socialist tradition. And thus the present disowns the past."[261]

The Indeterminacy of the Peasant and Back to the Land

Marx and his disciples all premised the successful transition to communism on the appropriation, by the workers, of the means of production. Arguably, what transpired, in every subsequent 'communist' country, was state capitalism with a large bureaucracy. In Gorbachev's Russia, the Party's attempt to give the workers more industrial autonomy led to economic collapse

---

[260] Hegel, GWF (2001), p20.
[261] Taylor, Barbara (2016), pxvi.

as lumpenproletarian capitalism intervened with its customary ruthlessness.

There are reasons for thinking that a revolution is a particularly bad way for the workers to seize control of industry. Unless they are *already organised* in a division of labour to which they collectively consent, then someone will have to take charge of the reorganisation, and it will have to happen quickly, otherwise production will halt. If such a standstill happens everywhere, people will starve. Any given reorganisation (barring a unanimous vote) will have to be at least partly imposed; there will be winners and losers, and likely a degree of resentment and confusion. These are, after all, workers whose mental outlook has been conditioned by lumpenproletarian capitalism, and each may well bear the psychological scars of that.

Only prefigurativism can prevent such an outcome: if the workers are satisfactorily workplace-organised in advance of any revolution, they can continue the day after as they began the day before. Nothing need be interrupted; no one need be unhappy.

But it is difficult to see how that might work. It would require the workers to have complete power over their conditions of employment before any transition. In which case, the transition would be pointless. In other words, although prefigurativism looks like a solution, apparently it is not.

We said at the beginning of this book that the means of production has four levels.

(1) The non-human means of production. The *growth* of plants and animals, fully independently of any use humans might make of them;

(2) The *harvesting* of the product of (1) by humans, either (a) by hunting-gathering or (b) on farms, using farming technology;

(3) The *processing* of food for consumption by industries alongside or outside the farming industry;

(4) The *production of everything else* – shoes, batteries, clocks, etc. - which obviously requires the production of food in (1) as its precondition.

Factories, of the sort Marx and Engels had in mind in their lionisation of the proletariat, belong to (3) and (4), and are subject to all the problems we have just outlined. If we are to hold onto the idea that communism involves the appropriation of the means of production, we must begin with levels (1), (2) and (3). In this case, contrary to initial appearances, it *can* be prefigurative. In other words, 'the revolution' must begin in the countryside.

From the point of view of orthodox Marxism, there are issues with this. Marxism has traditionally been fond of urban centres and factories. It has had little time for "the idiocy of rural life", as Marx himself put it. [262] Peasants are a non-class without a significant future. Their backward-looking, too-intimate relation to the Earth supposedly makes them particularly unsuited to lead a radically modernising uprising. We need to discuss this before we can proceed.

The 19th century Industrial Revolution, whose success *The Communist Manifesto* sees as underwriting Marxism[263], only became possible because of a prior agricultural revolution (or revolutions), beginning in the Netherlands at the end of the fifteenth century and quickly spreading to Britain. It started

---

[262] Although to be fair, "as Hal Draper pointed out, it was based on a mistranslation of the German term *idiotismus:* 'In the nineteenth century, German still retained the original Greek meaning of forms based on the word *idiotes:* a private person, withdrawn from public (communal) concerns, apolitical in the original sense of isolation from the larger community.'" (Finn, Daniel, 'Marxism and the Agrarian Question' in *The Jacobin* August 2024)

[263] The proletariat is the "special and essential product" of modern industry (1967), p91 .

with land enclosures, in what Marx described as 'primitive accumulation', and Karl Polanyi saw as a revolution of the rich against the poor.[264]

Polanyi remarks, "What we call land is an element of nature inextricably interwoven with man's institutions. To isolate it and form a market for it was perhaps the weirdest of all the undertakings of our ancestors. Traditionally, land and labour are not separated; labour forms part of life, land remains part of nature, life and nature form an articulate whole."[265]

He identifies three historical stages in 'the commercialisation of the soil'. The first – agricultural capitalism - began in Tudor times and effected conversions and enclosures. The second began at the start of the eighteenth century – a 'primarily rural' industrial capitalism – which needed sites for its mills and workers' settlements. The third began in the nineteenth century with the rise of industrial towns. He thinks that the Marxist categorisation of the peasantry as reactionaries, accentuating, by contrast, the alleged progressiveness of the proletariat, is partly to be explained by the fact that the former found their sponsors in the landed classes, while the latter were more in tune with the emerging advocates of the free market.

> "The trading classes sponsored the demand for mobilisation of the land. Cobden set the landlords of England aghast with his discovery that farming was 'business' and that those who were broke must clear out. The working classes were won over to free trade as soon as it became apparent that it made food cheaper. Trade unions became the bastion of anti-agrarianism, and revolutionary socialism branded the peasantry of the world an indiscriminate mass of reactionaries."[266]

---

[264] Polanyi, Karl (2024), p41.
[265] Ibid, p207.
[266] Ibid, p213.

This altered slightly in the second half of the nineteenth century, when the destructiveness of unrestricted free trade became generally apparent. The peasants were then granted a semblance of political power, but, of course, they were disinclined to overlook their indebtedness to the landed gentry who, for various reasons, had stood by them in earlier decades. They were often, therefore, a reactionary force, but perhaps more by accident than essence.

The German Ideology talks of "the isolation and consequent crudity of the peasants". In *The Eighteenth Brumaire*, they are "a vast mass, the members of which live in similar conditions … The identity of their interests begets no unity, no national union, and no political organisation, they do not form a class." In fact, nowhere in Marx do they appear in a particularly positive light. The proletariat – men with heavy machinery – are the superheroes of history, and there is scant room for anyone else.

There are two significant ironies here.

Firstly, in most revolutionary communist uprisings since Marx, it has been the peasants, not the industrial working classes, who took the initiative and destroyed the old order.[267] As AJP Taylor put it, in 1967:

> "Peasants, it seems, make revolutions. The proletariat do not. Or, to imitate Marx in a still more sweeping generalisation, revolutions occur in backward

---

[267] The Marxian amalgamation of 'bourgeoisie' and 'capitalist' may have its roots in the antagonisms that emerged after the French Revolution, which was carried out by the 'Third Estate' (a combination of peasants and the emerging middle classes) against the *Ancien Régime*. When the dust cleared, the bourgeoisie was in power, and the peasants were back where they started. As Polanyi puts it: "Since 1830, if not since 1789, it was part of the Continental tradition that the working class would help to fight the battles of the bourgeoisie against feudalism, if only – as the saying ran – to be cheated by the middle class of the fruits of victory" (2024), p202. What better reason to view the bourgeoisie as the embodiment of every new evil (including capitalist evils)?

countries, not advanced ones. Hence, with the advance of capitalism, the twentieth century has been singularly free from social revolutions."[268]

For the prominent twentieth-century libertarian, George Woodcock, this is one of the chief ways in which Marxism is to be distinguished from Anarchism:

> "The Marxist rejects the primitive as representing a stage in social evolution already past; for him, tribesmen, peasants, small craftsmen, all belong with the bourgeoisie on the scrapheap of history. Communist *realpolitik* may at times demand a *rapprochement* with the peasants, as now in the Far East, but the end of such a policy is always to turn the peasants into proletarians of the land. The anarchists, on the other hand, have placed great hopes in the peasant. He is near to the earth, to nature, and therefore more 'anarchic' in his reactions."[269]

What are we to make of all this? Are the peasants intrinsically reactionary, or are they even more progressive than the proletariat?

The truth may be yet more complex. Patrick Joyce points out what ought to be obvious, that "peasant society is deeply various", but also that:

> "Among the privileges of those who are powerful is the privilege to control how they wish to be known and seen by others. And how such people see themselves is

[268] Taylor, AJP (1967), p44. As Leszek Kołakowski noted in 2002, "What in the twentieth century perhaps comes closest to a working-class revolution were the events in Poland of 1980-81: the revolutionary movement of industrial workers (very strongly supported by the intelligentsia)."
[269] Woodcock, George (1986), p24.

in relation to what they are not, the powerless, who have historically usually been peasants. This control over how people are seen takes many forms: legal, political and aesthetic among them. Those who have little or no power must reckon with this, for the world comes to be 'objectively' seen through the lens the powerful hold up, so that peasants must contend with a truth about themselves which they have not themselves made."[270]

The second significant irony has to do with the fact that, on one reading of Marxism, which defines proletarian-capitalist relations in terms of surplus value, there is no such thing as the peasant – or, at least, the peasantry is less widespread than might appear. Thus:

(1) The land enclosures of the first agricultural revolution, which brought feudalism to an end, signalled the emergence of capitalism. They were the conversion of the commons into private property for the generation of profit.
(2) To put it another way, the 'owners' of the newly enclosed land sequestered it for capitalist purposes; they were capitalists. To the extent that their victims became homeless, they constituted a class of (in the language of the day) 'vagabonds'. To the extent that they were employed by the new owners to work the land, they became 'peasants'.
(3) These 'peasants' were employed on the basis of working the land for the production of commodities for sale at market: whole animals, parts of animals, quantities of vegetables, fruits and cereals, processed items such as drinks and loaves of bread.

---

[270] Joyce, Patrick 2024), p34.

(4) In other words, the 'peasant' sold his labour power to the capitalist, and the capitalist sold the fruits of the peasant's labour in the market. The difference – the profit - was the surplus value that the capitalist extracted from the peasant.

(5) But the extraction of surplus value from a worker for the production of commodities sold at a profit is simply an orthodox Marxist description of the relation between capitalist and proletarian.

(6) Therefore, in this setup (and on the Marxist definition), the 'peasant', as distinct from the 'proletarian', does not exist in the post-enclosure modern economy. Assuming the success of the first agricultural revolution in bringing the commons into the capitalist system, there are only urban proletarians and rural proletarians.

The empirical validity of this argument depends on the persistence of feudalism. We have already seen that Ganshof thought some elements of it survived into the nineteenth century and later, even though it mostly ended with the *Ancien Régime*. For Shoard, in England, it "effectively came to an end with abolition of feudal tenures and the Court of Wards [in 1646]."[271] Joyce thinks that England "is the odd man out, the early emergence of capitalist social relations having led to the trinity of large landowner, commercial farmer and waged agricultural labourer", although he quickly adds that this is "an oversimplification."[272] Even where we have what looks like a significantly 'feudal economy', as in Russia at the end of the nineteenth century, we still have the question of how to decode the overlap between the feudal 'serf' and the later 'peasant'. Alexander Chayanov, the great Soviet theorist of the agrarian economy, proposed that peasants were essentially subsistence farmers: they operated on the basis of a 'consumption-labour-

---

[271] Shoard, Marion (1987) p53.
[272] Joyce, Patrick (2004), p24.

balance principle' to the effect that labour will increase until it fulfils (balances) the requirements (consumption) of the household. Obviously, in at least some places and countries (including England again), that cannot have been the case. On the M—C—M' model the distinction between proletariat and at least part of the peasantry is chimerical: rightly considered, there are only proletarians.[273]

But, of course there is another way of characterising classes within Marxism. The thrust of historical materialism is that the means of production produces classes as a function of its total deployment. In the factory, the means of production would be conveyor systems, press brakes, lathes, forklift trucks, fixed-location machines of various types. On a farm, it would be ploughs, teams of horses, scythes, seed drills, abattoirs, knives, harvesting equipment. As we indicated above, in terms of the four levels of the means of production that we identified above, the 'peasant' would typically be involved in levels 1, 2 and 3, the 'proletarian' in levels 3 and 4 – which is to say, there would be some overlap, but not enough to make the two classes coincident: defined by the means of production, the peasantry would be mostly distinct from the proletariat, despite the identity (in places) of their economic status within the M—C—M' system.[274]

The problem with this solution is that, if we can only identify and describe a social class in terms of the means of production

---

[273] Marx's attempt to solve this problem in *The German Ideology* gets us nowhere. "The antagonism between town and country can only exist within the framework of private property. It is the most crass expression of the subjection of the individual under the division of labour, under a definite activity forced upon him - a subjection which makes one man into a restricted town-animal, the other into a restricted country-animal, and daily creates anew the conflict between their interests. Labour is here again the chief thing, power over individuals, and as long as the latter exists, private property must exist." Etc. This is more a description of the problem than an explanation.

[274] Marx's solution to this is to say that, during a crisis, the 'two classes' would recognise a common cause and coalesce to resist the ruling classes, but this defines them in terms of a means of securitisation of which they are both outside.

240

that generates it, we could easily end up multiplying classes indefinitely. So, for example, assuming the means of production in a tyre factory differs significantly from that in a cotton mill, why should workers in those two places be considered part of a single social class? The same applies in the countryside: where their jobs do not overlap, arable workers use a different means of production to those involved in animal husbandry, so are *they* two different social classes? The M—C—M' schema which was meant to override those divergences, cannot be marshalled to resolve the problem without at least partially abolishing the concept of the peasant. But by now, that might look like a price worth paying.

Is there any way beyond the apparent impasse? Common sense suggests that there is (or was[275]) a real class of peasants, wholly distinct from the proletariat.

The answer arguably lies, as we might expect, in the means of securitisation, which is naturally different in town and village: in large urban settings, it needs to cope with anonymised individuals whose whereabouts may frequently change, so the detective, the policeman and the spy are central. In the latter, where residential fixity is the norm, and there is likely to be a significant degree of personal mutual familiarity, the squire, the schoolteacher, the parson and longstanding custom are central, and gossip may even play a part.

To be 'lower class' (whether proletarian or peasant) means to be 'locked out' - and, just as significantly, *locked down* - in a variety of ways: by geography, by income, by educational attainment, by race or ethnicity, by culture. You have been secured *against*. To be higher class is to have the means of securitisation - or at least, parts of it - working *for* you; to a

---

[275] In the developed world, many of the jobs peasants would have done in Marx's day have now, of course, been taken over by machines, and rural populations have largely decamped to town and cities, so the class does not really exist in a significant sense anymore.

greater or lesser extent, you possess what is quite literally – Saint Peter notwithstanding – 'the power of the keys.' In short, what the peasant and the proletarian have in common is a relative position in society. They are both at the bottom of the pile, albeit in different ways.

But those 'different ways' are far from insignificant, because there is an important respect in which Marx was right to see the peasantry as a reactionary force. Joyce defines them partly in terms of their strong, age-old sense of place, of 'dwelling', centred on the family house, but also including "the other houses that might surround the main house, animals, crops, and so on. What we call the 'farm', in fact, the farm unfolding, as it were, in layers from the dwelling house to the fields, then the mountains, the forests, the wastelands."[276] A distinctly non-modern sense of time is an equally significant component of the peasant identity: "The dwelling is also a constitutive part of the relationship between past and present generations, between the living and the dead."[277]

By contrast, the nineteenth-century factory-worker was uprooted from his place and time: the factory may only recently have been built, and the urbanisation it often generated replaced the geographical landscape of 'mountains, forests, wastelands' with tenements, roads, offices, shops and more factories. The vaster the new infrastructure became, the more interchangeable individual workers became, and the less connected they could feel to their 'dwelling'. Marx himself covered much of this, of course, under the rubric 'estranged labour', in the *Economic and Philosophic Manuscripts*. But if the peasant and the proletarian are equally victims of capitalist exploitation, then the latter cannot fully explain it.

It is important to note, though, that this dissociation from place might only apply to the first generation of proletarians,

[276] Joyce, Patrick (2024), p67.
[277] Ibid. p67.

when exploitation and poverty are at their height. Even then, neighbourhoods and institutions may still be important and, of course, over time, those become increasingly inseparable from the physical infrastructure. Trade union marches often used repetition of routes as a means of asserting a connection to the local geography.

In his 2017 *The Road to Somewhere*, David Goodhart divides political actors in Britain and elsewhere into 'Somewheres' – individuals rooted in their nation and locality - 'Anywheres' - cosmopolitan individuals who do not feel especial allegiance to the society in which they happen to be living - and 'Inbetweeners', whose attitudes lie midway between the two. 'Anywheres', he thinks, are generally liberal, university-educated and urban. 'Somewheres' live in the provinces or the countryside, are socially conservative in outlook, and tend to value tradition and continuity.

Apart from the fact that Goodhart sees 'Anywheres' as politically liberal and well-educated city-dwellers – about 20-25% of the population in Britain - his distinction could have been designed to distinguish the Marxian proletariat from the peasantry. *The German Ideology*, for example, describes the proletariat as a class of "men in their world-historical, instead of local, being ... World-historical, empirically universal individuals in place of local ones": these 'anywheres' have become anonymised, and the physical landscape into which they were born has been transformed irreversibly, but without their consent or approval. They have become 'anywheres' by compulsion. They are looking for a new 'somewhere', a future society of moral fairness. A 21st-century equivalent might be homeless people.

It is certainly not clear that 'Anywheres' are (also) urban middle-class liberals. Resistance to the gentrification and homogenising of urban spaces is often led by middle-class liberals: Laura Oldfield Ford, Iain Sinclair, Fran Lebowitz and

Billy Talen are the tip of a middle-class intellectual iceberg dedicated to resisting the corporate takeover of (their own) cityscapes. On at least one level, they are clearly 'Somewheres'.

No, the purest 'Anywheres' are likely very wealthy individuals who own several properties dotted around the world, who travel frequently on business, and whose primary dwelling is significantly isolated from its neighbourhood, and gated. Such individuals are far less numerous than Goodhart assumes. They would not turn up to protest the 'Disneyfication' of their locality, because they would likely have interests in common with those initiating it. All in all, they are probably right-wing - when they think about politics at all.

To return to the point, there is no convincing reason why the countryside should be considered intrinsically reactionary. In developed societies, and increasingly, everywhere, the town-countryside, rural-urban distinction is a fiction designed to bolster one central prop of capitalism: which turns out to be the farming industry. How could it be otherwise? As an old Russian proverb puts it: 'the rich would have to eat money if the poor did not provide food.'

The misconception that towns and cities are the principal site of worker-capitalist relations, and that those relations do not even exist in the countryside (where they are replaced by farmer-farm labourer relations, a vague descendant of lord-serf, landlord-peasant relations), is a back-to-front assessment that has many elements, and may well pre-date capitalism.

The prominent eco-activist, George Monbiot, devotes the penultimate chapter of his 2022 *Regenesis* to discussing it. He begins by noting that the ancient world tended to think in terms of a bygone 'golden age', from which humankind fell. Since this was a pre-city state of affairs, it implied the primordial moral superiority of the countryside to the city, an attitude reflected, for example, in the stories of Adam and Eve, Cain and Abel, and in Theocritus' *Bucolics* and Virgil's *Eclogues*. This rosy-eyed 'ruralism' persisted broadly unchanged throughout the medieval period, and appeared in the Renaissance in Spenser, Marlowe, Lodge, and Sidney, among others. Shakespeare treated it with a degree of irreverence, but it took George Crabbe's 1783, *The Village* to really call it into question (by which time, the enclosures were well under way). However, Monbiot thinks Crabbe was already too late.

> "The pastoral story is one that urban civilization tells against itself without a flicker of disquiet: the shepherds and their sheep are good and pure, while the city is base and venal. Why do we see sheep farmers tending to their flocks in a blizzard as more romantic figures than office workers trudging through the same storm? Perhaps because the poets' herds have trampled such a trail through the grass that departing from it requires a deliberate cognitive effort."

In the modern age, Monbiot thinks, the fallacy is sustained partly by children's books and television. The relevant elements of the former are a genial farmer and a few talking animals, ensuring that, from our earliest years, "we learn that the livestock farm is a place of comfort and safety, a harmonious world removed from stress and conflict."[278] When we grow older, television cements the prejudice. "On British TV, at least once a week, often at peak time on a Sunday evening, weary urban people lose themselves in a bucolic fantasy of livestock farming."[279] As with sheep farmers in Britain, so with cow herders in the USA. "The West, once the indigenous people who lived there had been extirpated, became white America's Arcadia."[280]

---

[278] Monbiot, George (2022), p216.
[279] Ibid. p217.
[280] Ibid. p218.

The real business of the farmer today, Monbiot asserts, is not keeping animals or growing crops, but "takes place on the computer, filling in subsidy forms: livestock graziers in the UK are entirely dependent on the taxpayer." The same charge recently found its way onto the pages of *Private Eye* magazine.[281]

The problem, Monbiot goes on, is replicated globally: the world's governments spend over five hundred billion dollars each year on farm subsidies. Most of the money goes to the biggest and wealthiest farmers. "In the European Union, for example, money is paid by the hectare: the more land you control, the more cash you are given ... Taxpayers of all stations kindly donate their hard-earned income to the dukes, oil sheikhs, Russian oligarchs, corrupt politicians, and other aristocrats and tycoons who own great tracts of land."[282]

His overall judgement is, of course, damning:

> "The countryside is neither innocent nor pure. In some places, it is more corrupt than the city, its politics dominated by landed elites, hereditary power and a culture of deference. Pollution, now caused primarily by agriculture in many nations, is the physical manifestation of corruption... If we judged farming by the standards of any other industry, we would be incensed by their transformation into open sewers,

[281] "Farmers' chronic dependency [on government subsidies] has been revealed by cuts made to the old EU subsidy system in the budget last October. These cuts are predicted to have a huge negative impact on the profitability of many farms this year. Incomes on 'less favoured area' farms, for example, are forecast to fall by an average of 45 percent as a result of the subsidy cuts, and on mixed enterprise farms by 34 percent (Eve 1639). That the cuts have caused great financial distress should not have come as any great surprise to the government. As long ago as 2010, a study funded by the Department for Environment Food and Rural Affairs and carried out by the LEI research institute in the Hague found that, were the EU system of acreage payments ever to be withdrawn (which the government has now, effectively, done) British farms would be the *worst* affected." (*Private Eye*, 1647, 16 April-1 May 2025).
[282] Monbiot, George (2022), p219.

alongside the destruction of much of the rest of life on Earth. But the cultural power of the industry insulates it from both criticism and regulation. We grant farming an uncontested political space offered to no other profession."[283]

What are we to make of this? If Monbiot is right, the countryside evokes ambiguous sentiments because, while it is the primary site of capitalism's struggle for hegemony, it is largely camouflaged.

Some of the concealment is based in reality. The ordinary farmer is highly visible, but usually, the ordinary farmer is not particularly committed to capitalism: he or she is not aiming for infinite returns (no one would buy a farm for that reason), and he can literally live without capitalism. On the other hand, the owners of Cargill, Aria, Banham Poultry, *et al.* are virtually invisible: they certainly never appear in children's books or on feel-good TV, yet they make all the big money. The ambiguity is intensified because the countryside is subject to a tug-of-war: capitalism seeks to dominate it; it sees food production as an economic opportunity. But civil society recognises food security as a necessity: the world is unpredictable and a state's citizens will always need feeding.

Their agendas of the two forces may sometimes coincide, but not frequently, and never entirely. Somewhere in the middle – between civil society and predatory corporations - we have ordinary farmers, subsidised by the former as a kind of insurance policy, and encircled by the latter in their lust for profits. And then we have environmental and animal welfare campaigners, bringing a different, deeper and more existential level of concern to the mix.

---

[283] Ibid. p223.

These four forces can only avoid open conflict so long as one or more of them turns a blind eye to the others;[284] however, such a standoff suits capitalism better than its three rivals. A 2024 report by World Animal Protection indicated a rise of 209 factory farms in Britain since 2017, totalling 1821.[285] Compassion in World Farming's Factory Farming Map shows a 12% increase in the number of UK factory farms between 2016 and 2023, with a 20% increase in large pig and poultry units.[286] Meanwhile, agriculture is suffering the same corporate creep. According to War on Want:

> "As of 2022, at least 40% of the global trade in agricultural commodities is controlled by just ten corporations. In fact, this percentage may be even larger: global supply chains are opaque and much of the information is supplied by the companies themselves, which are among the most powerful and least transparent in the global supply chain."[287]

In other words, just as we might expect, capitalism is winning.

Self-sustaining agricultural countersocieties might provide a means for environmental resistance and communism to go hand in hand. As we suggested at the beginning of this section, if orthodox Marxism has any mileage in it at all, 'the revolution' must begin in the countryside. Prefigurative politics would work here, but, in the longer term, it could not succeed in transforming the wider society without support – as we have repeatedly suggested - from other, more vanguardist forms of

---

[284] So, for example, Monbiot observes that, according to a University of Illinois survey, 90 per cent of Americans eat meat, but 47 per cent want to ban slaughterhouses. (2022, p217)

[285] https://www.worldanimalprotection.org.uk/latest/news/confined-in-cruelty/

[286] https://www.ciwf.org.uk/our-campaigns/factory-farming-map/

[287] https://waronwant.org/profiting-hunger/3-corporate-capture-agriculture

activism. The entire movement would have to proceed on a number of different united fronts – including conventional political party politics - as described above.

Conclusion

In this book, I have argued that Marx's theory of historical materialism is flawed: history is driven far more by the means of securitisation than by the means of production. The former explains why, in every society, there are 'haves' and 'have nots' whose nature as such overrides any of their additional features. Before any community invests in the means of production, it must feel secure enough to believe such investment is worthwhile. Otherwise, it can always subsist on what we have called the 'first level' of the means of production: the biological, non-human production of plants and animals; ie, it will revert to hunter-gathering. There were many such reversions in pre-history.

The means of securitisation has a defensive and a proactive aspect, and in practice, particular instances of the means of securitisation can be deployed in both roles. The conflictual interaction between different types of securitisation device (forts versus siege-engines, for example) spurs further technological advances which, usually indirectly, drive advances in the means of production, and scientific progress more generally.

Capitalism has existed in every complex society since ancient times, but it has mostly kept a relatively low profile. The reason it has recently become dominant is because it only acquired full control of the means of securitisation after the democratising invention of firearms. Class structures, internecine conflicts and power differentials prior to the Industrial Revolution can be almost entirely explained in terms of the means of securitisation.

The means of production, as we have said, enters at a later explanatory stage.

Capitalism - defined as 'an inadvertent economic system premised on the private pursuit of unlimited monetary wealth by means, at least to begin with, of the scalable production of commodities, in the form either of goods or services, and the hypothetical perfectibility of the means of securitisation' - has achieved hegemony by parasitizing science, partly to flood the world with captivating consumer goods, but also to bring about exponential improvements in the means of securitisation, with which it has installed itself in a veritable fortress. That fortress will inevitably become bigger and more prison-like as time goes on, since capitalism is also defined by its pursuit of 'the perfectibility of the means of securitisation'. Face-recognition technology and other means of surveillance are likely to be collated by AI, and citizens increasingly tracked, manipulated and controlled. China currently leads the way here, but other countries are already following in its footsteps.

Human nature has always been conditioned by the means of securitisation. Modern capitalism, where securitisation devices are ubiquitous, has generated an 'indoor society' where humans are anxious, and often mentally unwell. They feel safer within the mini-forts capitalism has provided for (most of) them, partly by way of fettering society as a whole. But they never feel entirely secure.

By the same process, many people have also become self-centred, aggressive, reactionary and cruel. This is the sense in which Hobbes was correct in the seventeenth century, and John Gray is right in the twenty-first. But it is not the last word about human beings, as modern evolutionary psychology has shown. Humanity's murderous potential is one of the many factors progressives have always had to contend with, but it is possible to imagine a shared future without it.

In countries where capitalism had to fight for dominance against a long-established social system with laws and customs, it was restrained as rival powers brought those laws and customs to bear against it. Our present civil liberties and rule of law are ultimately the outcome of that long process of struggle (as, eg, workplace unions created cooperatives, or the landed aristocracy allied with the peasants to confront capitalism, or as vigorous radical movements occasionally had to be appeased with moral concessions). Those rights and liberties were not provided by capitalism, rather they are the legacy of the limits that were imposed on it by the eventual losers, limits against which it often kicked and yelled. They continue to hem it in, for all their fragility. The other side of the coin is that capitalism, despite appearances to the contrary, is, and has always been, a system under duress.

Limitarianism, as it turns out, and as Marx himself seems to have partly recognised, is the 'tipping' measure required to turn a capitalist society into a post-capitalist society, and eventually into a communist society. It recalibrates the capitalist mindset, and ensures that wealth is not sucked upwards, leaving a vacuum at the base.[288]

But Limitarianism is only one part of what needs to be implemented in the short term. The necessary components can only be installed by a broad alliance of countersocieties, prefigurative political movements, independent 'vanguardist' parties, and mainstream conventional political parties. None can succeed alone, and even together, they may have a long struggle ahead.

As a system, capitalism has sometimes been a force for good, mitigating the arbitrary power of tyrants, however, as it stands, it constitutes a barrier to human development. We have the

[288] Cf. Robeyns, Ingrid (Ed.) (2023), Icardi, Elena, 'A Neo-Republican Argument for Limitarianism' (p247-70), and Neuhäuser, Christian, 'The Self-Respect Argument for Limitarianism' (p271-96).

means to move beyond it, but, as we said at the beginning, that may mean right and left coming together a lot more than they seem capable of doing at present.

Which might seem a forlorn hope. In the USA, seventy-seven million people recently voted for Donald Trump. Across the world, right-wing parties are on the rise. Part of the explanation may be that the left has temporarily lost the battle of ideas: it has abandoned morality, the family, religion, science - and, above all, rational common sense, which it sees as intellectually gauche.

But that misses the point. The fact is that the right has been parasitized by neoliberalism. At its heart, it is arguably about tradition: longstanding institutions, scepticism of novelty, a consolidation of the few gains it thinks we have jointly achieved. It is not epitomised by Milton Friedman, Friedrich Hayek or even Margaret Thatcher; its best British representatives are probably Edmund Burke, Harold Macmillan and John Betjeman.[289] Most right-wingers, even today, probably have very little love for capitalism; their affections lie far more with Orwell's old maids biking to Holy Communion through autumn morning mists. Nevertheless, neoliberalism has done its best to make them untalkable-to, partly by using the press and social media[290] to polarise a handful of very specific issues: gender politics, 'reverse racism', immigration. The result is that, instead of being two halves of a community engaged in an ongoing dialogue – one wanting to power ahead, the other

---

[289] Cf. eg. this letter from Dr Stephen Watkins in the *New Statesman*, 22 February 2023: "In 1962 I was a Conservative. I believed privilege could only be justified by service, high taxes on very high incomes were necessary to prevent an entrepreneurial economy becoming a rentier economy, and Keynesian growth would finance public service improvements and a welfare state that steadily reduced inequality. I was suspicious of ideologically driven, large-scale change. These were the mainstream policies of the Macmillan government at the time. In 60 years I have moved from centre right to hard left without changing my opinions."
[290] Russia's notorious 'web brigades' are probably relevant here.

urging caution - left and right have now, in many countries, become island-republics of diametrically opposed militants armed with fixed inventories of known-issues-and-their-simple-solutions.

We have spoken throughout of our ultimate goal in terms of Immanuel Kant's Kingdom of Ends, but roughly the same ideal was expressed in the 20th century by Erich Fromm. Inspired by Christian and Jewish theology, Fromm distinguished two types of individual social existence: 'being' and 'having'.

> "Having refers to *things* and things are fixed and *describable*. Being refers to *experience*, and human experience is in principle not describable. What is fully describable is our *persona* – the mask we each wear, the ego we present – for this persona is, in itself, a thing. In contrast, the living human being is not a dead image and cannot be described like a thing. In fact, the living human being cannot be described at all. Indeed, much can be said about me, about my character, about my total orientation to life. This insightful knowledge can go very far in understanding and describing my own or another's physical structure. But the total me, the whole individuality, my suchness that is as unique as my fingerprints are, can never be fully understood, not even by empathy, for no human beings are entirely alike. Only in the process of mutual alive relatedness can the other and I overcome the barrier of separateness, insofar as we can both participate in the dance of life."[291]

The predominance of 'having' lies at the root of Fromm's four 'unproductive' personality types, first described in *Man for*

---

[291] Fromm (1997), p71. Italics in original.

Himself (1947): 'receptive' (or needy), 'exploitative', 'hoarding' and 'marketing'. In *Having and Being*, he insists that, under modern capitalism, the last has begun to predominate.[292]

> "I have called this phenomenon the marketing character because it is based on experiencing oneself as a commodity, and one's value not as 'use value' but as 'exchange value.' The living being becomes a commodity on the 'personality market.' The principle of evaluation is the same on both the personality and the commodity markets: on the one, personalities are offered for sale; on the other, commodities. Value in both cases is their exchange value, for which 'use value' is a necessary but not a sufficient condition... Since success depends largely on how one sells one's personality, one experiences oneself as a commodity or, rather, simultaneously as the seller and the commodity to be sold. A person is not concerned with his or her life and happiness, but with becoming saleable. The aim of the marketing character is complete adaptation, so as to be desirable under all conditions of the personality market."[293]

The sole 'productive' personality type is grounded in 'being', and characterised by relatedness, transcendence, rootedness, identity and freedom. It treats others as ends, not means.

In the first half of this book, we depicted a capitalist society through the metaphor of a walled battlefield. We should now add that there are things outside those walls that could help us, and that the walls themselves are by no means as impenetrable as we have often been led to suppose. To begin with, we need to concentrate our attack at capitalism's weakest points: its tax

---

[292] Ibid. p120.
[293] Ibid. p120-21. Fromm rightly connects this to Marx's theory of alienation.

avoidance, its lobbyism, its attempts to erode the moral foundation of society by egregiously rewarding the already rich.

Capitalism is now a fully secured system, and it has nearly all the tools of attack and defence at its disposal. It can loudly claim that dissenters will make society less secure, and that only it can preserve people's health and safety, etc. In the last resort, it can manufacture crises designed to foment insecurity and pin the blame elsewhere.

Although it is a system with a limited life cycle, it can, and does, keep reincarnating. In every one of its lifetimes, however, it will always plough the same furrow.

Fortunately, it is not unbounded, as some thinkers have asserted. It is contained within a structure of rights, obligations, civil liberties and institutional social norms. Those can be turned against it.

We must ensure that we take advantage of every opportunity open to us, as soon as it appears, and that we do not get in each other's way. The altersociety will always provide new troops, even though the master society will usually take them back after a few years' service. But better apprised of the reality, we can also go back to first principles and consult socialism's 'lost' thinkers. Who remembers Thomas Spence, or Henry George, or Johann Silvio Gesell, or Gustav Landauer? How many people have never heard of Parecon, The Wörgl experiment, the Tempestry Project or the Transition Towns movement? I said in the introduction to this book that I would discuss ways and means of getting beyond capitalism, but the truth is, the entire leftist tradition is already replete with good ideas. We simply need to recover them.

What we have proposed in the second part of his book is the creation of a political movement, loosely grounded in a ten-point manifesto, subsisting everywhere across the political landscape – in countersocieties, in political parties (mainstream and outlying), in third spaces, in neighbourhood associations, in trade unions, in cooperatives, in friendships and families, never hiding, in open dialogue with everyone, capable of coming together at speed, especially when radical direct action looks like being hijacked and repurposed by the enemies of progress. If you, the reader, can assent to even five of the ten measures listed at the head of this section, them you are one of us.

Capitalism has used science to give the world lots of apparent benefits. Those benefits would probably have arrived anyway, because, as we have shown, there is no necessary sympathy between the two enterprises, and on occasion, there may even be enmity. In return, capitalism has given us Holocene extinction; it has securitised us for its own safety, which - since it has created a dangerous, alienated society - is now perceived to be *ours* as well; it has given us a plethora of mental illnesses, pathological behaviours, deep anxieties.

It lies within our power to turn all that around. Little by little, we can reclaim the world outside the system; we can call a halt to the destruction, and perhaps repair much of it; given enough time, we can rediscover 'the dance of life', as Erich Fromm called it, the richness of a truly human community.

Can't we?

Let us begin.

Appendix 1: The Problem of Yanis Varoufakis's Mother

In *Technofeudalism: What Killed Capitalism* (2023), Yanis Varoufakis describes what he calls 'the duality of labour', whose two components comprise surplus value.

> "Well before I read a word that Marx or any other economist had written, I thought I could discern several dualities buried deep in the foundations of our societies. My first inkling of such a duality hit me one evening when Mum complained to Dad that, at the factory where she worked as a chemist, she got paid for her time but never for her enthusiasm. 'My wage is crap because my time is cheap', she said. 'My passion to get the right results the bosses get for free!' Soon after, she resigned and got herself a job as a biochemist at a public hospital. A few months into the new job, she told us happily: 'At least at the hospital, I love that my efforts benefit patients, even if I am as invisible to them as I used to be to the factory owners.'
>
> "Those words stuck with me. Mum had inadvertently introduced me to the duality of waged labour. The wage she was paid for her time and formal skills (the certificates, degrees) reflected the 'exchange value' of the hours she spent at work. But that's not what injected true value into whatever was being manufactured in her workplace. That was added to what was produced at the factory or the hospital through her effort, enthusiasm, application, even flair – none of which were remunerated... Labour is split between commodity labour (Mum's time, bought by

her wage) and experiential labour (the effort, passion and flair she put into her work).

"… What I call experiential labour, the part which can never be sold, Marx called simply labour. And what I have labelled commodity labour, Marx defined as labouring power." (p10-11)

This thesis gets a more formal treatment in *Technofeudalism*'s first Appendix.

"Surplus value is the difference that an employer retains after producing and selling a unit of commodity X. More precisely, it is the difference between (a) the value infused into a unit of X by the *experiential labour* necessary to produce it and (b) the value of the amount of *commodity labour* that the employer had to buy to produce that same unit of X." (p219)

While 'commodity labour" is "the bundle of labour time and skills a worker leases to an employer." (p217)

The biggest problem here arguably lies outside the text: it is that the capitalist is never allowed a right of reply: in anti-capitalist books, anti-capitalist arguments are generally presented as part of a long-established tradition of successful arguments.

But the capitalist in the first cited passage might well say he hired Ms Varoufakis on the understanding that she would do her best. (She may even have given assurances to that effect at the job interview.) Her 'passion to get the right results', he would continue, is irrelevant. Given that that passion 'can never be sold', it simply factors out of the equation. Her story suggests there is something morally wrong about her treatment, but it is difficult to see what alternative the capitalist has. He cannot have hired her on the basis of something she cannot sell.

Equally, getting the right results *is* part of her job. If those results are only possible thanks to a certain level of 'enthusiasm, application, even flair', then she must be being paid, not necessarily for those qualities *per se*, but at least for the temporary appliance of them to her work, because it would be senseless to hire someone who does not possess the job's necessary prerequisites, much less to pay them a wage. In any case, a consistent set of wrong results will probably get her fired, and (in the absence of extenuating factors) justly so. Her 'certificates, degrees' should be sufficient to enable her to make good – which is why such qualifications exist.

In sum, she either *does* need to bring her passion to the job, or she does not. If the former, then it is a prerequisite, and, explicitly or not, she *is* being paid for it; if she does not, then she is doing something redundant.

… Nevertheless, most of us will intuitively sympathise with Ms Varafoukis. The suspicion lingers that she has put her finger on something important.

If so, the problem must lie elsewhere.

I have argued in this book that the 'wrongness' of capitalism cannot be grasped in a reductionist account such as focuses only on the relationship between the individual worker and the capitalist. It only becomes evident when capitalism is considered holistically, as a *system* of capital*ists* engaged in a process whose goal is the elimination of other players – by fair means, if possible (but that is rarely possible) – and in which the winner takes literally all. To appreciate what is behind Mrs Varoufakis's complaint we can make a start by looking at her workplace.

Which might sound like a tall order, but we can proceed on the reasonable assumption that, as regards its moral features, it probably resembles every capitalist workplace ever created. To begin with, she will be surrounded by other workers, at least some of whom will have an understanding of capitalism as a system. They will be aware that they are dispensable, and that, thanks to a variety of factors over which they have no control – not the least of which is their employer's overriding determination to turn a profit – they could suddenly find themselves out of a job, or having to accept a reduction in wages, or having to retrain. They will be aware that, should some of those things happen, they may find themselves in competition with their fellow workers. They will cope with that foreboding in different ways. Some of them will work harder than they are contractually obliged to do, and they will resent the lack of recognition that comes from above; others will do the bare minimum, and will inspire resentment from their workfellows. The shop floor will not usually be a happy place.

The best employees will be those – like Ms Varoufakis – who do their best simply for its own sake, in a kind of Kantian devotion to abstract duty. But they will be rare. Some workers will decide, quite rationally, that advancement comes, not from making a good effort, but from being *seen* to do so by those who count. When it comes to dealing with unforeseen difficulties, they will tend to take the path of least resistance.

The characteristics of an accomplished capitalist are cunning and ruthlessness – intelligence is not absolutely necessary, though it is not entirely gratuitous – and capitalists will regularly overlook talent, and promote either individuals made in their own mould, or sycophants. They may well pay their employees irrationally: the most challenging jobs may not be the best remunerated, and at the far end of the scale, there will often be what David Graeber called 'bullshit jobs'.[294] A low-level distrust will likely pervade the company, especially given the

---

[294] Graeber, David (2018): "A bullshit job is a form of paid employment that is so completely pointless, unnecessary, or pernicious that even the employee cannot justify its existence even though, as part of the conditions of employment, the employee feels obliged to pretend that this is not the case." (p9-10)

divide between work and home, where different values will almost certainly preside.

Workers will also be aware that their jobs are dependent on the wider market, and that good ethics is not, in the long term, usually good business. If they are committed to quality in production and customer transparency, they may find themselves facing crises of conscience from time to time. They will know that a system in which the pursuit of profit is primary is unlikely to fret systematically about honesty and integrity, except as PR stratagems. Better to conform than risk unemployment.

In the earlier stages of his career, the capitalist may well be a hard worker, and may even be a very decent individual. Additionally, he may only be concerned to make a limited amount of money. But insofar as he is successful, he will accrue more private property, and he will notice that his disposable income has not increased as much as hoped. To use the modern term, he has become 'asset rich, income poor'. But in a system premised on the private pursuit of unlimited wealth, he only has himself to blame for that.

Meanwhile, he will be aware that his employees cannot see him as an ally. Given that they are both dependent on him and resentful of him, he will probably feel justified in regarding them with a measure of contempt. On paper, they may or may not be more 'intelligent' than him – in the sense of possessing better educational qualifications – but there is a more practical, more important sense in which the reverse is the case: for all their supposed 'talents', they will never reach his point on the social ladder, nor can they afford the kind of things he can afford. (If they could, they would: after all, anyone can set up a business.) Aristotle had a word for this type of intelligence in the *Nicomachean Ethics:* the intelligence predominantly possessed by the successful capitalist is *Phronesis,* practical wisdom, as opposed to *Nous*, the knowledge of abstract intellectual objects.[295]

Secondary education ends in adolescence, and higher education a decade, at the latest, afterwards. But while academic qualifications may show evidence of hard work, they are not usually vocational (and, in any case, a person may wish to switch careers). This is where the *Curriculum Vitae* comes in – a list of academic and 'other' achievements (which may be more or less bogus, misleading, or incomplete). To complement it, you usually need a reference. If you are a poor employee, high praise may enable your employer to jettison you, and vice-versa. Any regular subscriber to the fortnightly current affairs magazine, *Private Eye,* will wonder how it is that, in the UK, so many incompetent, cruel or deceitful individuals come to hold jobs commanding huge salaries. The fact that we live in a 'CV Society' goes a long way towards explaining why.

A scale of intelligences underlies all this – intelligence conceived as *Phronesis*, but this is a world in which *Phronesis* always publicly trumps *Nous* - in which the likes of Rupert Murdoch, Elon Musk and Michael Platt occupy lofty positions. Successful capitalists will write books called, *How I Succeeded Massively (And How You Can Too!)*, give TED talks, preach to fans at business conferences, and garner regard as gurus with arcane knowledge to impart. Science graduates will be sucked into finance, and will be seen as all the cleverer for having made the switch. The key to advancement is never to admit to mistakes, never apologise, and always sell yourself. Very few people will

---

[295] The so-called Theory of Multiple Intelligences first became part of educational theory in the 1970s, but it is implicit in the writings of Thomas Carlyle, Herbert Spencer, and Ayn Rand, and has probably always pervaded capitalist culture. The successful capitalist is 'intelligent' in the most significant way possible, and other supposed intelligences are less valuable.

have the gumption for such a thing, but those very few will usually profit.[296]

The overall aim of the capitalist game is to make money and defeat your competitors. It is a game because it has a goal (though it keeps shifting), a set of (putative) rules, a start-point, a series of rewards and penalties along the way, and winners and losers, but, equally, because, mostly, for the capitalists themselves, it is not a matter of life and death: if a business fails, no one is executed, no one goes to prison, and assuming the right safeguards are in place, the business owner need not even lose his or her personal property.

It is also a game (in a way that most people's lives and interactions are not) partly because the most successful capitalists will continue to accrue wealth beyond the point where it ceases to add anything significant to their lives. Like all games, it is addictive, and there is even a manner in which it is social. Even at the highest level, it will bring the players into contact with each other, albeit sometimes indirectly via lawyers, accountants, competitors, vassals, etc. It is not unheard of for some of the world's most successful capitalists to say that they are not driven by the desire to make more money.[297] They simply 'enjoy what they do', just as a successful poker play might: they have a natural flair for the game, and they feel most fulfilled when they are playing it. Meanwhile, because the stakes are so high and the game itself so brutal, the system is pervaded by aggression, insecurity, resentment, bitterness, and an all-

---

[296] Politicians generally are good at this, but in recent years the problem has worsened. But obviously, it is not just politicians. In *Capitalist Realism*, Mark Fisher recalls a middle manager of his acquaintance who "asserted with full confidence a story about the college and its future one day… then literally the next day would happily propound a story that directly contradicted what he had just said. There was never a question of his repudiating the previous story; it was as if he only dimly remembered there ever being one."

[297] Cf, eg, James, Oliver (2007), p63, 93.

pervading sense of bogusness. People become selfish because it helps them navigate the system.

No one can usually see your great wealth in itself, but to be appreciated as a successful capitalist, one needs visibility as such: conspicuous consumption has evolved since Thorstein Veblen noticed its centrality at the end of the nineteenth century[298], and nowadays, it is tied to brands, ie, symbolic representations of highly securitised companies. Even the most valuable status symbols - yachts and private jets - will come from prominently named manufacturers.

Brands are important because they can signify different grades of prestige – the commodities on which they appear as labels appear in differently priced ranges, plus counterfeits – and so can be widely distributed. They never work well singly, but only in combination, so to show my high status as a capitalist, it will never be sufficient for me to have just a few items of a prestigious brand. *All* my significant goods and accessories must be prestigiously branded. For many, this singularity is unattainable, but the important thing is that it admits of degrees of fulfilment.

There is a significant overlap here between branded fashion and modern art: both are products of a socially established consensus about what counts as culturally sophisticated. In the absence of brands, Veblen's original leisure class were apt to make serious gaffes: Jay Gatsby's fake library is symptomatic of one such, but the danger of being regarded as 'nouveau riche', or an 'arriviste', or a 'parvenu', or of 'getting one's living from trade' was never insignificant.

Brands did away with that. They simply shuffled the problem out of existence by restricting the realm of conspicuous consumption to a fixed set of commodities, and thus (no doubt

---

[298] Adam Smith dealt with a similar phenomenon in Part IV of his 1759, *The Theory of Moral Sentiments.*

partly as an unintended consequence of that) democratising it: the various brands have to be well known in order for them to signify anything, and that can only happen if they are widely available but pricey.

This availability, trumpeted by intensive advertising, turned the new relatively fixed, limited range into an approved consensus. Nearly everyone can participate. But for those who cannot get on the brand ladder – most of the young, for example - there is everyday fashion, which can, of course, be given a rebellious, anti-establishment expression[299].

Everyday fashion's drawback is that, whereas at the level of high-end brands, the consensus about what is apposite changes slowly, at the lower end of the 'conspicuous consumption' scale (where it is not so much 'conspicuous' as 'not inconspicuous'), it is much more unstable. The point of street fashion is to 'keep up', which isn't necessarily as easy or cheap as it sounds – so we get 'fast fashion' and the disposal of perfectly serviceable goods on the grounds that they jar with the latest caprice.

Overall, taking all the above into account, what we end up with is a society of relatively atomised individuals whose interrelations are based on *show*. What underlies the show is irrelevant, providing the show can be maintained.

We are now almost back where we started. We saw how, in the workplace, work becomes a performance, the point of which is to give the *impression* of work to the right people; we saw how the system promotes a certain type of intelligence (the capitalist's) at the expense of other kinds; we have now seen how everyone has been suborned into a democratised form of conspicuous consumption whose main feature is *staging*.

This is recognisably 'postmodernism', the culture Frederic Jameson recognised as the expression of late capitalism. It establishes a world in which the ersatz can no longer be

---

[299] At the time of writing, Nike is running an advertising campaign with the slogan 'rebellious by design.'

distinguished from the genuine, and moral and intellectual values become relative. We mentioned above that to succeed here, you should not acknowledge your mistakes, and never apologise. But in fact, there *are* no mistakes, and nothing to apologise for, because there are no longer any indisputable facts of the matter.

We are all compensated, during our short lifetimes, by having access to goods which we do not need, but which advertisers persuade us we do, and whose large-scale acquisition is driven by the endemic one-upmanship which makes the capitalist system so fractious. György Lukács and Jean Baudrillard described some of its features, but the former erred in finding its source in the worker-commodity relation (in which workers themselves become reified commodities), and the latter in the consumer-commodity relationship. Both thought the essence was to be located in the sort of reductionist account that Marx provided, and which finds its most recent major expression in the story of Yanis Varoufakis's mother. Baudrillard in particular erred in thinking that there is no objective truth about the way things are.[300]

None of the above might matter so much if science was left untouched, but, as we have said, one problem with capitalism is what it does to the notion of the truth, and it would be surprising if that did not have ramifications at the highest levels.

Under late capitalism, the university becomes overly timid, and ambitious research is avoided. One will find little discussion of this in academia itself: its denizens are all too busy writing unadventurous papers in order to secure grants. In

---

[300] Eg, Baudrillard, Jean (1988) p 182: "It is always the aim of ideological analysis to restore the objective process. It is always a false problem to want to restore the truth beneath the simulacrum." For Baudrillard, the cause of 'hyperreality' was entirely obscure: there was no underlying reality – at least, that could be discerned anymore. We have tried to show that, on the contrary, 'hyperreality' is a product of very specific relations in the workplace.

order to find out what is really going on, one has to listen to someone who left the system.

One such individual is Sabine Hossenfelder, and she explains her career path in a YouTube video called 'My dream died, and now I'm here.'[301] She gained her PhD in Physics in the 1990s, but virtually all of what she says is relevant today, perhaps more so.

She graduated with excellent results, and looked forward to charting significant new scientific territory in the way the eminent physicists of Europe had done in the early 20th century. She was employed by a prestigious research institution on a scholarship (a scholarship because she was a woman, and it meant they did not have to pay her). Her disillusionment began when she was asked to write part of a textbook for which the head of the institution would take credit (even though nearly everything it contained was produced by his students). She refused. He tried to fire her, but his attempt failed: technically, thanks to the scholarship, she was not employed by the institution.

Over the years, she realised she was not dealing with an anomaly: this was the norm.

> "The real problem is that the easiest way to grow in academia is to pay other people to produce papers on which you, as the grant holder, can put your name. That's how academia works. Grants pay students and postdocs to produce research papers for the grant holder. And those papers are what the supervisor then uses to apply for more grants. The result is a paper production machine, in which students and postdocs are burnt through to bring in money for the institution. After my PhD, I applied for another scholarship and got

---

[301] There are too many similar videos on YouTube to imagine that Hossenfelder's experience is atypical.

that and then I got a postdoc job, and a grant, and another job, and another job, and another grant, and so on. And I began to understand what you need to do to get a grant or get hired. You have to work on topics that are mainstream enough but not too mainstream. You want them to be a little bit edgy, but not too edgy. It needs to be something that fits into the existing machinery. And since most grants are three years or five years at most, it also needs to be something that can be wrapped up quickly. The more I saw of this, the more I realised this wasn't how I wanted to spend my life. The other thing that happened was that the more I saw of the foundations of physics, the more I became convinced that most of the research there wasn't based on sound scientific principles."

Books such as Charles Piller's recent *Doctored: Fraud, Arrogance and Tragedy in the Quest to Cure Alzheimer's*, Suzanne O'Sullivan's *The Age of Diagnosis: Sickness, Health and Why Medicine Has Gone Too Far*, show the effect of capitalism on science. All too often, the system is not alert enough to notice faulty methodology and malign outcomes.

In addition to the inbuilt difficulty of doing anything worthwhile in such an environment, we should add the surveillance culture, described by Mark Fisher, that has overtaken academia in the last few decades. Academics – and, in fact, teachers generally - are performance-managed for the completion of short-term goals unimaginatively conceived and rigorously imposed.

"Initially, it might appear to be a mystery that bureaucratic measures should have intensified under neoliberal governments that have presented themselves as anti-bureaucratic and anti-Stalinist. Yet

268

new kinds of bureaucracy – 'aims and objectives', 'mission statements' – have proliferated, even as neoliberal rhetoric about top-down, centralised control has gained pre-eminence ... The drive to assess the performance of workers and to measure forms of labour which, by their nature, are resistant to quantification, has inevitably required additional layers of management and bureaucracy. What we have is not a direct comparison of workers' performance or output, but a comparison between the audited representation of that performance and output."[302]

Part of that involves the production of papers for journals, described above. But does anyone seriously believe that the journals culture which has characterised academia now for well over half a century, really serves to advance the limits of knowledge? As Dan Davies puts it, in *The Unaccountability Machine:*

"A not-wholly-unfair analysis of academic publishing would be that it is an industry in which academics compete against one another for the privilege of providing free labour for a profitmaking company, which then sells the results back to them at monopoly prices. It is, as you'd expect from that description, highly profitable and passionately hated by the academics."[303]

Within a system such as the one we are describing, it should not surprise us that Postmodernism is the normative paradigm. Knowledge and truth are relative concepts.

---

[302] Fisher, Mark (2022), p40.
[303] Davies, Dan (2024), p20.

And now we really have come full circle. Our conclusion must be that the reason Yanis Varoufakis's mother felt dissatisfied is not because she was providing *gratis* something she had no capacity to sell. It is because, as someone who was sincerely trying to do her job to the best of her ability, she did not belong in a system where work is generally no more than a convincing performance. Add to that the fact that, in the 1960s and 70s (as today), women in skilled roles were often the victims of sexism.

Of course, despite everything above, her case is far from unique. The reader may well recognise something similar from his or her own experience. Which – paradoxically: just because of the recognition - is why we can have hope for humanity.

Appendix 2: A Brief History of Religionless Religion

The present work has argued that the next genuinely progressive step in human history will involve the irruption, within the present system, of countersocieties untethered from a hard materialist outlook. That some of those will be communist or anarchist in tenor is inevitable, especially as both those movements are, at root – and were, before they became infected with the capitalist ideology – 'religious' in outlook. Marx, of course, disparages 'feudal socialism' in *The Communist Manifesto*, but the various European peasants' revolts, the Diggers, the Levellers and the early Anabaptists are not so easily dismissible. A good picture of their revolutionary ardour and potential can be found in the well-researched 1999 historical novel, *Q*, pseudonymously written by 'Luther Blissett', while, the Canadian author, Erica Lagalisse, has recently shown that Anarchism began in various 'occult' movements from the Renaissance onwards, most of them heterodoxically Christian. She laments the modern-day 'sophisticated' radical antipathy to religion: "To refrain from telling the non-atheist activist they are wrong (while continuing to think they are)," she says, "simply because he or she is a person of colour, is altogether different than deconstructing one's colonial mentality, which treats the religious as Other in the first place."

We seem to be caught on the horns of a dilemma. On the one hand, there is no point in re-inventing the wheel: we already have several large-scale countersocieties, untethered from a hard materialist outlook, in the form of the major world religions. On the other hand, there are good reasons to see much of religion as reactionary and obscurantist. If religions, as they currently exist, are to be progressive phenomena, they may need to be entirely re-purposed, and that looks like a well-nigh impossible undertaking. According to most estimates, eighty-five per cent of the world's population identifies with a religion.

But that misconstrues the problem. Religions are by no means homogenous: mostly, they are riven by internal dissent, a large proportion of which, today, is predicated on liberal/ progressive vs. fundamentalist/ conservative lines. It can be shown that the latter branch in both dichotomies is the less plausible: forward-looking believers do not have to conform to a pre-existing template; backward-looking ones do, and, thanks to the way history works – there really is no going back to the past – the sought-after conformity is forever unachievable: things always have to be left undone. Modern-day Christian fundamentalists oppose homosexuality as they are supposedly required to do by the Book of Leviticus, but do not advocate plucking out one's own eyes as required by the Book of Matthew.

It might seem a hugely ambitious undertaking to show that nearly all 'religion' is, in essence, progressive, but that is only because capital has accustomed us to think otherwise. In fact, religion is easily the thing capitalism fears most. Religion represents an older, very different, and potentially disruptive, if not lethal, worldview. Capital meets the threat it represents by means of a double tactic: on the one hand, it tries to destroy it; on the other, it tries to co-opt it. The contradiction between these enterprises to some extent mirrors the contradictions in capital itself, but they are prevented from cancelling each other out by being contained within two different spheres: a nationalist, military-ceremonial sphere attempts the co-option; an intellectual sphere (including Marxism, etc., under the capital's spell) undertakes the attempted demolition.

Reactionary religion is partly the creation of capital. Nearly all scholars accept nowadays that 'religion' is itself a colonial concept: it was imposed on the spiritual beliefs of other cultures in a (mostly well-intentioned) attempt to make sense of the unknown (animism, polytheism, etc.) in terms of the known: the Judaeo-Christian-Islamic paradigm. Ninian Smart, writing in the mid-20th century, identified seven 'dimensions' of religion – ritual, mythical, ethical, doctrinal, experiential, communal, and material – acknowledging, at that point in history, a template into which other worldviews had already been inserted. As Jonathan Z Smith says, "Religion is not a native term; it is a term created by scholars for their own intellectual purposes." Lagalisse perhaps overstates the case when she says, "In the context of the colonial encounter, Christendom granted other communities and traditions the name it had only ever given itself – religion – and reincarnated itself as 'secular'", but the advantage of looking at the issue in that way is to underline the fact that it has a political as well as a theoretical dimension.

Before the rise of capitalism, 'religion' was different, and arguably did not even exist as such. What existed was either what we now call 'spirituality', more or less assisted by external 'religious' institutions, or formal cultic observances designed to verify loyalty.

That might seem at odds with history. It is common for modern faiths in their conservative incarnations to preach the religious unimpeachability of their origins – Ancient Israel for Judaism, the Eucharistic communities of Acts and Paul's letters for Christians, the Muhammad-era Ummah in Medina then Mecca for Muslims, Kartarpur for Sikhism, and Ayodhya for Hindus.

But none of those inchoate communities resemble the religions that presently romanticise them, nor could they. The early religion of Judaism was probably polytheistic, with Yahweh at its head; the early Christians expected the end of the world in their lifetimes, and had neither an Old nor a New Testament; the earliest Ummah had no Qur'an, and probably did not conceive the necessity of such a thing until Muhammad died; Muhammad himself may never have conceived it. (The idea that a religious text contains the words of God is perfectly consistent with a belief that it has no relevance for later generations of believers.) In Sikhism, the community at Kartarpur was pre-5K's; in Hinduism, Ayodhya is a mythical realm, but Hinduism and Buddhism evolved together, and the religions we call as such today are at least partly the reified products of a recent encounter with the West, as outlined above. Both have been redesigned to conform to modernist requirements.

The idealisation of origins is intended to suggest an essence to which each religion must conform. It is essentially a Christian idea, and in its most rigid form it is Protestant. As for the books of any given religion, in all cases, they only appear when the original vibrancy of the movement has run its course, and partly as a response to that – as a way of recovering the unrecoverable. They are Hegel's Owl of Minerva, mentioned above.

The collapse of religion in the old sense begins with the rise of capitalism, with John Calvin in Christianity, and Muhammad ibn Abd al-Wahhab in Islam. It is effectively completed by the later 'discovery' of Eastern religions in colonialism, and their subsequent reinvention according to the template provided by Christianity, as described above.

The high point of capital's attempt to destroy religion may have come in the first decade of the 21st century, when fundamentalist atheism briefly became highly fashionable. This had the effect of neutralising the religious progressives/liberals, so that only the hardliners were left - which in turn made religion a better target. The whole process could have succeeded, had it not been for the fact that it soon became clear, as it was bound to, that religion was not the only, or even the worst problem. The worst problem, as the nineteenth-century thinker, Max Stirner, had insisted all along, was 'fixed ideas', of which there were a theoretically infinite number. Identity politics, Brexit, Putinism, New Right-ism, and a host of other *idées fixes* casually emerged from the background and took their place in the massed ranks of obscurantist philosophies. The problem was exacerbated by the fact that many of the New Atheists were Humanists, and Stirner's critique of Humanism as a fixed idea was even more trenchant than his critique of orthodox religion as such.

So where are we now? We are both at the end of materialism *and* at the end of religion (in the sense it has been defined since the advent of capitalism).

Barbara Ehrenreich's *Dancing in the Street* may give the best account of what we might hope for. Her analysis begins in ancient Athens with Euripides's, *The Bacchae*, where King Pentheus sets himself up against the female devotees of the god Dionysus. Ehrenreich argues that the play's central conflict – law, order and sobriety versus collective joy – is one of the major themes of human history. The modern age, since the Protestant Reformation, has tilted the scales decisively against collective joy.

The Christian expression of collective joy reached its climax in medieval carnivals, which were genuinely democratic. At the end of that period, however, the elites withdrew from the festivities - "whether out of fear, or in an effort to maintain [their] dignity and distance from the hoi polloi" is an open question – but "since the participants were now solely, or almost solely, members of the subordinate group, their unity inevitably presented a challenge to the ruling classes." In short, henceforth, collective joy had to be suppressed.

She describes the historical consequence of that in Chapter 7 entitled, 'An Epidemic of Melancholy'. "Beginning in England in the seventeenth century," she says, "the European world was stricken by what looks like an epidemic of depression. The disease attacked both young and old, plunging them into months or years of morbid lethargy and relentless terrors." And of course, it is something from which we're still suffering.

The modern world – the 'postfestive' world, she calls it – is characterised by (a) *spectacles* (often with a significant military element) provided by the elites for the edification of the less-well-off, who usually play a purely passive role (b) *meetings* ("experienced in a sitting position and conducted according to strict rules of procedure"), and (c) by the conversion of potential merrymakers into an *audience,* a homogenised mass of immobile nonparticipants.

While capital has achieved the greatest repression of collective joy, it is not exclusively to blame. "The aspect of 'civilisation'," Ehrenreich says, "that is most hostile to festivity is not capitalism or industrialism ... but social hierarchy, which is far more ancient. When one class, or ethnic group or gender, rules over a population of subordinates, it comes to fear the empowering rituals of the subordinates as a threat to civil order." We are up, of course, against the means of securitisation.

Ehrenreich does not consider whether significant expressions of collective joy before the Reformation might have been tied to a specific form of pre-capital religion, and whether they might be impossible to revive without it. Modern communists and socialists have always excoriated religion for entrenching social division, but there is nothing necessarily quietist about religion: if I believe that this life is not all there is, and that our social positions cannot survive our physical deaths, then – unless I think that God has instituted the present political order – I may be highly uncooperative. And of course, the reverse is true: if I think I am a purely transitory life form, I may conclude that, as a short-term being, I should have short-term goals; generally speaking, that I might have most to gain by cooperating with the present system - especially if that system looks firmly established. But then, we covered all this in Part One.

Bibliography

➢ Al-Gharbi, Musa, *We Have Never Been Woke: The Cultural Capital of a New Elite* (Princeton 2024)

➢ Althusser, Louis 'Ideology and Ideological State Apparatuses (Notes towards an Investigation)', in *Lenin and Philosophy and Other Essays* (London 1971)

➢ Anderson, Benedict, *Imagined Communities: Reflections on the Origin and Spread of Nationalism* (Verso 2nd Ed. 1991)

➢ Aristotle, *The Nicomachean Ethics* (Penguin 2020)

➢ Arrighi, Giovanni, *The Long Twentieth Century: Money, Power, and the Origins of Our Times* (Verso 1994)

➢ Badiou, Alain, *In Praise of Love* (Serpent's Tail 2012)

➢ Baier, Annette, *Moral Prejudices* (Harvard 1995)

➢ Balibar, Étienne, *Politics and the Other Scene* (Verso 2002)

➢ Barrow, Clyde W, *The Dangerous Class: The Concept of the Lumpenproletariat* (Michigan 2020)

➢ Barthes, Roland, *Mythologies* (Noonday Press 1972)

➢ Baudrillard, Jean, *Selected Writings* (Polity 1988)

➢ Beatley, Timothy, *Biophilic Cities: Integrating Nature into Urban Design and Planning* (Island 2010)

➤ Bengtsson, Staffan, 'Out of the frame: disability and the body in the writings of Karl Marx' (Scandinavian Journal of Disability Research, 2017 Vol. 19, No. 2, 151–160)

➤ Benjamin, Walter, *Charles Baudelaire: A Lyric Poet in the Era of High Capitalism* (NLB 1973)

➤ Bevins, Vincent, *If We Burn: The Mass Protest Decade and the Missing Revolution* (Wildfire 2023)

➤ Blissett, Luther, *Q* (Arrow 2004)

➤ Bloch, Marc, *Feudal Society* Vols. 1 and 2 (Routledge 1965)

➤ Boggs, C, 'Revolutionary Process, Political Strategy and the Dilemma of Power', in *Theory and Society* 4(3) (1977).

➤ Bourdin, Jean-Paul, *Marx and the Lumpenproletariat* (Actuel Marx, No 54(2), 2013)

➤ Bowles, S and Gintis, H, *A Cooperative Species: Human Reciprocity and Its Evolution* (Princeton 2011)

➤ Bowyer, Jack, *A History of Building* (Orion 1973)

➤ Brooks, David, *Bobos in Paradise* (Simon and Schuster 2000)

➤ Burkett, Paul, *Marx and Nature: A Red and Green Perspective* (Haymarket 1999)

➤ Camus, Albert, *The Rebel* (Penguin 2013)

➤ Chaline, Eric, *Fifty Machines That Changed the Course of History* (Quid 2014)

➤ Chaney, Sarah, *Am I Normal?: The 200-Year Search for Normal People (and Why They Don't Exist)* (Wellcome Collection 2022)

- Claeys, Gregory, *Utopianism for a Dying Planet: Life after Consumerism* (Princeton 2024)

- Cohen, GA, *Karl Marx's Theory of History* (Oxford 1978)

- Collier, Paul, *Left Behind: A New Economics for Neglected Places* (Penguin 2024)

- Coverley, Merlin, *Psychogeography* (Pocket Essentials 2006)

- Coverley, Merlin, *Utopia* (Pocket Essentials 2012)

- Crewe, Ben, '"Sedative Coping": Contextual Maturity and Institutionalization Among Prisoners Serving Life Sentences in England and Wales' (*The British Journal of Criminology* Vol 64, Issue 5, Sept 2024, p1080–1097)

- Davies, Dan, *The Unaccountability Machine: Why Big Systems Make Terrible Decisions* (Profile 2024)

- Davies, James, *Sedated: How Modern Capitalism Created Our Mental Health Crisis* (Atlantic 2021)

- Dean, Jodi, *The Communist Horizon* (Verso 2012)

- Debord, Guy, *The Society of the Spectacle* (Good Press 2022)

- Deleuze, Gilles and Guattari, Félix, *A Thousand Plateaus* (New York 2004)

- Diamond, Jared, *Guns Germs and Steel* (WW Norton 1997)

- Dixon, Chris, *Read Write Own: Building the Next Era of the Internet* (Penguin 2024)

- Draper, Hal, 'The Concept of the Lumpenproletariat in Marx and Engels' (*Économies et Sociétés* December 1972)

➢ Dunbar, RIM, 'Neocortex size as a constraint on group size in primates' (*Journal of Human Evolution*, 22 (6), p469-93, 1992)

➢ Easton, Malcolm, *Artists and Writers in Paris: The Bohemian Idea, 1803-1867* (Edward Arnold 1964)

➢ Ehrenreich, Barbara, *Dancing in the Streets: A History of Collective Joy* (Granta 2008)

➢ Engels, Friedrich, *The Peasant War in Germany* (Allen & Unwin 1926)

➢ Feyerabend, Paul, *Against Method* (New Left Books 1975)

➢ Fisher, Mark, *Capitalist Realism: Is There No Alternative?* (Zero Books 2nd ed. 2022)

➢ Foster, John Bellamy, *Marx's Ecology: Materialism and Nature* (New York 2000)

➢ Foucault, Michel, *Discipline and Punish: The Birth of the Prison* (Penguin 2020)

➢ Frank, Andre Gunder, *Lumpenbourgeoisie and Lumpendevelopment: Dependency, Class and Politics in Latin America* (Monthly Review Press 1970)

➢ Freedman, Sam, *Failed State: Why Nothing Works and How We Fix It* (Macmillan 2024)

➢ Freeman, Jo (aka Joreen), 'The Tyranny of Structurelessness' (https://www.jofreeman.com/joreen/tyranny.htm)

- ➤ Friedman, Milton, 'A Friedman Doctrine: The Social Responsibility of Business is to Increase Its Profits' (New York Times, September 13 1970)

- ➤ Fromm, Erich, *Man for Himself: An Inquiry into the Psychology of Ethics* (Routledge 2020)

- ➤ Fromm, Erich, *To Have or to Be?* (Continuum 1997)

- ➤ Fromm, Erich, *The Sane Society* (Routledge 1956)

- ➤ Fukuyama, Francis, *The End of History and the Last Man* (Penguin 2020)

- ➤ Ganshof, FL, *Feudalism* (Harper 1964)

- ➤ Gilligan, Carol, *In a Different Voice* (Harvard 1982)

- ➤ Goldacre, Ben, *Bad Pharma: How Medicine is Broken, And How We Can Fix It* (Fourth Estate 2012)

- ➤ Goldacre, Ben, *Bad Science* (Fourth Estate 2008)

- ➤ Golding, William, *Lord of the Flies* (Faber and Faber 1954)

- ➤ Goldwater, Robert, *Symbolism* (Harper & Row 1979)

- ➤ Graeber, David, *The Utopia of Rules: On Technology, Stupidity, and the Secret Joys of Bureaucracy* (Melville House 2016),

- ➤ Graeber, David, *Bullshit Jobs: A Theory* (Simon & Schuster 2018)

- ➤ Gramsci, Antonio, *Selections from Prison Notebooks* (Lawrence and Wishart 1971)

- ➤ Gray, John, *Straw Dogs* (Granta 2002)

- ➤ Greer, Germaine, *The Female Eunuch* (Fourth Estate 2012)

➤ Habermas, Jürgen, *Moral Consciousness and Communicative Action* (Polity 1990)

➤ Habermas, Jürgen, *The Theory of Communicative Action* (Polity 1986)

➤ Hahn, Emily, *Romantic Rebels: An Informal History of Bohemianism in America* (Cambridge 1967)

➤ Haidt, Jonathan, *The Anxious Generation: How the Great Rewiring of Childhood is Causing an Epidemic of Mental Illness* (Penguin 2024)

➤ Hardt, Michael and Negri, Antonio, *Empire* (Aakar 2016)

➤ Hardt, Michael and Negri, Antonio, *Multitude* (Penguin 2006)

➤ Harvey, David, *Paris, Capital of Modernity* (London 2003)

➤ Harvey, David, *The New Imperialism* (Oxford 2003)

➤ Harvey, David, *Spaces of Global Capitalism* (Verso 2006)

➤ Hayek, Friedrich, 'The Use of Knowledge in Society' in *The American Economic Review*, September 1945

➤ Hayes, Nick, *The Book of Trespass: Crossing the Lines That Divide Us* (Bloomsbury 2020)

➤ Hegel, GWF, *Philosophy of Right* (Batoche 2001)

➤ Hegel, GWF, *The Phenomenology of Mind* (George Allen & Unwin 1971)

➤ Heidegger, Martin, *Being and Time* (Blackwell 1980)

➤ Held, Virginia, *The Ethics of Care: Personal, Political, and Global* (New York 2006)

➢ Hickel, Jason, *Less is More: How Degrowth Will Save the World* (Penguin 2022)

➢ Hobbes, Thomas, *Leviathan* (Cambridge 1991)

➢ Holten, Matthew, *Moneyless Society: The Next Economic Evolution* (Clearsight 2022)

➢ Horkheimer, Max and Adorno, Theodor W, *Dialectic of Enlightenment: Philosophical Fragments* (Stanford 2002)

➢ Hossenfelder, Sabine, 'My dream died, and now I'm here' at YouTube
https://www.youtube.com/watch?v=LKiBlGDfRU8&t=116s

➢ Huston, Simon, Wadley, David, and Fitzpatrick, Rachael, 'Bohemianism and Urban Regeneration: A Structured Literature Review and *Compte Rendu*' in *Space and Culture*, 2015, Vol 18(3), 311-323.

➢ Jacobs, Jane, *The Death and Life of Great American Cities* (Random House 1961)

➢ James, Oliver, *Affluenza: How to Be Successful* and *Stay Sane* (Penguin 2007)

➢ Jameson, Fredric, *Postmodernism, or The Cultural Logic of Late Capitalism* (Duke University Press 1991)

➢ Jeffries, Stuart, *Grand Hotel Abyss: The Lives of the Frankfurt School* (Verso 2017)

➢ Jones, Lucy, *Losing Eden: Why Our Minds Need the Wild* (Penguin 2020)

➤ Joyce, Patrick, *Remembering the Peasant: A Personal History of a Vanished World* (Penguin 2024)

➤ Jung, Carl, *Modern Man in Search of a Soul* (Routledge & Kegan Paul Ltd 1933)

➤ Kamenka, Eugene, *The Ethical Foundations of Marxism* (Routledge 1962)

➤ Kant, Immanuel, *Critique of Practical Reason* (Cambridge 2015)

➤ Keucheyan, Razmig, *The Left Hemisphere: Mapping Critical Theory Today* (Verso 2014)

➤ Kinsella, N Stephan, *Against Intellectual Property* (Ludwig von Mises 2010)

➤ Kittay, Eva, *Learning from My Daughter. The Value and Care of Disabled Minds* (Oxford 2020)

➤ Klein, Naomi, *The Shock Doctrine: The Rise of Disaster Capitalism* (Penguin 2008)

➤ Kojève, Alexandre, *Introduction to the Reading of Hegel: Lectures on the Phenomenology of Spirit* (Basic Books 1969)

➤ Kołakowski, Leszek, 'What is Left of Socialism' (*First Things*, October 2002)

➤ Kropotkin, Peter, *Mutual Aid: A Factor in Evolution* (Affordable Classics Limited 2018)

➤ Kuhn, Thomas, *The Structure of Scientific Revolutions* (Chicago 1962)

➤ Laclau, Ernesto and Mouffe, Chantal, *Hegemony and Socialist Strategy: Towards a Radical Democratic Politics* (Verso 2001)

➤ Lagalisse, Erica, *Occult Features of Anarchism: With Attention to the Conspiracy of Kings and the Conspiracy of the Peoples* (PM Press 2019)

➤ Lamont, M, *The Dignity of Working Men: Morality and the Boundaries of Race, Class, and Immigration* (Harvard 2009)

➤ Le Goff, Jacques, *La Civilisation de l'Occident Médiévial* (Paris 1964)

➤ Lenin, VI, *What is to Be Done? Burning Questions of Our Movements* (Lenin Internet Archive 1999)

➤ Lewis, CS, *The Allegory of Love: A Study in Medieval Tradition* (Oxford 1936)

➤ Locke, John, *Second Treatise of Government and A Letter Concerning Toleration* (Oxford 2016)

➤ Lukács, Georg, *History & Class Consciousness: Studies in Marxist Dialectics* (The MIT Press 1971)

➤ Mandel, Ernest, *Late Capitalism* (London 1975)

➤ Mannheim, Karl, *Ideology and Utopia: An Introduction to the Sociology of Knowledge* (Routledge 1936)

➤ Marcuse, Herbert, *An Essay on Liberation* (Beacon 1969)

➤ Marcuse, Herbert, *Negations: Essays in Critical Theory* (Penguin 1972)

- Marx, Karl, *Economic and Philosophic Manuscripts of 1844* (Progress 1977)

- Marx, Karl and Engels, Friedrich, *The Communist Manifesto* (Penguin 1967)

- Marx, Karl, *Capital: Critique of Political Economy* (Penguin 1990)

- Marx, Karl, *The German Ideology* (Prometheus 1998)

- Marx, Karl, *The Poverty of Philosophy* (Legare Street Press 2022)

- McLellan, David, *Karl Marx: His Life and Thought* (Macmillan 1973)

- McLellan, David, *Marx* (Fontana 1975)

- Mészáros, István, *Marx's Theory of Alienation* (Merlin 1970)

- Monbiot, George, *Captive State: The Corporate Takeover of Britain* (Pan 2000)

- Monbiot, George, *Regenesis: Feeding the World without Devouring the Planet* (Penguin 2022)

- Montinelli, Lara (Ed.), *The Future is Now: An Introduction to Prefigurative Politics* (Bristol University Press 2024)

- Moreno, Carlos, *The 15-Minute City: A Solution to Saving Our Time and Our Planet* (Wiley 2024)

- Morrow, Elizabeth and Meadowcroft, John, 'Violence, self-worth, solidarity and stigma: how a dissident, far right group solves the collective action problem.' (*Political Studies.* https://doi.org/10.1177/0032321716651654)

- Moulier-Boutang, Yann, *Cognitive Capitalism* (Polity 2012)

- Nairn, Tom, 'Globalisation and Nationalism: The New Deal' in *Open Democracy* (March 2008)

- Nelson, Anitra, *Beyond Money: A Postcapitalist Strategy* (Pluto 2022)

- Nicholson, Virginia, *Among the Bohemians: Experiments in Living 1900-1939* (Penguin 2002)

- Noddings, Nell, *Caring: A Feminine Approach to Ethics and Moral Education* (California 1984)

- Nunes, Rodrigo, *Neither Vertical nor Horizontal: A Theory of Political Organization* (Verso 2021)

- Oborne, Peter, *The Triumph of the Political Class* (Simon & Schuster 2007)

- Ollman, Bertell, *Alienation: Marx's Conception of Man in Capitalist Society* (Cambridge 1971)

- O'Sullivan, Suzanne, *The Age of Diagnosis: Sickness, Health and Why Medicine Has Gone Too Far* (Hodder & Stoughton 2025)

- Paulré, Barnard, 'Introduction au capitalisme cognitif' (cited in Moulier-Boutang 2012).

- Peckham, Robert, *Fear: An Alternative History of the World* (Profile 2023)

- Piller, Charles, *Doctored: Fraud, Arrogance and Tragedy in the Quest to Cure Alzheimer's* (Icon 2025)

- Polanyi, Karl, *The Great Transformation* (Penguin 2024)

➢ Project Society After Money, *Society After Money: A Dialogue* (Bloomsbury 2020)

➢ Raekstad, Paul, and Gradin, Sofa Saio, *Prefigurative Politics: Building Tomorrow Today* (Polity 2020)

➢ Raworth, Kate, *Doughnut Economics: Seven Ways to Think Like a 21st-Century Economist* (Random House 2017)

➢ Ransome, Arthur, *Bohemia in London* (Oxford 1984)

➢ Richardson, Joanna, *The Bohemians: La vie de Bohème in Paris 1830-1914* (Macmillan 1969)

➢ Ridley, Matt, *How Innovation Works* (4th Estate 2020)

➢ Robeyns, Ingrid (Ed.), *Having Too Much: Philosophical Essays on Limitarianism* (Cambridge 2023)

➢ Robeyns, Ingrid, *Limitarianism: The Case Against Extreme Wealth* (Allen Lane 2024)

➢ Roemer, John (Ed.), *Analytical Marxism* (Cambridge 1986)

➢ Rosenberg, Alex, *Philosophy of Science: A Contemporary Introduction* (Routledge 2000)

➢ Roszak, Theodore, *The Making of a Counter Culture* (California 1969)

➢ Rousseau, Jean Jacques, *Emile: Treatise on Education* (London 2016)

➢ Rousseau, Jean-Jacques, *The Social Contract* (Penguin 2012)

➢ Saito, Kohei, *Slow Down: How Degrowth Communism Will Save the World* (Weidenfeld & Nicolson 2024)

➤ Saint-Paul, Gilles, *Bobos in Paradise: Urban Politics and the New Economy* (HAL 2015)

➤ Sayer, Andrew, *Why We Can't Afford the Rich* (Policy Press 2015)

➤ Schmitt, Carl, *Political Theology: Four Chapters on the Concept of Sovereignty* (Chicago 2006)

➤ Segal, Lynne, *Radical Happiness: Moments of Collective Joy* (Verso 2017)

➤ Shoard, Marion, *This Land is Our Land* (Collins 1987)

➤ Siegel, Jerrold, *Bohemian Paris: Culture, Politics, and the Boundaries of Bourgeois Life, 1830-1930* (Viking 1986)

➤ Sitrin, Marina, *Horizontalism: Voices of Popular Power in Argentina* (AK Press 2006)

➤ Small, Hugh, *The Future of Anarchism* (Knowledge Leak 2019)

➤ Smil, Vaclav, *Invention and Innovation: A Brief History of Hype and Failure* (MIT 2023)

➤ Smil, Vaclav, *Numbers Don't Lie: 71 Things You Need to Know About the world* (Penguin 2020)

➤ Smith, Adam, *The Theory of Moral Sentiments* (Cambridge 2023)

➤ Smith, Adam *The Wealth of Nations* (Everyman 1991)

➤ Sombart, Werner, *Der moderne Kapitalismus* (Munich 1927)

➤ Spufford, Francis, *Red Plenty: Inside the Fifties' Soviet Dream* (Faber and Faber 2011)

➤ Standing, Guy, *The Precariat: The New Dangerous Class* (IB Tauris 2021)

➤ Stephenson, Carl, *Mediaeval Feudalism* (Cornell 1956)

➤ Stirner, Max, *The Ego and Its Own* (Cambridge 1995)

➤ Strayer, Joseph R, *Feudalism* (New York 1965)

➤ Suleyman, Mustafa and Bhaskar, Michael, *The Coming Wave: AI, Power and Our Future* (Vintage Digital 2023)

➤ Susskind, Daniel, *Growth: A Reckoning* (Penguin 2024)

➤ Sweezy, Paul and Baran, Paul A, *Monopoly Capital: An Essay on the American Economic and Social Order* (Monthly Review Press 1966)

➤ Taylor, AJP, 'Introduction' to *The Communist Manifesto* (Penguin 1967)

➤ Taylor, Barbara, *Eve and the New Jerusalem: Socialism and Feminism in the Nineteenth Century* (Virago 2016)

➤ Thompson, EP, *The Making of the English Working Class* (Gollancz 1963)

➤ Toffler, Alvin, *Previews and Premises* (William Morrow & Co 1983)

➤ Toffler, Alvin, *The Third Wave* (Bantam 1980)

➤ Treadwell, J and Garland, J, 'Masculinity, Marginalization and Violence a Case Study of the English Defence League', *British Journal of Criminology*, 51 (4), 621-34 (2011).

➤ Tronto, Joan C, *Moral Boundaries: A Political Argument for an Ethic of Care* (New York 1993)

➤ Varoufakis, Yanis, *Technofeudalism: What Killed Capitalism* (Bodley Head 2023)

➤ Veblen, Thorstein, *The Theory of the Leisure Class: An Economic Study of Institutions* (Allen & Unwin 1957)

➤ Ward, James, *A New Theory of Justice and Other Essays* (Cool Millennium 2012)

➤ Ward, James, *21st Century Philosophy* (Cool Millennium 2012)

➤ Wark, McKenzie, 'The Vectoralist Class' in *e-flux Journal* Issue #65 (May 2015)

➤ Weber, Max, *The City* (Free Press 1966)

➤ Weikart, Richard, 'Marx, Engels, and the Abolition of the Family' (History of European Ideas, Vol. 18, No. 5, pp. 657-672, 1994)

➤ White, Lynn, *Medieval Technology and Social Change* (Oxford 1966)

➤ Wilkinson, Richard G and Pickett, Kate, *The Spirit Level: Why More Equal Societies Almost Always Do Better* (Allen Lane 2009)

➤ Wilson, Edward O, *Biophilia* (Harvard 1984)

➤ Wittgenstein, Ludwig, *Philosophical Investigations* (Blackwell 1958)

➤ Woodcock, George, *Anarchism: A History of Libertarian Ideas and Movements* (2nd Edition, Penguin 1986)

➢ Wright, Erik Olin, *Class Counts: Comparative Studies in Class Analysis* (Cambridge 1996)

➢ Ypi, Lea, *Free: Coming of Age at the End of History* (Penguin 2021)

➢ Slavoj Žižek, *The Sublime Object of Ideology* (Verso 1989)

➢ Slavoj Žižek, *Žižek on Lenin: Revolution at the Gates – The 1917 Writings* (Verso 2004)

➢ Zuboff, Shoshana, *The Age of Surveillance Capitalism* (Profile 2018)

Acknowledgements

I am grateful to the University of Sussex for allowing me (free!) use of their library in my capacity as an alumni: this book would have been far more expensive to produce without it.

I would also like to thank Ravensbrook Shortfall Haddison, my editor at Cool Millennium, for her good judgement, dry sense of humour and patience; plus all of her colleagues, especially Craig Bough, Munificence Poynter and Slim Goofy McGee. I owe a special debt of gratitude to M Tiff-Bonk, at Radley Welt, and to Duffle Coat Jones, Peeps van de Pows, and Maudlin Samovar at Beefy Mount. I am particularly indebted to 'Gatling Gun' Keith Forest for introducing me to the Glaswegian section of the Rods and Cones. I am equally obliged to my agent, Jumbo Blimey, of Rabbity Stock Harp Chute Ltd., and his minders, L J Mickerty Stomp, 'Guru' Paul Walters-Pryce, Scrutiny Shouttup and Tarry Slurp. I would also like to thank my international publishers, 'Royal' Caspar Flatpack (in Chad), Topphoss Biffo (in Mongolia) and Carpark Hootem Jr. (in Iceland).

I owe a special debt of gratitude to Prince Lionel Mardvark for allowing me 'access' to his fridge in Santa Nella (although, since I have never been to America, I never actually used it – the thought was there). For their encouragement, typographical skills and enthusiasm, I would like to thank my dear friends, Ronnie Flapjoint, Julie Elbownoise, Plumeboat Glyff and Alfredo Blisterpack. Love also to Chiralee Beknothtethen-Clamp and Peenix Plowerfower, both of whom are still in prison.

I cannot pass over this opportunity to thank my editors, Twissmote Pockmark-McDyke, Dixie Bamberflash and Kelvin Pu for their timely suggestions and massive thesaurus. Sadly no longer with us, though their suggestions were very helpful in the early stages, are Faye Bentos, Nora Lambtickle and Lambert Daftpratfinder. May you all rest in peace. For pointing out the difference between saddle stitch, PUR and singer sewn binding, I am very grateful to Pat Flagcrap, although Bingo Dripbutt's timely advice on the pertinence of solander boxes and slipcases was also invaluable. Thank you. Milky Trohns and Rodney Fanackapan helped me with my research at every step of the way, and Jeanette Windshield plays the trombone.